Language Testing

Language Testing

THE CONSTRUCTION AND USE
OF FOREIGN LANGUAGE TESTS

A Teacher's Book

ROBERT LADO, Ph.D.

Dean of the Institute of Languages and Linguistics
Georgetown University

McGRAW-HILL BOOK COMPANY
New York   St. Louis   San Francisco

© Robert Lado 1961
All Rights Reserved
First published 1961 *by Longmans, Green and Co Ltd*
New impression 1962
American impression 1964 by McGraw-Hill Book Company

PRINTED IN THE UNITED STATES OF AMERICA

Library of Congress number 64-22726

ISBN 07-035750-1

6789101112 HDVB 7654321

to

CHARLES CARPENTER FRIES
and
HERSHEL THURMAN MANUEL
and to L.A.L.

ACKNOWLEDGMENTS

I owe much to Charles C. Fries, founder of the English Language Institute, whose insights into language and language teaching and learning have stimulated my work along lines that have yielded valuable knowledge. *Teaching and Learning English as a Foreign Language* and *The Structure of English* by Fries would be particularly useful reading in connection with the discussions and experience presented here.

I also acknowledge with gratitude my introduction to the field of measurement by H. T. Manuel, whose work on the *Inter-American Tests* attracted me to research on testing. The interest shown by my colleagues at the English Language Institute and in other departments of the University of Michigan and elsewhere was helpful in the long undertaking of developing new tests and writing the book.

The final writing of the material was made possible by a sabbatical leave from the University of Michigan supplemented by a travel grant from the Horace H. Rackham School of Graduate Studies. To them, and more specifically to the administration and colleagues who processed the applications and shared the work involved, my humble tribute and gratitude.

Mr. Bonifacio P. Sibayan of the Philippines made the invaluable contribution of reading the typescript critically in detail and discussing with the author every point that did not seem clearly presented or fully thought through. Many improvements resulted from Mr. Sibayan's constructive criticisms.

PREFACE

This book is a comprehensive introduction to the construction and use of foreign language tests. It incorporates modern linguistic knowledge into language testing as one of its chief contributions. The development of modern linguistics during the past thirty-five years permits the analysis of the problems that students have in learning a foreign language with an accuracy and precision that can result in vastly improved testing instruments and programs.

The theory of language testing evolved from the experience that led to this book is discussed in Part I. Specific techniques for testing the "elements of language," namely pronunciation, intonation, stress, grammatical structure, and vocabulary, appear in Part II. Part III presents the testing of auditory comprehension, reading, writing, speaking, and translation, which are labeled "integrated language skills." Part IV, "Beyond Language," discusses possible ways of testing cross-cultural understanding and other higher values. The last part deals with the refining and use of language tests. This part includes norms, validity, reliability, item analysis, equivalent forms, designing experiments, and diagnostic, achievement, and aptitude testing.

The material is primarily intended for teachers of foreign languages and of English as a foreign language. Test makers will be interested in its linguistic content and point of view. Prospective language teachers will gain valuable insights from its perusal, and scholars interested in research and experiments on teaching and learning language will want to read it. Linguists who are not acquainted with modern testing can use the book as an introduction to the field as it concerns foreign languages. The author hopes that teachers and graduate students will be encouraged to conduct language learning experiments and to report them in the professional journals so that increasingly we may speak on the basis of knowledge rather than from opinion and hypotheses alone, valuable as these are at proper stages in the development of man's thought.

The style has been kept as non-technical and as simple as possible because of the variety of backgrounds of the intended readers. Linguistic terminology is not always familiar to the average teacher and test maker; and testing terminology is not often familiar to language teachers and linguists. The chapters will vary in difficulty, but they can be read with understanding by the average reader for whom it is intended.

We are indebted to the following for permission to quote copyright material:

Professor J. B. Carroll for material from *Construction and Validation of a Test Battery for Predicting Success in Spoken Language Courses* by J. B. Carroll, S. M. Sapon and S. E. Richards (Report No. 1, 1954—The Harvard Language Aptitude Project); Ginn and Company, Boston, for material from *An Investigation of Second-Language Teaching* by F. B. Agard and H. B. Dunkel; and Mr. Leo Rosten for material from *The Education of Hyman Kaplan* by Leonard Q. Ross, published by Constable and Co. Ltd. and Harcourt, Brace and World Inc., copyright 1937.

June, 1959

This is the American edition of *Language Testing* which was first published in 1961 by Longmans, Green and Co Ltd of London. The book, in spite of the usual restrictions of foreign publication, awakened strong interest in the United States, so it was the decision of the McGraw-Hill Book Company to make an edition readily available to the American public as a companion volume to *Language Teaching: A Scientific Approach* by the same author.

This is the complete text of the London edition of *Language Testing* without abridgment or change. It is sincerely hoped that this edition will be as well received in the United States as was the London edition in other parts of the world.

Washington, D.C.

1964   ROBERT LADO

CONTENTS

Part I

GENERAL INTRODUCTION AND THEORY
OF FOREIGN LANGUAGE TESTING

A*   ix

CONTENTS

Part II

TESTING THE ELEMENTS OF LANGUAGE

Part III

TESTING THE INTEGRATED SKILLS

Part IV

BEYOND LANGUAGE

Part V

REFINING AND USING FOREIGN LANGUAGE TESTS

CONTENTS

GENERAL INTRODUCTION AND THEORY OF FOREIGN LANGUAGE TESTING

Chapter 1

LANGUAGE

1.1 INTERNATIONAL COMMUNICATION AND THE STUDY OF LANGUAGES

The great advances in transportation and communication made by man have brought home to all but the most isolated of men the value of world languages for international communication. They have also shown the value of local languages for effective communication with the native speakers of these languages.

In previous centuries it was reasonable and proper to study languages exclusively for the purpose of reading their literatures. The jet airliner that spans the oceans in a matter of hours and flies regularly over the North Pole, radio, television, and the telephone, and safer and more comfortable ships, trains and automobiles have multiplied travel and international communication a thousandfold and have made the study of languages for basic communication with native speakers a mark of the twentieth century.

The speed and frequency of international communication have outstripped the speed of teaching and learning languages and demand more effective methods of teaching. The systematic investigation of science is needed to advance the teaching of languages.

With the need for more effective teaching of languages goes the need for more effective testing of their use. Language testing also requires the advances and methods of science to meet present and future demands. This book is a comprehensive discussion of foreign language testing, bringing together modern experience and scientific knowledge.

1.2 LANGUAGE AS A SYSTEM OF COMMUNICATION

Since language is so ever present in human activity and thinking and since it flows so easily from the tongue of native speakers, it is possible on one hand to oversimplify it in our thinking and in our plans to study it. Thus we often hear people who, upon meeting a native speaker of a different language, naively ask to be taught that language and wait right then for the process to begin. For the same reason we see people buying books that promise to teach a language with great ease even without a teacher.

Language is more than the apparently simple stream of sound that flows from the tongue of the native speaker; it is more than the native speaker thinks it is. It is a complex system of communication with various levels of complexity involving intricate selection and ordering of meanings, sounds, and larger units and arrangements.

On the other hand, in spite of the fact that language uses the same sound waves as the noise that the physicist studies, and writing the same ink and paper that can be studied as chemical substances, these chemical and physical properties of the substance in which language is cast are not human language strictly speaking, and it is confusing to think of them as part of language. Their study often helps us understand language and thus they are of interest to the student of linguistics, but they are not language.

Language has been defined in various ways by linguists and others. Rather than attempting a full definition here, we will identify language by pointing out some of its most distinctive features. Language is primarily an instrument of communication among human beings in a community. A community that speaks the same language is a *speech community*. Languages differ from each other in such ways that the members of one

2

speech community usually do not understand the speakers of other speech communities. The fact that languages differ from each other is accepted as a normal state of affairs, and when the speakers of one community wish to communicate with those of another they usually study their language or find someone who knows it.

Certain uses of language are felt to be aesthetically more satisfying than others and are called literature in a strict sense. These artistic uses of language are not independent of the ordinary uses of language for basic communication; they are related aesthetically to them.

Language in its most common, pervasive, representative and apparently central manifestation involves oral-aural communication. We therefore say that language consists of oral-aural symbols of communication, arbitrary in their association to particular meanings and units and arbitrary in their particular shape for a given language.

Language as an instrument of communication among the members of a speech community who are also members of the same culture is best suited to convey the meanings current in that particular culture. These *cultural meanings* are roughly uniform for the members of the community and are thus readily conveyed and understood. Beyond these cultural meanings are *individual meanings* not readily communicated through standard forms of a language. Individual meanings require explanations, metaphors, analogies, and other indirect approaches if they are to be communicated through language. Some meanings and features of meaning become so frequent in their use in language or so attached to language distinctions that they can be described in terms of a language without recourse to full cultural reference. These can be called *linguistic meanings*.

Linguistic, cultural, and individual meanings are independent of the facts that science discovers or proves. They are in a sense facts in their own right, to be studied by science as such.

Languages are often represented by various systems of writing. Certain aspects of these systems of writing can be studied somewhat independently of the languages they represent, but their essential features are relevant insofar as they relate to a language.

Languages which are no longer spoken have to be studied through written records left to us, but the written records do not in themselves constitute the central part of language.

The study of language is necessary for the effective study of literature. The study of language, on the other hand, can proceed without the study of literature until it reaches the level of the study of artistic creation in a language.

1.3 THE MOST COMPLEX OF MAN'S TOOLS

When we use language even in an ordinary conversation we are wielding a most complicated tool with amazing dexterity and ease. We keep track of the general thread of our conversation, select whether to say something, ask something, tell our listener to do something, admire something; we choose the particular words to fit the situation, the listener, the type of sentence; we give proper endings to the words, place them in the proper place in the sentence; we connect each sentence and part of sentence with what has gone on before; within each word we select the proper sounds and order them in the proper sequence; we place the stress where it belongs; we modulate the tone of what we say to make the sense we intend, and we add variations to our voice to show our changing mood and attitude. We do all this while considering the effect of what we say upon our listener. In trying to please, or to attack, we think ahead to support what we want to prove or to counter what we do not approve. And this is done at the rate of several hundred movements of the articulators per minute.

Man as we know him is incapable of performing the complex operation of language at its normal speed without reducing most of it to habit. Habit carries most of the operation of the complex mechanism of language, leaving our attention free to dwell on the message and the attitudes of speaker and listener. The lowly power of habit is the support of the distinctively human gift of language. We can in this sense speak of language as a conventionalized, highly complex system of habits which functions as a human instrument of communication.

4

1.4 LANGUAGE, CULTURE, AND THE INDIVIDUAL

When an individual communicates with another in a common language he emits certain sounds (or writes certain symbols) that in particular distributions have particular meanings some of which he intends to convey to his listener and others that go along through the habit patterns imposed by the language. The sounds and their arrangement and the units which they constitute we call *form*; the permitted environments in which each form appears constitute its *distribution*; and the meanings, intended and habitual, are the *meaning*. When the listener who speaks the same language hears these forms in this distribution he grasps the same linguistic meanings encoded by the speaker in his utterance.

If these two individuals are of the same culture, the cultural meanings that each will encode in language for communication will usually be those which are common to other members of the cultural community. The listener thus grasps from the linguistic utterance the cultural meanings encoded in it by the speaker.

Beyond the culturally bound meanings of language each person perceives meanings which are his own through the particular life experience that is his. The ordinary forms of a language and the ordinary meanings of a culture do not accommodate these individual meanings. If the word *dog* has a pleasant connotation for one who remembers a dog he had as a boy, when he uses this word in a message for one who remembers dogs as animals that frightened him or injured him, the individual meaning of the speaker will not be transmitted to the listener, who will on the contrary add his unpleasant individual meaning to the linguistic and cultural meaning of *dog*.

Figure 1.1 is intended to show these elements in a schematic way. Individual meaning is outside of the system of language and outside of the coverage of this book. Cultural meaning is part of language. Since cultural meanings, however, have not been fully described in any culture we will usually have to be content with minimal features of cultural meaning of wide currency in a particular culture. Linguistic meaning is part of

5

language, for without linguistic meaning there is no language. The description of linguistic meaning has received much attention in dictionaries and grammars. Much of it remains vaguely described, yet we will have to deal with it if we are to test language in operation.

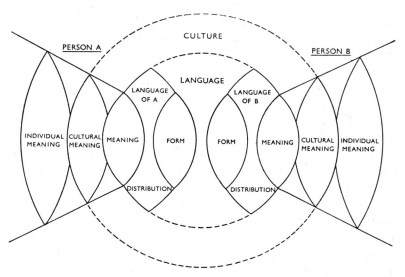

Fig. 1.1. Language, Culture, and the Individual

1.5   THE STRUCTURE OF LANGUAGE

To study language we usually begin with *utterances*. An utterance is a stretch of talk by one speaker beginning after silence and ending with silence. Obviously, an utterance thus defined can be as short as a single word or as long as a speech. For our present purposes in understanding language this is satisfactory.

Utterances can transmit an almost infinite number of meanings and combinations of meanings, yet all the meanings conveyed through language in any utterance are transmitted through a limited number of different sounds (or written symbols). The minimum sound unit that can change one utterance into another in a language is called in linguistics a *phoneme*. Phonemes are therefore units of sound, not letters, although in alphabetic writing a letter sometimes represents a phoneme.

6

We have thus far pointed out the largest unit of language that we need to deal with, the utterance, and the smallest unit of language that we need to handle at this stage, the phoneme. Between these two extremes lies the whole range and hierarchy of language units and their patterns of arrangement.

Phonemes have no specific meaning. They identify particular utterances which have meaning. The smallest language unit that has specific meaning is the *morpheme*. The word *cap* is a morpheme since it cannot be made smaller and keep any part of its meaning. The prefix *un-* in *uncap* is a morpheme since it has a meaning and cannot be cut any further in this word without losing its identity and meaning. The plural ending *-s* of *caps* is also a morpheme. A free morpheme, that is a morpheme that operates in certain positions as part of phrases and sentences and not exclusively as part of other words, is a *word*. Some words are made up of a single morpheme, for example *cap*. Others are made of two or more morphemes, for example *uncap*, *caps*. Some words are made up of two free morphemes, that is, of two words; these are *compounds*.

Groups of words that operate as a single structure but not normally as free utterances that initiate conversations are *phrases*. Groups of words that occur freely as complete utterances and are not made up of more than one normal free group of words are *sentences*. Sentences that occur as part of other sentences are *clauses*.

Phrases that cannot be made smaller without losing their structural identity or permitted shape are minimal phrases. Minimal phrases are enlarged by *modification structures*. Modification structures are phrasal structures in which one word functions as *head* and others as *modifiers*. The head of a phrase has the same structural function as the total phrase in a particular sentence structure.

In many languages there are also phonemes of pitch. These are features of pitch that serve to identify particular words and utterances and to distinguish them from others. When these phonemes of pitch occur as part of words only, they are called *tonemes* or *tones*. When pitch phonemes occur as part of phrases and sentences they are called *intonation phonemes* and the

7

meaningful sequences of pitch phonemes are *intonation phrases*, *contours*, or simply *intonations*.

1.6 EACH LANGUAGE IS A STRUCTURALLY DIFFERENT SYSTEM

1. Unity in the variety of the languages of the world. When we compare a large number of languages from the point of view of their structure and organization we see that the baffling variety of the languages of mankind shows remarkable similarities. Even when we compare the languages of primitive peoples still in the Stone Age with the languages of highly developed civilizations we observe striking correspondences within their variety. They all have phonemes, morphemes, words, sentences and certain sentence types, certain parts of speech, sequences, meanings, etc. Where we least expect it a pattern may turn out to be signaled the same way in Chinese and English, or in Japanese and Finnish, or in Korean and Spanish.

2. The differences are not merely a matter of words or variations of form. Perhaps because we sense the common basis of language within the diversity of languages we tend to assume erroneously that the differences are merely a matter of different words for the same meanings, different sounds for the same units of sound, and a few formal variations for the same grammatical units.

Even when words are borrowed from one language into another they are no longer the same words. They will not be used in the same situations. They will be subject to restrictions and limitations of use in one language that are different from those of the other. Similarly, the sounds of one language are not merely different physical sounds but represent different signaling units of sound. Even when a sound is borrowed from one language into another, it becomes a different unit or part of a unit with different restrictions of use and coverage. And the same is true of the grammatical constructions of different languages.

3. Each language is a structurally different system of communication. Within the common characteristics and striking correspondences among languages, each language is a unique system of communication, self-contained within its own

8

structure. Sounds, words, sentences are meaningful within this frame of each language structure and system.

Because of this uniqueness of each language system within the common basis of human language it is possible to observe that two closely related languages such as Spanish and Portuguese, for example, have very different vowel systems, while two unrelated languages such as Spanish and Japanese have strikingly similar vowel systems.

The vowel units of English, Japanese, and Spanish will serve to demonstrate the fact that languages differ not only as to the shape of the sounds but actually as to the contrasting units used to identify words.

English: / iy i ey e æ ə a ɔ ow u uw /
Japanese: / i   e   a   o   u /
Spanish: / i (ei)e   a   o(ou) u /
( ) indicates a diphthong.

The remarkable similarity in the system of vowel units of Japanese and Spanish is diminished but not eliminated by the fact that Japanese has what amounts to long and short vowels in contrast, while Spanish does not. Differences in the physical shape of the vowel units are not discussed here because they are readily admitted. What is invariably overlooked by the layman is the fact that each language has different vowel units or phonemes and that all utterances in a language are built upon the vowel units of the particular language.

Each language uses only a limited number of the possible arrangements of its phonemes, morphemes, words, etc., and no two languages use exactly the same set of possible arrangements. Thus English uses such sequences as /st- sp- sk-/ as in *student, Spanish, school,* in word initial position, but Spanish does not use them in this position. In Spanish such sequences must be preceded by a vowel as in *estudiante, español, escuela.*

Similarly, each language uses its own patterns of arrangement and form for its grammatical meanings. Thus English uses a word order arrangement with or without a function word and intonation to signal many of its questions while Spanish uses intonation chiefly, and Japanese uses a function word primarily.

Thus also, Japanese and English use a word order signal in many modification structures while Spanish uses agreement of forms and part of speech signals for its modification structures. And Japanese and English, although using word order primarily, use a different word order in many cases.

Each language, then, is a system of communication in which the sounds, words, arrangements, etc. are meaningful under the particular conditions of the system which is known functionally through experience by the speakers of the language.

1.7 SELECTED REFERENCES

There are excellent books dealing comprehensively with language and linguistics. *A Course in Modern Linguistics* by Hockett is recent, comprehensive and readable. It is used as a textbook. *An Introduction to Descriptive Linguistics* by Gleason is also used as a standard textbook. Bloomfield's *Language* is a classic. For many years it was the standard text in basic linguistics courses. Some of its chapters are now dated. It is considered difficult reading. Sapir's *Language* is of earlier date but remains thoroughly readable and full of valuable insights into human language. It can be read quickly by the uninitiated as an introduction to more complex treatments.

1. Bloomfield, Leonard. *Language* (New York: Henry Holt and Company, 1933).

2. Gleason, Henry A., Jr. *An Introduction to Descriptive Linguistics* (New York: Henry Holt and Company, 1955).

3. Hockett, Charles F. *A Course in Modern Linguistics* (New York: The Macmillan Company, 1958).

4. Sapir, Edward. *Language*: An Introduction to the Study of Speech (New York: Harcourt, Brace and Company, 1921).

Chapter 2

LANGUAGE LEARNING

2.1   LEARNING THE NATIVE LANGUAGE

Much remains to be known about how we learn our native language. Detailed studies of individual children report when particular sounds were first uttered and when particular words were first understood and used. In general these studies are limited by their view of language as isolated words and sounds without relation to the total system of contrasts that is a language. Studies which take into account the relevant structure of language are few.[1]

Before the child learns specific words he uses noise with a rudimentary system of intonation and loudness. He uses utterances of a sort which show certain differentiation akin to the intonation of the language of his parents. His use of intonation seems to develop ahead of other elements and units of language for several years, and young children are as a rule able to use effective intonation patterns at a complex level of the intonation system before they have mastered many words or the entire stock of the segmental phonemes of the language.

The intonation utterances become differentiated in single words so that the child produces communicative utterances that consist of a single word in an intonation contour. These intonation-word utterances have a very vague and general meaning. If a child says, "Mama," it might mean, 'I am sleepy; put me to bed,' 'I am hungry,' 'I am tired,' 'Where are you?' or anything else that he is used to having mother solve for him (if we can be this specific about the thoughts and feelings of a child). If a

---

[1] Werner F. Leopold, *Bibliography of Child Language* (Evanston, Illinois: Northwestern University Press, 1952) is a comprehensive list with annotations by an author who has also published studies of his bilingual children.

child says "Bread," again it might mean, 'I am hungry; I want some bread,' 'Look at that piece of bread,' 'I want a big piece of bread,' 'Sister has a piece of bread and you didn't give me any,' or anything else connected with bread and the thoughts and feelings of a child.

As long as the child learns a word like *mama* and another like *bread* which have no common phonemes it is doubtful that he has learned phonemes. When he learns to say and distinguish *mama* and *papa* he approaches the use of phonemes although even in this case the contrast is not in one element only. Not until he uses minimally contrasting words such as *two* and *do* can he strictly be said to have learned phonemes. Even then the number of phonemes used by the child is smaller than that of the full language, and he will use variations of his phonemes which actually constitute different phonemes in the language. The child does not add phonemes individually to his stock but adds classes of phonemes; for example he may learn velar /g/ and /k/ at about the same time.

Progress comes not merely in the addition of new words but in the use of groups of words and sentence-like utterances. He may use a sentence like "Don't do that," or "Stop that," before he actually differentiates the elements of these sentences.

Major progress comes in the form of pattern learning, that is, learning sentence and word patterns which permit him to build new sentences by analogy. This takes place before he can analyze and differentiate the elements of the sentences he uses. Pattern and analogy come to his aid early and are powerful elements in language learning.

A major problem in learning is the matter of the boundaries and restrictions of the forms, patterns, and meanings he learns. He has an uncanny talent to imitate new sounds and new words, and he has an uncanny memory to remember new words, which he often enjoys using. But he has a great deal of trouble knowing how far these patterns and these meanings can go. As adults we forget this process of learning and wrongly assume that once we have told somebody that the yellow disc of the moon is called *moon* he will know when to use *moon* without hesitation. A child may use *moon* for both the moon and a flashlight, which seems similar enough to the moon. A child pointing to a drawer in a dresser may ask, "What is this?" When he is told that it is a drawer, he may point to another drawer in the same dresser and ask "Is this a drawer?" Then he may point to a third drawer, to the drawers of a desk, and to a trunk, asking, "Is this a drawer?" This he does as a sort of game, but in the process he is finding out how far this word *drawer* can go.

This problem of distribution is observed when a child who otherwise speaks well invents a regular preterite where there is none and says, "I *knowed* it." He learns the regular preterite of most verbs and quite unaware of a limitation attaches it to *know* which the memory of the speech community has kept as *knew*. We do not notice the many cases in which he has by analogy created a preterite that is all right.

When he has learned to build new sentences using the patterns of the constructions of the language, the phonemes, and higher units, within a limited vocabulary, he has learned the language. The more elaborate and artistic variations are learned later. The top level of achievement in these dimensions is not a matter of general culture but depends chiefly on individual talent and training.

2.2   LEARNING A FOREIGN LANGUAGE

1. Habit. We observed that the complex process of communication through language as we know it is made possible by the system of habits which operates largely without our awareness. These habits are deeply set in the nervous system of the individual and in his muscular, intellectual, and emotional processes. To change any part of this system of habits is a major undertaking. To set up a parallel system in learning a foreign language is an equally formidable task.

If we consider the diagram of Figure 1.1 we can see that the rapid-fire movements of the tongue in the process of speech have behind them the distribution of the units of speech in the language, the linguistic meanings, and the cultural and individual meanings. When a speaker says something to a listener he puts together some cultural sequence of meanings through linguistic meanings and on to the sentences, phrases, words, morphemes,

13

and phonemes. He does this mostly without thought, and a listener of the same language reacts to it with the same speed and equally without awareness of the process.

2. Transfer. If we now place two speakers of different languages facing each other in a similar diagram, when the listener hears an utterance in a foreign language he is learning, his set of native language habits cannot be eliminated at will, and he hears units of sound, words, phrases and sentences that are those of his own language; that is, he distorts what he hears to fit the rapid-fire perceptions that he habitually hears. Similarly when he attempts to speak in the foreign language he thinks of the general meaning, the general thread of what he wants to say, but the encoding into language units down to words and phonemes he handles the only way he has ever been able to handle them: through the habits of his native language.

The result, of course, is that he transfers the entire sound system of his native language to the foreign language both for speaking and for listening. That is, he transfers the phonemes, their distribution, the patterns of syllables, of words, the patterns of sentences, the meanings. When his attention is called to what in the foreign language constitutes an error, he has no easy way to understand the error; he is not aware of what he has done, and he may not even perceive it.

2.3 A FEW EMPIRICAL OBSERVATIONS AND THEIR POSSIBLE SIGNIFICANCE

1. Experience shows that when the native language has one phoneme in a phonetic area in which the foreign language has two, the learner finds major difficulty learning to pronounce the two phonemes of the foreign language; and what is less well known, he has difficulty hearing the difference even when his hearing is quite normal. This fact can easily be demonstrated by experiment. List ten short words containing either the vowel /iy/ as in *eat* or /i/ as in *it*. Read them aloud to a group of speakers of Spanish, Japanese, Portuguese, or any other language that does not have a phonemic contrast in this phonetic area. Ask them to write number 1 if they hear /iy/ and number 2 if they hear /i/. Then tell them to correct their papers by giving them the right answers yourself. Native speakers of English in the room will score either ten or nine correct out of the ten words. They will wonder why you give such a simple test. The speakers of Spanish, Japanese, etc. will score eight, seven, six, or even less depending on how long and how well they have studied English. Fairly advanced students of English as a foreign language will miss two or three out of the ten items. Even teachers of English who have studied the language for many years will often miss some items. This is proof of the existence of the problem and dramatic demonstration of the unbelievable persistence of the native language habit pattern.

The fact that by comparing the linguistic structures of the native and the foreign languages we can predict the learning problems of our students seems to prove that the assumption of transfer of the native language habit patterns is at least substantially correct.

2. When the foreign language has two phonemes such as English /d/ and /ð/ as in *day* and *they* which are phonetically similar and when these two sounds exist in the native language not as separate phonemes but as variants of only one phoneme (Spanish /d/ has a stop variant initially before vowels and a fricative variant resembling English /ð/ between vowels), the student has very great difficulty pronouncing the distinction and hearing it. He pronounces the variant of his one phoneme that fits the phonetic environment in each case, but he cannot pronounce the other variant, which would operate as the other phoneme. He hears only one phoneme regardless of the distinction made in the foreign language.[1]

3. When the foreign language has a phoneme which is not structurally equivalent to any phoneme in the native language and which is not phonetically similar to any other phoneme in the native language there is a learning problem of less persistence than those reported above. Finnish has fewer consonants than English. Consequently Finnish speakers have difficulty learning those English consonants which do not exist in their native language, but they have less difficulty with these than

[1] See *Linguistics Across Cultures* by Robert Lado for a more detailed description.

with other sounds which are phonetically more similar to those of Finnish.

4. In general when the native language of the student has more phonemic distinctions in a phonetic area than the foreign language, he finds little difficulty adjusting to the simpler phonemic pattern. Even when the phonemic distinctions of the native language are transferred to the foreign language they do not produce phonemic problems but merely distortions that give their speech a foreign flavor but not different linguistic meaning.

5. In general when the student goes from a simpler phonemic system to a more complex one he has difficulty producing and hearing the distinctions that constitute greater complexity.

6. In matters of significant items of word order, function words, and correlation of forms the student will transfer the form of his native language with its meaning to the foreign language. For example, if the native language of the student indicates a modifier by position after the head in a modification structure, and the foreign language indicates this type of modifier by a position before the head, the student will have persistent difficulty placing the modifier before the head; time and again he will place the modifier after the head as he does habitually in his native language. In listening and reading he will take as head what is modifier and as modifier what is head. If he is a Spanish speaker he may understand *milk chocolate* to be a kind of milk and *chocolate milk* to be a kind of chocolate, instead of the opposite, which is their sense in English.

7. When a linguistic meaning such as the relation of modifier to head is signaled one way under certain conditions and a different way under other conditions, and when the native language of the student has only one way to signal this type of linguistic meaning, the student will have great difficulty using the proper form. In English, for example, some modifiers precede the head, others follow it. In Japanese most modifiers precede the head, even phrasal modifiers whose counterpart in English would necessarily follow the head. Consequently, Japanese speakers learning English will tend to put all modifiers before the head.

16

8. General observation. Similar observations could be stated in the form of rules or laws about intonation, stress, sentence patterns and the other units and patterns of linguistic structure. All of these can be summed up in the general observation that where the native language of the student and the foreign language differ structurally there is a learning problem and the nature and description of this problem depend on the comparison of the two language structures. When the transfer of the native habit system produces distortions in the foreign language which can produce differences in meaning, there is a serious learning problem.

On the other hand, where the two languages do not differ structurally, that is, where the transfer from the native language will function as the foreign language structure with native speakers of the foreign language, there is no particular learning problem.

9. Corollary. Learning the problems, that is, the structural matters that differ between the two languages, is learning the foreign language. The non-problems will be picked up by simply being exposed to these patterns in the foreign language. Actually they are transferred from the native language and since they function satisfactorily they do not have to be learned anew.

2.4   HOW WE LEARN A FOREIGN LANGUAGE

Although we have made considerable progress in the linguistic understanding of problems in learning a foreign language, we know very little of the psychology (emotional, memory, process, order) of learning. Teaching methods have been largely the collected practice and teaching habits of particular teachers who reacted to the memory of their own experience in learning, the example of their own teachers, and the fashion which seemed prevalent or attractive at a particular moment in the history of language teaching. It would be interesting and profitable to analyze the psychology of language learning underlying each of the more widely known methods, regardless of whether or not its author ever consciously worked out the psychology of language learning underlying his views.

In the grammar-translation method, for example, the assumption is that the student learns by memorizing rules of correct grammar and by translating from one language to the other. This learning assumption is woefully incomplete; that is, it says nothing specifically about how the student learns anything in particular.

Regardless of method, we need to know the elements to be learned, the order in which they are learned, and other matters of importance.

1. Elements. Among the general elements to be learned there is the linguistic form to be produced and heard, to be remembered, and to be established as a habit at the speed of speech for production and recognition in whatever environments it fits and in which it is permitted. There is also the meaning to be grasped, limited, remembered, and established as a habit at normal speaking delivery and/or effective reading speed.

2. Order of learning. Sometimes the student learns a form —a word or a construction—before learning its meaning. Later, coming in contact with the same form in a situation which makes sense to him or completes the partial sense which he could not accept previously, he discovers that finally he knows what this form means. In general this is a case in which the student already knows the meaning as part of his experience, and the final clarification is only a matter of associating this form with the meaning he already knows. In other instances he remembers a meaning but cannot recall the form that conveys it.

There is a stage in which he can encode meanings by consciously putting together the various elements and units that constitute the utterance. At this stage he speaks haltingly, with long pauses at places where normally there should be none. When reading, he slowly puts together each word, phrase, clause, and sentence by parts. For many students of foreign language this stage is the highest ever attained. Not coming in contact with native speakers of the foreign language they and their teachers are apt to feel that this slow, halting process is in fact knowing the foreign language. Sometimes those who do discover that knowing the language means a much faster and smoother delivery and perception are nevertheless not able to attain this stage of mastery because teaching methods often stop before it. Practice that forces the student to produce and understand the language at normal speed is necessary at this stage.

3. Age. Adults and older people have the problem of transfer of the habits of the native language more severely than younger people. Adults and older people have maximum difficulty in hearing the sounds of the foreign language and in producing them. They have maximum difficulty in remembering the sounds they finally learn to hear and to produce, and they have the same difficulty establishing the new sounds as habits of speech. To such learners the use of written symbols for clarification and as an aid to their memory seems to be a definite help.

Younger people, as young as three and four years old, have great facility imitating foreign sounds and remembering them. The three- and four-year-olds have no use for written symbols as an aid to pronunciation. Elementary school children learning a foreign language could learn its pronunciation without recourse to writing. Teaching them the writing system of the foreign language is an end in itself and not an aid to speaking. High school children are at a transition stage in which limited use of special symbols can be an assistance.

2.5 **SELECTED REFERENCES**

There are many books treating the teaching of foreign languages. For the purpose of understanding foreign language learning a very helpful book is *Teaching and Learning English as a Foreign Language* by Fries. For the analysis of the linguistic problems of learning a foreign language there is *Linguistics Across Cultures* by Lado.

1. Fries, Charles C. *Teaching and Learning English as a Foreign Language* (Ann Arbor: University of Michigan Press, 1945).

2. Lado, Robert. *Linguistics Across Cultures* (Ann Arbor: University of Michigan Press, 1957).

Chapter 3

LANGUAGE TESTING

3.1   RELATION OF LANGUAGE TESTING TO LANGUAGE LEARNING

The same basic understanding of the facts of language learning applies to language testing. What the student has to learn constitutes the corpus of what we have to test. Since the student has to learn language, it is language that we must test.

There are some differences in strategy between language learning and language testing that will be taken up in the chapter that follows. There is also a difference in economy that we will mention now. Testing time is precious time. We must test in one hour what has been learned in a month or a year or five years.

As the content of a test we can and usually must select a sample of the things that have to be learned. The sample should ordinarily be randomly selected. Since some things are easy to master because they are already known from previous language training in mastering the native language, we will generally eliminate these from the corpus. We will attempt to test the learning problems, on the grounds that knowing the problems is knowing the language. We say specifically that testing the problems is testing the language.

3.2   TESTING THE NATIVE LANGUAGE

In learning the native language the basic patterns of sound, of word formation, of sentence construction are learned by all the speakers unless they have a particular speech defect or other impediment. We can test these basic elements at various ages to see if a child is developing normally in his use of the language. But beyond this growth that goes with age, the central core of language is learned by all native speakers and therefore need not be tested merely to discover mastery.

1. Problems. The problems to be tested with native speakers are those resulting from dialect differences, faulty logic, inadequate vocabulary, writing skill and style. These problems are marginal to the central core structure of a language.

2. Dialect differences. Languages normally evolve differences from one region to another and from one social class to another. The forms of language become associated with the region where they are used and with the social class which uses them. Thus if a person uses a form which is heard characteristically in a certain region, we assume that he is from that region or was educated in that region. Similarly, when we hear a language form that is characteristic of a certain social class we assume that the speaker is of this social class or was educated in it. Furthermore, whatever social attitudes there may be toward that social class or region will be applied to the speakers of those dialects.

Consequently language learning in the native language has often been a matter of learning the forms of a dialect that enjoys social prestige at a particular time and place. Language testing in the native language therefore often consists of testing the student on the forms that are characteristic of the dialect that has social prestige and is considered "correct" and standard. These forms are usually a reduced number of items that have acquired notoriety. Since these are matters of habit, they can be tested over and over again.

Unfortunately a good portion of these items that are considered correct are artificial forms not used in everyday educated speech, and the forms that are condemned as incorrect are often perfectly current forms. In any case, these tests deal with marginal problems of usage.

3. Faulty logic. Inconsistencies in logical sequence are a mark of underdeveloped language use, yet these may be more a matter of intelligence or the lack of it than of language mastery.

4. Lack of vocabulary. Range of vocabulary is related to intelligence, and beyond the basic vocabulary common to children of a particular age is more an indicator of superior intelligence than of language mastery.

5. Writing. Since writing is not one of the parts of language and culture that is learned by all members of the culture but must be taught as a separate skill, one finds all stages of mastery in writing the native language. Hence it is possible to test central as well as marginal elements of writing in the native language. As we will see below, however, even these central elements in learning to write the native language will usually be different from those that trouble the student who is learning to write a foreign language.

6. Style. Whether or not a language form which is otherwise correct, is appropriate and aesthetically elegant for a particular situation is a matter of style. Since the structural part of language is soon mastered by native speakers, the area of style looms large in any advanced test for native speakers. When dealing with composition, often we are concerned heavily with matters of style. In a foreign language, style will remain a marginal problem in most cases since there will be more central problems to be tested even at advanced stages of mastery.

3.3 THEORY OF FOREIGN LANGUAGE TESTING

The theory of foreign language testing is based on present linguistic understanding of language and on observations concerning the role of habit in learning a foreign language. This theory is congruent with psychological knowledge and thinking but constitutes an organization of the problem that is not found in psychology textbooks at present.

1. Theory. The theory of language testing assumes that language is a system of habits of communication. These habits permit the communicant to give his conscious attention to the over-all meaning he is conveying or perceiving. These habits involve matters of form, meaning, and distribution at several levels of structure, namely those of the sentence, clause, phrase, word, morpheme, and phoneme. Within these levels are structures of modification, sequence, parts of sentences. Below them are habits of articulation, syllable type, and collocations. Associated with them and sometimes as part of them are patterns of intonation, stress and rhythm.

The theory assumes that linguistic and cultural meanings communicated through languages are also structured and associated to the formal elements specifically stated above.

When the communicant speaks his native language he goes from individual stimulation and meanings which are not part of the units of language to cultural and linguistic meanings that are. He encodes these cultural and linguistic meanings in the forms that are associated to them in the language. When these forms are uttered, the listener perceives them and through them he grasps the same linguistic and cultural meanings that the communicant encoded. The individual meanings the listener grasps in addition are not part of the language. (See Figure 1.1.)

The individual is not aware that so much of what he does in using language is done through a complex system of habits. When he attempts to communicate in a foreign language that he knows partially, he adopts the same linguistic posture as when using his native language. He thinks of the over-all meaning and proceeds to encode it in the linguistic forms of the foreign language. He may concentrate consciously in addition on one or another matter of grammar or pronunciation or vocabulary, but the bulk of the encoding goes to his habit system and here it is channeled through the system of habits of his native language. This in psychology is known as transfer. He transfers the habit system of his native language to the foreign tongue.

When this transfer occurs, he produces the sounds of his native language and the sentence patterns of his native language, in short the entire structure of his native language in the foreign one, except those few units and elements he is able to keep under conscious control and those he has mastered to the point of habit. If his attention is brought to something he has missed and already knows at the conscious level, he will correct himself but may miss something else instead. Several repetitions may produce enough immediate memory to result in satisfactory production, but when the same problem is met elsewhere it may be missed again.

When this transfer occurs, some of the units and patterns transferred will function satisfactorily in the foreign language and will not constitute a learning problem. Other units and patterns will not function satisfactorily in the foreign language. Against these the student will have to learn the new units and patterns. These constitute the real learning problems.

These learning problems turn out to be matters of form, meaning, distribution, or a combination of these. They can be predicted and described in most cases by a systematic linguistic comparison of the two language structures. Where several elements of the native language structure are factors, it is sometimes difficult to predict exactly what the problem is going to be. In such cases a special exploratory test or set of interviews can answer the question.

In listening to or reading the foreign language the same transfer takes place, only the sequence is reversed as the listener is exposed to the forms first, which he interprets through his native language units to the meanings of his own language and culture, except for those which he can keep in his conscious attention or which he has already mastered as a linguistic habit.

The theory assumes that testing control of the problems is testing control of the language. Problems are those units and patterns that do not have a counterpart in the native language or that have counterparts with structurally different distribution or meaning.

The problems in speaking are not necessarily the same as the problems in listening. For example, the question, " Does he speak? " is often a problem in speaking for some foreign students because they add an " s " ending to *speak* and say, " Does he speaks? " In listening, this is not a problem because the correct ending is given by the native speaker and it does not confuse the student.

The theory assumes also that the student does not know these units and patterns that are problems unless he can use them at normal conversational or reading speed in linguistically valid situations, that is, situations that parallel those of language in use. Definitions, for example, are not valid linguistic situations because native speakers are able to use forms and structures that they cannot define, and other speakers are able to define structures that they cannot use. Stating grammatical rules is not a valid linguistic situation. Lists of words are not in themselves valid situations.

Chapter 4

VARIABLES AND STRATEGY OF LANGUAGE TESTING

4.1   VARIABLES

1. The elements. The matter to be tested is language. Language is built of sounds, intonation, stress, morphemes, words, and arrangements of words having meanings that are linguistic and cultural. The degree of mastery of these elements does not advance evenly but goes faster in some and slower in others. Each of these elements of language constitutes a variable that we will want to test. They are pronunciation, grammatical structure, the lexicon, and cultural meanings. The first of these, pronunciation, is itself made up of three separate elements, namely sound segments, intonation and its borders, and stress and its sequences which constitute the rhythm of a language.

Within grammatical structure there are two main subdivisions, namely morphology and syntax. Syntax will be given priority in testing. Morphology will be treated as much as possible in connection with syntax.

The testing of the lexicon and of cultural meanings will be treated as separate variables although they are closely related.

2. The skills. The elements of language discussed can be profitably studied and described—and tested—as separate universes, yet they never occur separately in language. They are integrated in the total skills of speaking, listening, reading, and writing. That is, granted that a person's pronunciation may be ahead or behind his knowledge of vocabulary, when he speaks we can lump both together in stating what his ability to speak the foreign language is. There are then these four skills, the mastery of which does not advance evenly. We have thus four more variables to be tested, namely the degree of achievement in

25

speaking, understanding, reading and writing. A fifth skill is the ability to translate, which should be tested as an end in itself and not as a way to test mastery of the language. Each of these additional five skills will be treated in separate chapters.

4.2 STRATEGY IN FOREIGN LANGUAGE TESTING

1. **Situation versus language.** If there were a high uniformity in the occurrence and use of the various variables and units of language we could simplify the testing of a foreign language a great deal. We could take any situation and engage the student in speaking, listening, reading, and writing and could give him an achievement score that would be the same if we chose a different situation, a longer topic, etc. This is not the case, however.

The situations in which language is the medium of communication are potentially almost infinite. No one, not even the most learned, can speak and understand his native language in any and all the situations in which it can be used. There is the technical language of the scientist in a particular field that is not understood by scientists from other fields of study. There is the language of the trained sailor which is not understood by the outsider. Even though all the classes in a large university may be taught in the same language it is doubtful that any professor could go into any and all the classrooms of his university and understand what is being explained. It is easy to find situations in which a person who speaks and understands a language natively fails to understand what is said because the subject matter is not within his experience.

At the same time it is easy to think of situations in which one would understand what a speaker means even without understanding the language. Leonard Bloomfield's example to illustrate the basic sequence of language between speaker and listener can also be used to illustrate a case in which communication takes place in spite of the lack of a common language. In Bloomfield's example, Jack and Jill are taking a walk. It is assumed that they speak the same language. Jill sees an apple in a tree nearby. She makes some noises with her vocal apparatus assumed to be language noises. Jack vaults the fence that separates them from the tree, fetches the apple and gives it to Jill who eats it. The situation here is so obvious that we can imagine Jack and Jill speaking two different and unrelated languages, yet when Jill looks insistently at the apple and makes language noises that are unintelligible to Jack, he still vaults the fence, fetches the apple and gives it to Jill who eats it.

We have no assurance that we have tested language merely because a situation has been understood. And we have no assurance that it is lack of knowledge of the language when a situation is not understood.

Strategically a situation approach that does not specifically test language elements is not effective. It has only the outward appearance of validity.

Furthermore, even if we could pick only valid situations and even if we could be sure that understanding these situations occurred through the language used, we would still have the problem of the great variety of situations which must be sampled.

The elements of language on the other hand are limited, and it is more profitable to sample these elements than to sample the great variety of situations in which language can be used.

2. Skills versus elements of language. Even when we decide to test the language as directly as possible, we still are faced with choices between integrated skills and separate elements. It is economical and more comprehensive to test the sound segments systematically than to test only a few sounds and a few grammatical patterns in a general test of auditory comprehension, yet even in testing the sound segments systematically we have to decide whether to test this element in speaking or in listening.

The decision in the choice of skill versus element will depend to a considerable extent on the purpose for which the test is made and the available time for testing, plus the conditions under which the test must be given. If we want a comprehensive diagnostic test of pronunciation to be used for pinpointing specific problems yet to be mastered by the student we would obviously choose a test that ranges over the sound system, a specific test of that element of language.

If on the other hand we merely want a general level score to tell us whether or not this student may go on to study other subjects using the foreign language as a tool, we may choose a skill test of auditory comprehension plus a test of reading, and perhaps one of writing. The test of auditory comprehension will have to choose a few sounds and a few structures at random hoping to give a fair indication of the general achievement of the student.

If we need to determine general proficiency without reference to listening alone or to any of the separate skills alone and if we have ample time for a comprehensive test we may choose to range over the several elements of language with some sections to test the integrated skills as well.

The conclusion here is that we need to test the elements and the skills separately and will choose one or the other or a combination depending on the purpose and conditions of the test.

3. Group testing versus individual testing. In general we will be interested in testing under practical teaching situations. In these we will have to handle considerable numbers of students under limited time and personnel. We will not be able to plan thirty-hour interviews for each student such as the anthropologist may conduct in his investigations. Even when we need to give individual tests we will attempt to devise techniques to do it in the shortest possible time to permit language teachers to use such a test.

A simple multiplication will show the necessity of using group tests or very short individual tests in a school situation. If we give a fifteen-minute individual test to one hundred pupils, the teacher would need to be giving these tests for three days working eight hours without rest. Three days of the examiner's time for a fifteen-minute test is not economical. On the other hand a modern group test of one hour duration will take only one hour of the examiner's time to administer. The matter of validity will be discussed fully in other chapters. It will not necessarily favor the fifteen-minute individual test over the one-hour group test.

4. Objective versus subjective tests. These terms are used to designate two types of scoring. Objective tests are those that are scored rather mechanically without need to evaluate complex performance on a scale. Subjective tests are those that require an opinion, a judgment on the part of the examiner.

In subjective tests there are differences in scoring by different examiners, hence the name subjective.

In general subjective tests permit the use of techniques that are natural and seem outwardly very valid. Objective tests have been criticized at times because in order to reduce the items to mechanical scoring they are rendered outwardly artificial.

This matter of objective versus subjective scoring is not one of two extremes; that is, tests are not either subjective or objective but range over a scale with completely objective scoring at one end and completely subjective scoring at the other. Often we have to choose between more apparent validity but less objectivity and more objectivity but less apparent validity.

This dilemma can be broken partly at least by locating and describing the linguistic problems to be tested with the accuracy that linguistic analysis makes possible. Knowing what an item is testing we are left free to choose objective techniques even if outwardly they seem less valid, for if they test the language problems in essentially valid linguistic situations they are valid items.

Chapter 5

CRITICAL EVALUATION OF TESTS

5.1   CRITERIA FOR THE EVALUATION OF LANGUAGE TESTS

The questions we ask about a test will vary in each case depending on purpose, time, subject, etc. In general, however, we must ask if a test is valid, reliable, scorable, economical, and administrable.

1. Validity. Does the test measure what it is intended to measure? If it does, it is a valid test. Validity is not general but specific. If a test of pronunciation measures pronunciation and nothing else, it is a valid test of pronunciation; it would not be a valid test of grammar or vocabulary because it does not test grammar or vocabulary.

Validity in language tests depends on the linguistic content of the test and on the situation or technique used to test this content. A test that uses a perfectly valid conversational situation but does not test the elements of the language is not valid. On the other hand, a test that tests the elements of the language but does it by lists or rules or technical names rather than in use in essentially communicative situations is not a valid test either.

Also, a test that has good language content and appears to use essentially linguistic situations will not be valid if it introduces a very heavy intelligence factor, or a heavy memory factor, or some other element that cancels out the language content and the valid situation.

Validity can be achieved and verified indirectly by correlating the scores on a test with those of another test or criterion which is valid. If the two sets of scores correlate highly, that is, if students who make high scores on the valid criterion test also score high on the experimental test and if those who score low on one also score low on the other, we say that the test is valid.

2. Reliability. Does a test yield the same scores one day and the next if there has been no instruction intervening? That is, does the test yield dependable scores in the sense that they will not fluctuate very much so that we may know that the score obtained by a student is pretty close to the score he would obtain if we gave the test again? If it does, the test is reliable.

Reliability is necessary for validity, because a test with scores which fluctuate very much does not test anything. Reliability, however, is general rather than specific. If the scores on a test are steady, that is, reliable, they are reliable regardless of what we test. If the scores of a pronunciation test are reliable they will remain reliable even if we use the scores as a measure of vocabulary although they are not valid as a measure of vocabulary and should not be used as such.

Reliability is measured by a correlation between the scores of the same set of students on two consecutive administrations of the test. This is known as the re-testing coefficient of reliability. Reliability is also measured by computing separate scores for two halves of the same test. The correlation between the sets of scores for the two halves of the test is the coefficient of reliability for one-half of the test. By a special formula[1] we can compute from the reliability of half of the test a close estimate of the reliability of the entire test.

3. Scorability. Can the test be scored with ease so that the users may be able to handle it? Subjective tests are not easy to score. The examiner who is conscientious hesitates, wonders if this response is as good as another he considered good, if he is being too easy or too harsh in his scoring. Objective tests are easy to score. Even objective tests vary in their scorability. A test that collects all the responses on a separate sheet that can be scored by a superimposed punched stencil or by a machine is more scorable than one which has the responses scattered in the pages of the test and not on the same column. The difference will affect the accuracy of the scoring and the time it takes to score a test.

4. Economy. This is a practical criterion. Does the test measure what we want it to test in a reasonable time considering the testing situation? If it does, the test is practical and economical.

---

[1] The Spearman-Brown correction formula is generally used.

5. Administrability. Can the test be given under the conditions that prevail and by the personnel that is available? That is, if we do not have a record player, a test on a record cannot be administered. In general we will think of the more representative situations. If tape-recorders are generally available in the schools of Japan, a tape-recorded test is satisfactory even if in a particular school there does not happen to be a tape-recorder at hand. We can assume that in Japan the school might easily obtain a tape-recorder.

If a test requires highly trained engineers to handle electronic equipment it is not administrable since most schools would not have the services of an engineer available every time the test is to be given.

Much of the above is simply a matter of good practical common sense. Some of the criteria, however, will require technical formulas that will be discussed in later chapters.

5.2   CRITICISM OF SOME GENERALLY USED TECHNIQUES

Perhaps because most testing is done by the teacher, who is primarily interested in teaching, there is not much imagination used in language tests. Translation and the written essay are used over and over in most of the countries of the world. Dictation is widely used and highly regarded. Objective tests are increasingly used but with apologies in many countries. Aural comprehension tests of foreign languages and of English as a foreign language are increasingly popular in the United States. Let us look at these types of tests critically.

1. Translation. *Ad hoc* translation tests are used to measure general achievement in foreign language, to give final grades in language courses, as a measure of proficiency to determine entrance in schools that require a foreign language. Such translation tests are easy to prepare and they have the outward appearance of validity.

Are they valid? The ability to translate is a special skill. People who speak a foreign language well are not necessarily those who translate most effectively, although there is a correlation between knowledge of the foreign language and the capacity to translate.

Some whose control of a foreign language is defective are nevertheless able to translate written material at considerable speed and reasonably well. Whether these differences are the result of the kind of training they received in learning the foreign language or whether they are the result of different native ability is irrelevant at this point. The fact remains that ability to translate shows wide differences with ability to speak, understand, read and write. Consequently, a translation test is not valid as a test of mastery of a foreign language. If properly constructed a translation test can be a valid test of the ability to translate.

In addition, the problem of scoring translation tests is a very serious one. Scoring a translation is a highly subjective affair. Do we score higher a translation that has captured the mood of the original and renders it in the foreign language even though the details of the utterances are not well translated? Or do we score higher a translation that is accurate in every detail but misses the mood and significance of the original? These are difficult questions to answer and they become more difficult when we are faced with scoring the actual translation in which the issues are more mixed than the simple choice presented here.

The scoring of translation tests can be made more objective, but such tests would lose the outward validity of the translation and become objective tests, which are generally distrusted by those who would favor translation as the best testing device.

2. Essay. Essay or composition tests are widely used and are highly respected. Somehow the prestige of writing an essay, especially on a topic that has prestige of its own, covers the multitude of weaknesses that essay tests have as indicators of language achievement.

The ability to write a good composition does not run parallel with the ability to speak, understand, read and even write a foreign language. If a student cannot write a good composition in his native language—a perfectly common case—we cannot expect him to write a good composition in the foreign language even if he has progressed a great deal in it.

Furthermore, a good composition can be written without using a single question pattern or a single request. That is, a composition is often a very poor sample of the elements of a language.

33

Finally, compositions are difficult to score and time consuming in whatever scoring is possible. Experiments have been made giving a set of compositions to different judges to score without seeing the scores given by the others. The range of grades given to the very same compositions by the various judges is usually very great. Essay tests, then, are not reliable.

This is not intended to condemn essay tests for all purposes. Essay tests are probably most effective as tests of the ability to write essays rather than as measures of proficiency in a foreign language.

3. Dictation. Dictation is favored by many teachers and students both as a teaching and as a testing device. However, on critical inspection it appears to measure very little of language. Since the order of words is given by the examiner as he reads the material, it does not test word order. Since the words are given by the examiner, it does not test vocabulary. It hardly tests aural perception of the examiner's pronunciation, because the words can in many cases be identified by context if the student does not hear the sounds correctly. The student is less likely to hear the sounds incorrectly in the slow reading of the words which is necessary for dictation. Spelling and a few matters of inflection and punctuation can be tested through dictation, but the complicated apparatus of dictation is not required to test these matters. Simpler techniques can be substituted.

4. Objective tests. Group objective tests are extensively used in the United States where they have received the greatest attention and support. In other countries they are increasingly coming into use. The usual objections to objective tests are that they are too simple, that they do not require real thinking but simply memory, and that they do not test the ability of the student to organize his thoughts.

The first criticism, that they are too simple, is in error. They may appear to be very simple, and usually the first few items of an objective test are purposely very simple, but the range of difficulty of objective tests can reach as high as any other test and usually goes higher in good tests than any student will go. In the construction of objective tests the usual concentration of items in the middle range of difficulty is pruned, leaving the difficult items and a few simple ones to increase the discriminating power of the test.

The second criticism, that they do not require thinking on the part of the student, depends entirely upon the type of item and the type of test. Objective test items can be excellent measures of the ability to think when they are properly devised. The criticism must then be reserved for those objective tests that encourage memory only, but it cannot be leveled on all objective tests.

The third criticism, that they do not test the ability to organize one's thoughts in a logical and effective sequence, is true. Special items could be devised that would test at least part of the ability to organize one's thoughts, but normally, objective tests are collections of unrelated items, each of which constitutes a miniature test in itself. To test the ability to organize thought, other types of test should be used in addition to objective tests.

Some of the criticisms of objective tests would not be made if we did not defend or attack objective tests as if the techniques of objective tests were everything. Actually the format of an objective test does not guarantee anything except that the scoring will be objective and that a good many items can be included in the test. In language tests in particular it is all too easy to be misled by the appearance of an item into thinking that it tests language when it does not.

When objective tests of language are properly made, they have two important values; they can test in a short time the entire range of the sound system of a language, or the major grammatical patterns, or a representative sample of the vocabulary taught during a whole year or several years.

Second, they can be scored with speed and ease. One hundred tests of one hundred items can be scored by one person in one hour or less. Scoring by machine is not of primary interest to us here, yet the fact that objective tests can be scored by machine makes them usable for masses of students on a scale that would be impossible otherwise. For the individual teacher, the use of objective tests means that more and more comprehensive tests can be given by him without imposing an impossible burden on himself.

35

5. Auditory comprehension tests. With a resurgence of interest in spoken language in the United States there has been an increased interest in auditory comprehension tests. Listening comprehension is one of the most important language skills, and techniques are now available to give group tests of auditory comprehension that are of the objective scoring type. The technique consists simply in reading out loud a paragraph or sentence or an essay and having the students check multiple-choice responses to show whether or not they understand what is read to them.

In general there is a tendency to be satisfied with the appearance of auditory comprehension rather than with checking the specific linguistic elements of auditory comprehension. Along this misleading road there is insistence that several voices should do the reading to insure comprehension in general and not simply by one speaker. The use of several voices does not detract from the value of a listening test; on the contrary it enhances it. But the matter of a variety of voices is rather marginal. The student has from his childhood been used to hearing a variety of voices in his native language and to overlooking these differences in getting at the language structure that signals the intended message. Transfer of this training should be and is successful. What he has not learned is to hear and to react to the language units of the foreign language. These are the ones that have to be tested, and these can be tested with a single voice. They will not be tested even with several voices unless the items have been properly prepared.

Again, as in the use of composition tests, mature essays read to the students to check their comprehension seem to have a prestige as language tests that they do not deserve as such. Tests using mature essays as auditory comprehension stimuli have been used which could be answered by the logical sequence of the essay without any but the vaguest idea of what the essay was about. Others have been used that tested nothing but elementary vocabulary.

The fact that format alone is not enough in language tests can be illustrated with a double example. The format will be the same in both, yet one is useless and the other is effective.

36

In the first example the examiner reads aloud the sentence, "John is watching the car." The student chooses between two pictures: one, a picture of a man watching a baby; the other, a picture of a man watching a car. In this item, although the student listens to a sentence spoken by the examiner and must choose between two pictures only one of which agrees with what was spoken, practically nothing is being tested. To choose between "watching a car" and "watching a baby" the student will be able to make an intelligent guess if he knows only the words *car* and *baby*. The sound differences between these two words are so complete that students who know only the sounds of their native language can hear the difference. We have thus an elaborate listening technique used to test a single word item which could be handled easily in a simple paper-and-pencil test.

In the second example, one that uses the same format and technique yet gets at an important linguistic problem, the examiner reads aloud the same sentence, "John is watching the car." The student, however, chooses between two pictures that force him to decide at a crucial point which one to select. The first picture shows a man *watching* a car. The second picture shows the same man *washing* a car. In this case the student must hear the difference between the *tch* of *watching* and the *sh* of *washing*. The test item in this case checks the student's control of a pronunciation contrast that is a problem to him if it is not a phonemic contrast in his native language.

Both these examples involve the same steps and outwardly seem to test aural control, yet one of them tests nothing that might be of particular significance in auditory comprehension, while the other directly tests a major learning hurdle.

5.3   BIBLIOGRAPHICAL NOTES

The most important single reference on tests and books on testing is the series of mental measurements yearbooks edited by Oscar K. Buros. The latest one of the series is *The Fifth Mental Measurements Yearbook*. This excellent volume lists tests, books on measurement and related fields, and gives signed original reviews and excerpts of signed reviews of the tests and books listed.

PART II

TESTING THE ELEMENTS OF LANGUAGE

Chapter 6

PRONUNCIATION: THE SOUND SEGMENTS

One night Mrs. Moskowitz read a sentence, from "English for Beginners," in which "the vast deserts of America" were referred to. Mr. Parkhill soon discovered that poor Mrs. Moskowitz did not know the meaning of "vast." "Who can tell us the meaning of 'vast'?" asked Mr. Parkhill lightly.

Mr. Kaplan's hand shot up, volunteering wisdom. He was all proud grins. Mr. Parkhill, in the rashness of the moment, nodded to him.

Mr. Kaplan rose, radiant with joy. " 'Vast!' it's commink fromm *diraction*. Ve have four diractions: de naut, de sot, de heast, and de vast."

Mr. Parkhill shook his head. "Er—that is 'west,' Mr. Kaplan." He wrote "VAST" and "WEST" on the blackboard. To the class he added, tolerantly, that Mr. Kaplan was apparently thinking of "west," whereas it was "vast" which was under discussion.

This seemed to bring a great light into Mr. Kaplan's inner world. "So is 'vast' vat you eskink?"

Mr. Parkhill admitted that it was "vast" for which he was asking.

"Aha!" cried Mr. Kaplan. "You minn 'vast,' not"—with scorn— " 'vast.' "

"Yes," said Mr. Parkhill, faintly

"Hau Kay!" said Mr. Kaplan, essaying the vernacular. "Ven I'm buyink a suit of clothes, I'm gettink de cawt, de pents, an' de vast!"

(Leonard Q. Ross, *The Education of Hyman Kaplan*, Harcourt, Brace and Company, New York, 1937, pp. 6–7.)

6.1 PHONEMICS AND PRONUNCIATION TESTS

Phonemics, the branch of linguistics that studies the structure of the sounds of a language to discover its system of significant sounds, provides a new basis for solving some of the knottiest problems in the testing of pronunciation. The theory of testing pronunciation upon which this chapter is based makes full use of phonemics. Ignoring phonemic units and considering only whether or not a sound occurs or does not occur in the native language as well as the foreign language does not account for what we know about the transfer of the native language system to the foreign one in foreign language learning.

1. Role of pronunciation. Three points of view are often observed toward the role of pronunciation. The first point of view denies its importance altogether and limits the study and testing of foreign languages to vocabulary, grammar, reading, writing, and speaking with the native language sounds. This point of view is in error as illustrated humorously by Mr. Kaplan in the above quotation and as illustrated over and over by intelligent speakers addressing a foreign audience reading their lectures in the native language sounds and failing to be understood.

A second point of view goes to the other extreme and assumes that nothing short of native pronunciation is adequate. This point of view though commendable is at best one of wishful thinking. Only young children can be expected to achieve *en masse* a completely native pronunciation of a foreign language. Adults in general will fall short of it with notable exceptions.

A third point of view adopts a criterion of intelligibility as the standard of pronunciation. This standard, however, is hard to define. Intelligible to native speakers, but what native speakers? A native speaker that has been in contact with foreign speakers will understand utterances that sound entirely foreign to another native speaker.

Phonemics provides the way out of this problem. When a student hears and speaks the foreign language using all the phonemic units of the language, that is, maintaining all the phonemic contrasts by means of the distinctive phonemic features, he "knows" the pronunciation of the language. These phonemic units, contrasts, and distinctive features are described by linguists in what is known as phonology.

Subphonemic sound differences used by foreign speakers through transfer from their native language will be designated "foreign accent." For ordinary communicative purposes, the main goal in foreign language study in the twentieth century, a foreign accent need not be eliminated, unless the learner is young and can eliminate it without having to pay an excessive price in time and effort at the expense of other aspects of the language.

Native pronunciation beyond phonemic accuracy is a goal for those who wish to teach the foreign language or engage in other activities which require such native accent. In these cases, nothing is lost by pursuing phonemic accuracy first, and then proceeding to native pronunciation without a trace of foreign accent.

2. Testing of pronunciation. Language tests follow somewhat the attitude of teachers toward pronunciation with one added point of view. There are first those tests and teachers that completely ignore the testing of pronunciation because they do not understand the role of pronunciation in language.

There are also those who do not test pronunciation, even though they realize its importance, because they do not know how to test pronunciation in an efficient and simple way. These will find help in this book and particularly in this and following chapters.

At the other extreme are tests and teachers who test pronunciation with a native accent criterion. Unless an utterance or part of an utterance sounds exactly like that of a native speaker it is considered incorrect. These tests are extremely difficult to give and particularly to score objectively because the examiner must be a trained phonetician and differences in hearing even among phonetically trained teachers will be reflected in the scores.

3. Phonemic point of view. Testing pronunciation with a phonemic criterion of accuracy is the new thing. It is defensible because it makes possible and practicable a communication point of view, because it permits certain new techniques that will be described below, and because it permits more accurate scoring by teachers of the language and by native speakers. Tests of phonetic accuracy beyond the phonemic criterion that has already proved highly productive require specialized phonetic training that is not within the scope of this book to attempt.

4. Production versus recognition. Although the sound system of a language is the same for the speaker and the listener, the techniques used to test recognition of the sound contrasts in listening will differ from those used to measure production of the sounds of the foreign language. Likewise, the description of the problems to be tested will not always be the same when testing production in speaking or recognition in listening. Hence, the discussions that follow will treat separately the problem of listening tests and that of production tests.

5. Informal classroom tests versus formal tests of pronunciation. Students like to show their teacher what they have learned and they learn more effectively when they know what they have and have not mastered. Teaching of foreign languages can be made sharper and more interesting by the use of many short tests given in the classroom as well as by the more formal tests given at the end of the course and at other points during the term. The informal test given by the teacher in the classroom can use a great variety of techniques that may not always be suited to the more formal testing done independently of the particular course to determine general proficiency or diagnose over-all problems of pronunciation. The instructions in informal classroom tests can be improvised orally by the teacher. Answer sheets can be prepared by the students themselves who may also score their own tests. The more formal language tests require grading of items, careful written instructions, highly efficient items treated and screened statistically. Because of these differences, it is better to treat informal tests of pronunciation and formal ones separately.

6. Age. Although the phonemic units and distinctions that constitute the sound system to be mastered are the same for the young student and the adult, the techniques that permit their testing will be different for very young scholars. If writing is more difficult for a boy than the foreign sounds themselves, we cannot test his mastery of the sounds through writing. Pictures and actions can be handled more freely and can therefore more properly be used to check his hearing of the sound system.

6.2 PRONUNCIATION PROBLEMS: WHAT TO TEST

According to our theory the thing to be tested is the phonological system—the phonemic system with its chief phonetic features and distribution of phonemes—in use for production and recognition. This system is operated through firmly set habits and transferred to the foreign language when the student is learning it. By a systematic comparison of the phonological system of the native language with that of the language to be learned we discover the learning problems. These learning problems constitute the content of a test.

Following are suggestions to illustrate how a bilingual teacher with an understanding of phonemics can prepare a list of the problems of his students.[1] These suggestions are not intended as a rigid step-by-step approach but as a simple summing up of important things involved in such work.

1. Stage 1. Find or prepare a linguistic analysis of the sound system of the language to be learned and a similar description of the language of the learner. It is crucial to find good descriptions. As a rule we will not be able to use the descriptions found in ordinary textbooks since except for those which have made use of scientific linguistic data the descriptions are not complete or accurately stated.

The descriptions must give all the segmental phonemes of each language, their significant phonetic features, and their distribution. They should also be stated according to parallel organization and description. If they are not parallel, one of the descriptions should be recast so that it does parallel the other.

2. Stage 2. Compare the two sound systems phoneme by phoneme in order to locate and describe the points of difficulty.

The comparison of each phoneme should include at least three queries. First, does the native language have a similar phoneme? For example, in comparing the sound system of English with that of Kusien, a language spoken by about 2,000 people in the easternmost part of the Caroline Islands, we would find that

[1] For a fuller treatment see *Linguistics Across Cultures* by Robert Lado.

English /b/ as in *bay* has no counterpart in this language. Similarly we would find that English /d/ as in *day* and /g/ as in *gay* are without parallel phonemes in Kusien. These English phonemes would constitute learning problems for speakers of Kusien learning English. These problems should therefore be included in the list of problems to be tested.

Second, if there is a phoneme in the native language of similar phonetic features we assume that the students will not have difficulty with the phoneme as a whole. We ask a second question, however, to discover if there might be trouble with some variant of the native phoneme that parallels the foreign one. We ask, therefore, are the variants of the native language phoneme similar to the variants of the foreign phoneme? If a variant of the native phoneme is phonetically similar to a different phoneme in the foreign language so that when transferred it would function as a different phoneme, we have located a very stubborn problem.

For example, in comparing English with Spanish we would check the phoneme /d/ as in *day* and would find a reasonably similar phoneme in Spanish: /d/ as in Spanish *de*. We would then inquire into the variants of these two Spanish and English phonemes. We would find that Spanish /d/ has a stop variant [d] as in *de* and a fricative variant [ð] as in *lado*. The fricative variant is more similar to English /ð/ as in *they* than to /d/ as in *day*. We have assumed that the Spanish speaker transfers his entire phoneme /d/ with both variants and thus automatically produces the fricative variant in the same environments in which he would use this variant in Spanish. Thus he will pronounce English *ladder* as *lather* because he normally uses the fricative variant between vowels in Spanish.

When checking the English phoneme /ð/ as in *they* we find that Spanish does not have a similar phoneme. The most similar one phonetically is Spanish /d/ which the Spanish speaker associates with English /d/. The Spanish speaker uses his /d/ phoneme for English /ð/ and produces the stop variant initially before vowels because that is the variant he automatically uses in Spanish. Thus when attempting to pronounce English *they* he will say what to an English speaker is *day*. These then are problems to be tested. As a matter of fact evidence from tests shows

43

this to be one of the most stubborn pronunciation problems for Spanish speakers learning English.

Third, in those cases in which we find a similar phoneme in the native language, and the variants are similar and do not become different phonemes in the foreign language we still might discover a problem of distribution. For this purpose we ask a third question. Is the phoneme similarly distributed? That is, does it occur in the same positions that it occurs in the foreign language? If a phoneme occurs in word final position in the foreign language but does not occur in this position in the native language the student will have trouble pronouncing the phoneme in this position, and he will have trouble hearing it in the same position.

For example, in comparing French with English we would find that French /ž/ as in *je* has a parallel English phoneme /ž/ as in *measure*. We would also find that their variants would not cause any particular difficulty. In asking the third question, however, we would notice that in French /ž/ appears at the beginning of words as in *je, jamais*, etc. but in English it does not appear in this position. English speakers will transfer their /ž/ phoneme with its restriction on distribution in initial position and will thus have difficulty with word initial /ž/ in French.

By comparing the combinations in which each phoneme appears we would discover also the sequences that will constitute difficulties. It is, however, more economical to describe syllable structure or some other sequence unit, and the comparison of the sequence patterns of the two languages will reveal these sequence problems. For example, if the foreign language permits closed syllables—syllables that end in a consonant—and the native language permits only open syllables—those ending in a vowel—the student will have trouble with closed syllables in learning the foreign language. Another example: if the foreign language permits consonant clusters of three consonants in final position and the native language permits only single consonants in final position, the student will have trouble with all final consonant clusters. If a particular consonant does not occur in final position in the native language and it does in the foreign one, this will constitute a learning problem.

44

3. Stage 3. Prepare the lists of problems to be tested. Since the problems will differ somewhat for production and for recognition, different lists are necessary to test the student's pronunciation in speaking and in listening.

4. Recognition. In listing the recognition problems we indicate the phonemes that are difficult to hear for speakers of a particular native language and the ones with which they are likely to confuse them. We usually list these problems in pairs. For example, the Spanish speaker has trouble hearing English /ð/ because he does not have a parallel phoneme in Spanish. He hears it as Spanish /d/, which he transfers as English /d/. So we list the problem as English /d/ confused with English /ð/ in listening. This confusion will be all in the direction of /d/ at first, but as he learns that there is a /ð/ phoneme, he will sometimes think he hears /ð/ when the speaker uses /d/.

5. Production. In speaking he will produce the native phoneme which may sound like another phoneme in the foreign language. We list the phoneme of the foreign language that the student misses, not the one he produces in error. The problem will be more complicated when one variant in the native language becomes one phoneme in the foreign language and another variant becomes a different phoneme. This is the case of Spanish /d/. Initially, after pause, and after /l/ or /n/, Spanish /d/ is a stop and functions as English /d/. In other environments it is a fricative and becomes English /ð/. The problem then is listed as English /d/ produced as /ð/ between vowels and after /r/. English /ð/ produced as /d/ initially, after pause, and after /l/ and /n/. In final position English /d/ becomes /ð/ or is omitted altogether.

Chapter 7

TESTING RECOGNITION OF THE SOUND SEGMENTS

7.1 RECOGNITION TECHNIQUES

The general technique for testing recognition of the sounds of a foreign language is simple: the examiner reads aloud one or more utterances, and he checks the students to find out if they have distinguished the problem sound or contrast. To test language in use, which is our aim, he checks only phonemic units and contrasts since the moment he checks phonetic differences within a phoneme he is checking technical linguistic training rather than language use.

The voice of the examiner, which constitutes the stimulus containing the problem being tested, can be presented live, that is, directly by the examiner. In ordinary classroom quizzes and tests, this is the most practical and satisfactory way to present the stimulus. The same person that teaches the class merely announces that they will have a test or an exercise; he will then give the instructions, and proceed to read the items.

With the advent and general diffusion of recording equipment it is also easy to have the stimulus, the voice of the examiner, recorded on magnetic tape or a disc. This permits the teacher to bring into the classroom the voice of some other speaker, giving the test a more realistic atmosphere. In cases in which the teacher has evidence that his or her own pronunciation is not up to standard he may wish to use a recorded test instead of his own voice. For this purpose, a tape-recorder is at present the most satisfactory instrument. Reasonably good reproduction is achieved on moderately priced machines which if operated properly by the teacher will render good service.

A caution is here in order. Probably too much has been made of the value of the native speaker of a language as the ideal teacher. As a result, good teachers of a foreign language who are not themselves native speakers may feel that they cannot give pronunciation tests to their own students. This is an unfounded feeling. If the teacher of a foreign language speaks it with all the phonemic contrasts and the distinctive phonetic features of these contrasts he can safely and confidently use himself as examiner. Phonetic features beyond these are not necessary for full communication in the language. At the same time, native speakers who do not speak a standard variety of the language are not satisfactory as examiners or teachers. Standard variety means any variety spoken by educated speakers of that language from any of the regions where it is spoken natively.

In some countries or cities or school systems which have a radio program for their schools, it is theoretically feasible to broadcast a daily or weekly quiz to all the language classes and have the students answer it in their classrooms. If the papers are corrected and handled by the teacher and the students it can remain an informal classroom test in spite of the formality of having the stimulus received by radio.

1. Group testing. Group testing is simple and valid in this kind of testing. When the live voice is used as the stimulus, the group of students taking the test should not exceed that which can clearly hear the voice of the examiner. The exact number cannot be prescribed here because it will depend on the acoustic conditions of the room and the volume and clarity of the voice of the examiner. If the students attend class in a room and hear the teacher well in their daily class activities they can be examined together at one sitting. Twenty-five students can be tested under ideal conditions. Fifty may be tested in a good classroom. It should be remembered that enough space between students will discourage copying and permit more concentrated listening by the students.

2. Individual testing. Sometimes it is convenient to give a listening test to an individual or two in the same classroom where the teacher or supervisor is directing the activity of other students. This is easily done by means of sets of earphones attached to a tape-recorder in the classroom. The teacher sets the machine, gives the instructions, and leaves the students taking the test silently as far as the rest of the class is concerned, yet hearing the stimulus through the earphones for the test itself. This device is convenient for make-up testing of students who are unavoidably absent when the test is given to the group.

7.2   SOUND TO GRAPHIC SYMBOL

PERCEPTION TECHNIQUE 7.1. **Sound to digits.** This technique admits of many variations. Essentially it consists of words that contain one sound or another of a troublesome pair or trio as the stimulus which the student must identify by the numbers 1, 2, or 3. The examiner tells the students to write 1 if they hear one of the sounds, and 2 if they hear the other of the pair that is being tested. Number 3 is used for the third sound if the test includes three sounds. The examiner then reads his list of words, pausing briefly after each to allow the students to write 1, 2, or 3. Reading each word once is enough, and it approaches speaking and listening more than reading each word twice.

An example will further clarify the technique. To test the contrast between English /iy/ as in *eat* and /i/ as in *it*, which is troublesome to Spanish, Japanese and many other speakers we prepare a list of ten words containing either /iy/ or /i/. Here is a set: *beat, trip, swim, keep, with, fleet, speak, miss, lead, key.* The examiner tells the students to write 1 if they hear a vowel like that of *eat* and to write 2 if the vowel they hear is like that of *it*. He then reads the ten words of his list, leaving brief pauses between words to allow the students to write their response.

This technique is very convenient and valid for informal classroom use. A test such as the above example can be prepared in a few minutes and administered and scored in a few minutes. The use of digits eliminates any factor of spelling, and these digits are familiar practically throughout the world.

The limitations of the technique should also be remembered so that it may not be used beyond its effective range. Since the sounds have to be identified by digits, only two or three sounds can be tested each time. A larger number of sounds tends to

48

introduce an undue memory factor and the student has trouble remembering whether this or that sound should be written with 8 or 9. Also, since the student has to be told the sounds that are going to be tested in order to identify them with the numbers he will write, he is able to give his conscious attention to the sounds, a condition that does not obtain in the ordinary use of the language, when he cannot be warned as to just what sounds will be spoken. A third limitation is the fact that single words are used as the stimulus instead of phrases or sentences as would be more frequently the case in conversation.

PERCEPTION TECHNIQUE 7.2. **Sound to letters.** In languages with a reasonably consistent alphabetic or syllabic writing in which learning to write could go hand in hand with learning to pronounce, a sounds to written symbols technique can be used to advantage for informal classroom testing. Again it can be varied in many ways, but it consists essentially in having a set of words or short sentences containing the troublesome sounds as the stimulus, and having the student mark the written word or phrase that matches what he hears.

Here are two examples from Spanish for English speakers. The examiner says in Spanish, *le*. The students choose from the three written words, *le*, *ley*, *leí*. The examiner says, *cero*. The students choose from *cerro*, *cedo*, *cero*. This is a multiple-choice technique.

A variation known in testing as matching can be illustrated with the same examples. In the matching type, the examiner gives all or nearly all the items that the students have in writing, only he gives them in a different order. For example, the examiner says, *le*, *leí*, *ley*, and the student writes 1 beside *le* in his paper, 2 beside *leí*, and 3 beside *ley*, thus showing that he heard the words correctly. If the student has only the three words to match, the third word tends to be wasted because it must match the only remaining choice. To overcome this minor limitation we usually add a choice or two that do not match any word given by the examiner. In the example above we might add the words *leeis* and *les* as decoys.

This technique is in one sense more flexible than technique 7.1 because the sounds being tested do not have to be announced to the students, and several occurrences of the sounds may be permitted in each choice without complicating the instructions.

Its chief limitation is the factor of spelling. We often do not know whether the error was caused by inaccurate hearing or by a spelling confusion. This factor of spelling is minor in languages which have a fairly regular spelling system as is the case with Finnish, Turkish, and Spanish. In English it is a heavy factor that cannot be ignored or taken lightly. For informal classroom tests in an approach that uses a limited vocabulary and introduces writing early, technique 7.2 may be used with profit even for English. In more formal tests the technique appears seriously limited, certainly for English, since the results could not be taken either as a good indication of pronunciation or of spelling achievement.

PERCEPTION TECHNIQUE 7.3. **Dictation.** This is a well-known technique. It consists of reading to the students a set of words or utterances and having the students write down what they hear. If the stimulus is made up of words or phrases containing the troublesome sounds and if the test words are not given away by the context, dictation can be used effectively as an informal classroom test.

Its advantages are that it can range freely over any and all sounds and that like technique 7.1 it can be prepared easily, does not require special answer sheets, and can be scored objectively. Its disadvantages are that a heavy spelling factor is introduced, requiring active mastery of spelling before hearing discrimination is achieved. In English this is a serious limitation for formal testing. In informal tests in which it is not essential that the teacher know whether the error was caused by spelling or sound it can be used. Another shortcoming is that the student has to write the entire word or utterance as his answer, and in so doing he wastes time with those parts of the words that are not crucial to the test. Writing itself is slower than listening, and the whole technique of dictation has to be used with caution for the sake of economy if for no other reason. Of course, dictation is preferable to no checking of the spoken language and it is preferable to passive listening alone.

PERCEPTION TECHNIQUE 7.4. **Sound to phonemic symbols.** When students are familiar with a phonemic alphabet of the foreign language it is possible to have the student listen to the spoken stimulus and either write the phonemic symbols of what he hears or check the phonemic representation of what he hears if it is given on his answer sheet. In every case, the stimulus must be words or sentences that contain the problem sounds and contrasts.

Several variations are possible. In one, the student merely writes the one symbol that represents the problem sound which has been identified as the only vowel of the word, the last vowel of the utterance, the first or last consonant, or in some other mechanical way. This variation is similar to technique 7.1 except that any sounds may be tested without previous mention of the particular sounds.

In another variation, several choices are given in phonemic symbols to the student, who numbers or marks the ones he thinks he hears the examiner say. This is similar to technique 7.2 only using phonemic symbols instead of ordinary writing. It has the advantage of eliminating the factor of spelling, but it introduces the factor of the phonemic alphabet which may not be equally well mastered by all the students. Consequently, a wrong answer could be caused either by inaccurate hearing or by inadequate knowledge of the phonemic symbols.

A third variation is dictation with phonemic symbols as the writing of the students. This technique in all three varieties has the advantage of forcing the student to use the symbols that represent the phonemic inventory of the language. In classes that use such an alphabet as part of the teaching equipment this technique is a very useful one. In classes which do not employ a phonemic alphabet it is useless. As a formal testing technique independent of any particular class it cannot be used because some students will be familiar with the alphabet and will have an undue advantage over those who are not.

Any phonemic alphabet may be used with this technique. For obvious reasons the alphabet used in the class will have to be the one used in the tests. A good phonemic alphabet is one that has a distinct symbol for each of the phonemes of the language and no more.

7.3   SOUND TO SOUND

In all the above techniques the student has to translate a sound —a phoneme—into a written symbol of some sort, be that a number, a letter, or a phonemic symbol. This has two general disadvantages, although the techniques are useful and should be used.

One of the disadvantages is that in using language we do not have to translate sounds into graphic symbols; we identify sound units that yield meanings (compare Figure 1.1). Hence, translation into graphic symbols is a burden that diminishes in some measure the directness and therefore the validity of our tests. The other disadvantage is that the graphic symbols impose restrictions on the usefulness of the techniques either because knowledge of the symbols becomes an important factor as in the case of letters and phonemic symbols or because use of the symbols limits the test to a very few sounds at a time as in the case of numbers.

In order to overcome these limitations, especially for the construction of formal tests of perception, an entirely different approach was developed. In this new approach the student has to compare sound with sound rather than sound with graphic symbol.

Native speakers of English are able to say instantly that *day* and *they* are different even though they may have never studied phonemics or phonetics. The same speakers will say that the /k/ in *kill* is the same as the /k/ in *skill*. Phonemically they are the same even though phonetically they are different. In other words, native speakers of a language tend to react phonemically when comparing sounds in their own language. We assume, therefore, that when foreign speakers learn the sound system well, they will also be able to react phonemically; that is, to perceive a difference between phonemes and to overlook differences that are not phonemic in the foreign language.

The essence of these techniques is to give a set of utterances orally to the students and ask them if what they have heard constitutes different utterances or the same utterance repeated.

PERCEPTION TECHNIQUE 7.5. **Minimal pairs.** In this technique we select minimal pairs of words or sentences containing the troublesome contrasts for a particular language background and we read the pairs aloud to the students. The students simply write "S" if they hear the same word or sentence repeated and "D" if they hear two different words or sentences. An example of ten items testing the contrast between /iy/ as in *eat* and /i/ as in *it* in English, a contrast that is a problem for speakers of Spanish, Portuguese, Japanese, Finnish, and many other languages, is as follows:

The examiner reads these ten pairs of words allowing a few seconds between pairs for the students to write "S" or "D" after each pair has been read: 1. *sleep*; *slip*. 2. *fist*; *fist*. 3. *ship*; *sheep*. 4. *heat*; *heat*. 5. *jeep*; *gyp*. 6. *leap*; *leap*. 7. *rid*; *read*. 8. *mill*; *mill*. 9. *neat*; *knit*. 10. *beat*; *bit*. On a simple test such as this, fairly advanced students of English will miss several items, while native speakers of English in the same room will not miss any or miss one or two occasionally.

The great advantages of this technique are its flexibility and validity. We can test a different problem in each item without having to forewarn the student. For example, item 1 might remain *sleep*, *slip*; item 2, become *chair*, *share*, testing the /š/–/č/ contrast; item 3, *boat*, *vote*, testing the /b/–/v/ contrast; item 4, *rise*, *rise* with a potential /z/–/s/ contrast with *rice*; etc.

A little more difficult and more valid than isolated words is the use of minimal pairs of sentences. Here is an example: 1. *Will he sleep? Will he slip?* 2. *They beat him. They bit him.* 3. *Let me see the sheep. Let me see the sheep.* The student does not know where the difference will occur if it does occur. If he has mastered this sound contrast he will have little or no difficulty determining which pairs are the same and which are different.

This is an excellent technique for classroom testing. For formal tests it suffers from the problem of all two-choice tests: the effect of wild guessing is quite heavy. Guessing reduces the reliability of the test. A test of 125 items showed a reliability of ·73, which is disappointing for a full-length test. As for validity, it is more valid than even extended observation of students in their everyday use of the foreign language in and out of class. In the ordinary use of the language it is difficult to know if the student has perceived the sound contrast, guessed at the meaning, or understood from the context rather than through the words containing the difficult sounds. In this technique, on the other hand, we are able to control the non-language factors and the language factors that are not primarily pronunciation.

PERCEPTION TECHNIQUE 7.6. **Triplets.** The examiner reads aloud three words or sentences that differ only by one of the troublesome contrasts. Some items have all three words or sentences the same in order to increase the possible answers and decrease proportionally the possibility of successful guessing. The student merely indicates which of the three words or sentences are the same if any. He does this by writing the numbers of the choices that are the same. If the first and the second are the same he writes 1 2. If the first and the third are the same he writes 1 3. If the second and the third, 2 3. If all three are the same, 1 2 3. And if no choice is the same as any other, that is if all three are different, he writes 0.

We see that with only three choices in each item the student has five possible answers. With an increase of one choice over technique 7.5, minimal pairs, we have added three possible answers and thus reduced the effect of guessing effectively and economically.

A 100-item test of this type showed a reliability coefficient of ·90, which is satisfactory even for formal testing of aural perception.

An earlier variation of this technique requires that the student write the numbers of the choices that are different rather than of those that are the same. This practice is fully satisfactory also.[1]

This technique is the most effective and satisfactory one to test aural perception that has been reported. It can test the entire system of segmental phonemes of a language in a reason-

---

[1] I favor marking the choices that are the same rather than those that are different because it approaches slightly closer the operation of language. The listener identifies what a thing is first, and then is able to tell what it is not. Each sound is different from many others, but is only the same as itself.

ably sized test. It can be used for any language. It requires no special answer sheets for informal classroom use. This aspect of language testing is as advanced as any in any field of testing.

PERCEPTION TECHNIQUE 7.7. **Quadruplets.** This technique is the same as technique 7.6, only instead of giving three words or sentences the examiner gives four. For example, the examiner says, *share, share, chair, share.* The student writes the number of the words that are the same, in this case 1 2 and 4. Minimally contrasting sentences can be used instead of single words.

Theoretically this type of item has the advantage of increasing the number of possible answers to 12 by adding one choice. The possible answers are 1 2, 1 3, 1 4, 2 3, 2 4, 3 4, 1 2 3, 1 2 4, 1 3 4, 2 3 4, 1 2 3 4, and 0. This results in a further reduction of the effect of guessing.

The technique has remained largely untried and untested, however. There is a potential memory factor that could invalidate it as a formal test. Some native speakers that were exposed to it felt that four choices tended to introduce a factor of learning during the test, that is, the cumulative effect of the choices tended, they thought, to give away the answer rather than to make it more difficult. There should be no reservations, however, in using it as an informal classroom test.

In the above the student is told that there will be only one set of choices that are the same in each item, not two. It is possible to say, otherwise, *share, share, chair, chair,* in which case the answer is 1 2, and 3 4, since the first two and the last two are the same though each pair is different from the other pair. This variation has not been tried because it imposes even more of a memory burden than the other. This variation would give fifteen possible answers per item: the twelve listed above plus 1 2, 3 4; 1 3, 2 4; and 1 4, 2 3.

PERCEPTION TECHNIQUE 7.8. **Comparing sounds to a model.** Essentially the same as 7.6 and 7.7 but differing from them mechanically, this technique consists in giving a word or sentence as a model and three words or sentences as choices which may differ from the model by a minimal phonemic contrast. The student writes the numbers of the choices that are the same as the model. Using the same words as before, the examiner says *share* as the model, pauses briefly, then says *share, chair, share*. The answer in this case is 1 3, because the first and third choices are the same as the model. The possible answers are eight, namely, 1, 2, 3, 1 2, 1 3, 2 3, 1 2 3, and 0.

This technique has been used in formal and informal tests successfully. The students, however, tend to complain that the memory burden is heavy. Native speakers manage these items correctly though some feel that they are complicated. It is not recommended that the technique be used in the same test following techniques 7.5: minimal pairs, 7.6: triplets, or 7.7: quadruplets. Considerable confusion arises among the students, who find it difficult to switch to the model type. If used in succession, a good number of examples are required to help the students change their mental sets.

7.4 TESTING THE RECOGNITION OF SOUNDS THROUGH MEANING

In all the techniques described thus far, the student is not required to understand the message of what he hears. Basically he has to be able to identify phonemes regardless of the meaning of the words and sentences in which they appear. These are valid and useful techniques. Now we will describe techniques to test recognition of the phonemic distinctions of a language through the meaning of the utterances used.

The examiner reads a word or sentence and the students indicate what they have understood. What the examiner says must contain the sounds that constitute the problem to be tested in an environment in which it could be one or the other of a difficult pair or one of a problem set of three or more sounds. The differences are in the form of the response, which can make use of pictures, writing, and, theoretically, actual objects and actions.

PERCEPTION TECHNIQUE 7.9. **Sound to pictures.** In this picture technique the examiner reads a word or sentence and the students choose from two or more pictures the one that fits the word or sentence. Various subtypes are possible and will be clear through examples.

A word and two pictures. The examiner says *sheep* and the students choose from the two pictures that follow:

A B

Fig. 7.1

Picture B fits the word given by the examiner. The student who cannot discriminate between the vowel of *sheep* and that of *ship* is at a loss in choosing his answer.

A sentence and two pictures. The examiner says *He is watching the window.* The students choose from the following pictures:

A B

Fig. 7.2

Students who do not hear the difference between the middle consonants of *watching* and *washing* are at a loss to select the right picture.

Three choices. To reduce the effect of guessing in two-choice items, a third choice can be added. The third choice in the following example represents a third contrast at the same point and in the same sound area. The examiner says *It's a pen.* The students choose from the following:

A   B   C

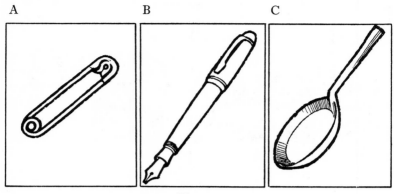

Fig. 7.3

To select the right answer the students have to discriminate between the vowels of *pen* and *pin* and between those of *pen* and *pan*.

Two unrelated contrasts can be used in the same item to increase the number of choices as in the next example. The examiner says *It's a sheep.* The students choose from three pictures.

A   B   C

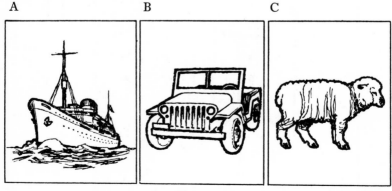

Fig. 7.4

The student must discriminate between the vowels of *sheep* and *ship* and between the initial consonants of *sheep* and *jeep*.

58

If he chooses *jeep* it indicates that he has trouble with the consonant contrast. If he chooses *ship* it indicates that he has trouble with the vowel contrast. If he chooses *sheep* he has either heard both contrasts or has made a lucky guess. If in other items testing the same problems he continues to choose the right answers we conclude that he does hear these sounds phonemically.

Composite pictures showing a room with people and objects can be used in testing aural comprehension in more general terms than exclusively for pronunciation. The restrictions imposed by the need of constructing a reasonable picture limit this type of picture unduly for any systematic testing of phonemic recognition. A few pronunciation items intermingled with other items in a comprehension test are possible in a composite picture. The item contrasting *pin*, *pen*, and *pan* could be tested in a composite picture. The item contrasting *watching* and *washing* could also be tested in the same picture. The examiner might say, *Where is the pen? Where is the picture? Who is watching the dishes?* The students would mark the pen, the picture, and the boy if they perceive the crucial discriminations in sound. We assume that they also know the words and the sentence patterns used, otherwise we would have to select simpler material. Young children could simply point at the objects in the picture if they are tested individually.

Fig. 7.5

It is possible to overestimate the value of pictures in testing. Pictures can be very ambiguous. There are many important words and sentences that cannot be pictured or that require highly abstract interpretation of pictures. Cultural differences in picturable objects may lead to unexpected humorous effects or may mislead altogether even if they are crystal clear to the students in your culture. In fact, the very use of pictures in everyday situations that our children grow up with as a matter of course may be a very foreign experience to children in other cultures.

As a result of these limitations, pictures have to be used with care. They must be carefully edited and tried with the students for whom they are intended. They must be simply drawn and carefully studied even before they are tried with the students.

In spite of these inconveniences, pictures are an important ingredient in present-day testing, and they are all but essential in testing young children. The use of a few picture items enlivens the interest of young students in a test and has the effect of convincing adults that the sounds being tested are important for communication and not simply to sound like a native of the foreign language.

7.5 PREPARING AND USING INFORMAL CLASS-ROOM TESTS OF RECOGNITION

The following things need to be done in preparing and using informal tests of sound recognition: work out the list of problems to be tested with accurate description of each; choose the words and phrases that contain the recognition problems in minimal pairs; produce the items; decide on the type of answer and answer sheet to be used; administer the tests; score the tests. Each of these things will require some comment.

1. List of problems. Before we begin to write a single item of a test we must have a complete list of the problems to be tested. This list must give the phoneme that is a problem for recognition, the phoneme with which it will be confused by the foreign speaker of the particular background we are going to test, the distinctive phonetic feature or features that distinguish the two phonemes and are not heard by the students, and the environments—distribution—in which the distinction is not heard. Some illustrative examples of the location and description of recognition problems were given above (6.2). A test cannot be much better than the list of problems from which it is made.

2. Finding words and phrases that contain the problems. Once the problems are listed we collect words and phrases that contain these problems in the environments in which they are troublesome. For techniques 7.1 through 7.4, those that require the student to identify the phonemes by means of written symbols representing them (sound to graphic symbol), we need single words and phrases that contain the problems. For techniques 7.5 through 7.9, those that require the student to compare sound with sound and those that require him to identify the meaning of the word or utterance, we need to find minimal pairs of words, phrases, and sentences. Finding minimal pairs that meet all the requirements of a good test is a laborious process. It takes a great deal of tedious searching for examples of the given specifications, and one must expect to make many false starts as a matter of course. Let us look at examples of the search for single items for techniques 7.1 through 7.4 and then at examples of the search for minimal pairs for the other techniques.

In some cases, for example when the sound is at the beginning of words and when the spelling of this sound is regular, we can go directly to a dictionary and find all the items available. This would be the case with word initial /b/ and /v/ in English. In fact, we would find so many items in this search that it would be a nuisance to read through the entire list of V and B words in a dictionary if we need only a few of each.

In most cases, the sounds may have to be in other than initial position at least in some instances, or they may not be as regularly spelled as /v/ and /b/. A method that helps to find examples in any position and regardless of multiple spellings is to substitute mentally one sound after another in a position of a word until a new word that meets our specifications is formed. When we exhaust the changes in one position we change sounds in another position. Notice that we are talking about changing sounds, not letters. For example, if we want to find examples with initial /ð/ in English we begin substituting mentally after the /ð/ the vowel sounds of English and we find *thee, the, they*, and *though*. We might then add a consonant after the vowel

/iy/ and find *these*. Changing /iy/ to each of the other vowels and substituting consonants after it we find *this, they've, they'll, they're, there, them, then, that, than, thus, those.*

If we need items with /ð/ between vowels, the process is the same, only a bit more complex. We might start substituting each vowel before the /ð/ and let the ending of words suggest themselves in the process. We might thus think of *either, other, this way.* Substituting the various consonants before each vowel and then adding /ð/ and whatever ending completes a word we might get *teething, seething, heathen, wreathing, neither, thither, wither, bathing, lathing, feather, leather, weather, whether, gather, fathom, lather, rather, further* (in some dialects), *southern, mother, another* (suggested when substituting /n/), *bother, father, farther* (in some dialects), *loathing.* These examples were collected by the process suggested. They are not exhaustive nor do they need to be.

The list of vowels used is from Mid-West American English. The symbols are not important and whichever are most familiar should be preferred if they are complete. The author used mentally /i, ɪ, e, ɛ, æ, a, ə, ɔ, o, ʊ, u/. Others may prefer /iy, i, ey, e, æ, a, ə, ɔ, ow, u, uw/. Those dealing with British English might prefer the symbols used by Daniel Jones or some other scholar. The consonant list used mentally by the author was /p, t, k, b, d, g, č, ǰ, f, θ, s, š, h, v, ð, z, ž, l, r, m, n, ŋ, y, w/.

Any of the standard phonemic alphabets is acceptable. What is not practical or safe is to attempt to use the ordinary alphabet for the English phonemes because the letters may represent different phonemes and some of the phonemes are not represented by single letters. It is useful for a teacher of a foreign language to memorize the list of phonemes of the language he teaches.

If we search for minimal pairs for techniques 7.5 through 7.9, we proceed exactly as we did thus far, only when we find a word with /ð/ we immediately substitute /d/ in place of /ð/ to see if there is such a word. For example, when we find *thee* with initial /ð/ we substitute /d/ and get "*d*," the name of the fourth letter of the alphabet. This is a minimal pair, /ðiy/ /diy/. The word *thee* we would discard because the vowel of it changes according to the sound that follows and according to whether or not it is stressed. When we find *they* we substitute /d/ and get *day*, an excellent pair in many respects. For *though* we get *dough*. For *these* the substitution of /d/ produces "*d's*," the plural of "*d*." For *this* the substitution of /d/ does not yield an English word. If we had to have a minimal pair here, we could, however, compare *disappointment* and *this appointment*. For *they've* we would find *Dave*, familiar simplification of *David*. We would not get minimal pairs for *that, thus, either, teething, heathen, thither, wither, gather, fathom, rather, further, southern, farther*, and some of the pairs for the others would be somewhat dubious.

When one of the words of a minimal pair is much more common and familiar than the other, the students who are not familiar with the less common word may miss the item because of this vocabulary factor rather than through inability to hear the sound contrast. These pairs should be used carefully then. If the student is warned that the words he hears may be unfamiliar to him, however, it may actually be desirable to include some items like these. If, in a comprehension item, the right choice is the familiar word, this will tend to make the item useless since the student would not be attracted to the unfamiliar word in the other choice even if he is not sure of the sounds he hears.

Another problem to avoid is that some minimal pairs do not occupy the same location in a sentence because they are not the same part of speech or because they are lexically incompatible with the same linguistic sentences. These pairs can be used in items that present only isolated words. Occasionally two sentences can be constructed that are grammatically very different but are the same in stress, rhythm and intonation, or that can be rendered the same in some particular context. These items may be used, of course, but the particular rendition that makes them a minimal pair should be clearly marked for the examiner so that he may not misread and render the pair useless.

When the test of pronunciation is through meaning and must be restricted to a limited vocabulary of a thousand words, or two, or three, it will be easier to go through the list and classify each word under the various pronunciation problems to be tested.

With such a list it is possible and desirable to exhaust the words that will fit each problem. Tests of recognition of sounds, however, should test the ability to hear not only those words which the student knows lexically but also the words that he does not know. To include a proportion of items that are beyond the student's vocabulary yet within the phonemic contrasts and patterns of the language is an excellent addition to a test.

3. Preparation of items. If we have followed the order of work thus far described we now have the complete list of the problems to be tested and the words and pairs of words or phrases that contain these problems. We now decide what type of item best suits our needs at the moment. The decision will depend on a good many factors that are not crucial. Thus the teacher should vary the technique to avoid overspecialization and monotony.

To prepare items with technique 7.1, with numbers, decide how many items you will need or will have time for. List the problems you want to test in this particular test. Put together the words that contain the problem, and make sure you do not use too many words with one of the sounds of a pair and not enough of the other. Be careful also not to have too many of the same sound together. Let the problems or the two sounds of the same problem alternate in a random order rather than in any regular pattern. This is done to avoid having a student discover the pattern and answer correctly without actually hearing the sounds.

For technique 7.2, with ordinary writing, we again decide the number of items we need to use or those we will have time for. We distribute the problems, and write the pairs of words in the order that we want the problems to appear or in a random order if there is no particular order required.

If this technique is varied to handle minimal pairs of sentences, and you want the items to be made up of sentences, proceed to write sentences that vary only as to the words of the pair. If the pair of words is *sheep* and *ship*, we can say, "Look at the sheep," for example, because *ship* would be equally possible instead of *sheep*. We could not say, "Sheep give wool," because *ship* would not be equally possible in the position of *sheep*.

Write down the word that the examiner is going to read, and on a separate list, write down the minimal pairs of words or sentences that the student will have before him to choose the right one. The right answer should sometimes appear first, sometimes second. If there are three or four choices, the right one should alternate its position in a random fashion. One way to achieve this is to have three or four numbered buttons and to pull one out for each item. The number of the button is the number of the position of the right choice. After the test is finished it is desirable to look back at the order of the position of the right choices to see if by chance some regular pattern did not develop. Also, when by chance too many items have the right answer in the same position it is wise to change some to avoid giving the good student a feeling of insecurity when he sees the right answer in the same position and wonders if he is making a mistake.

In preparing items for dictation under technique 7.3, perhaps the most important thing to remember is to control the context. The tendency is to prepare sentences that are reasonable and contextually complete, and as a result we are likely to give clues in the context that give away the answer. With the pair, *ether*, *either*, for the contrast between $/\theta/$ and $/\eth/$, if we write, "He didn't like it, either," we have given away the answer as far as the sound contrast is concerned. The word *ether* does not fit the context, and the word *either* is practically a requirement given its approximate sound with this negative sentence. The sentence, "He didn't like either," on the other hand, meets the specifications well. *Ether* could go in the place of *either* without forcing the language. The factor of spelling might be important here, but the example is satisfactory for the point we are illustrating.

Writing items for technique 7.4, comparing sound with sound, is no problem when only words or phrases are used since the words need not fit the same linguistic context. When the items are made of sentences, we must think up sentences that are compatible with both members of the pair, or think up different sentences grammatically which nevertheless have the same sound sequence except for the minimal sound contrast. A random placement of the right answers is important here also.

In the preparation of items for techniques 7.5 through 7.9, those that go through meaning, again both members of the minimal pair must be possible in the context of the item, even though the examiner reads only one of the members of the pair. As in other techniques, decide the number of items, distribute the problems, scatter the position of the right choice in a random order, and avoid giving too much context.

4. Types of answers and answer sheets for informal tests. The ideal answer sheet for an informal test is a plain piece of paper. This makes it possible for the teacher merely to tell the class to prepare a sheet of paper for the test without having to mimeograph or otherwise reproduce an answer sheet. A plain sheet of paper can be used with all the techniques that require the student to make a choice between two or more possibilities. The idea is merely to tell the student to write 1 for the first possibility, 2 for the second, 3 for the third, etc., or to write 1 2 if the first and second choices are the same, 1 3 if the first and third are the same, 2 3 if the second and third are the same, 1 2 3 if all three are the same, and 0 if no choice is the same as any other. For more complicated techniques the numbers will be different or differently arranged, but the idea is the same.

For technique 7.3, dictation, and for the dictation part of technique 7.4, a plain sheet of paper is the answer sheet. The student writes on the answer sheet either the letters or the phonemic symbols of what is read to him by the examiner.

In those techniques that give the students graphic choices on paper to select the one that best matches what the examiner says, we need the examiner's part, the student's part, and the plain sheet of paper to record the answers. The examiner's part may be written at the convenience of the examiner in informal tests. The student's part should be clear, unambiguous and easy to follow, since the problem we are trying to test is contained in what the examiner says. The student's booklet is only a means of getting at what he hears the examiner say.

Not much more can be suggested beyond the above. Individual words and phrases are probably easier to compare if they are listed and numbered vertically, for example:

Problem 99:   1-jeep
2-gyp
3-sheep
4-ship

If the examiner reads only *ship* the student writes 4 on his sheet. If the examiner reads more than one, the student writes the number of those he reads in the order in which they are read.

Pictures may be presented horizontally as in the illustrations given above or vertically. There seems to be no particular advantage to either even though theoretically giving the pictures in the same direction as the numbers that the student will write, that is, horizontally, would seem to be better.

With items which begin with a sentence and end with several words as completion choices it may be better to use a horizontal arrangement, which uses less space on a page. These items will be discussed later when dealing with elements of language other than pronunciation.

It might be easier to provide the students with printed or mimeographed answer sheets and to let them mark the answer sheets. This is more expensive and requires bringing supplies for the test and is therefore considered a more formal type of test form. These more formal types of tests will be discussed separately below. Even in the techniques that require a separate student's booklet, if the answers are not marked on the student's booklet but on a separate sheet of paper, the same booklets can be used again, and the teacher need have in class only the number required for the number of students in any one class.

In giving an informal test with answers on a plain sheet of paper, it is convenient to tell the class to write vertically at the left side of their sheets the numbers of the items that the test will have. When the students have done this, you are ready to begin reading the test items, giving first the number of each and then the item itself. For the item above, the examiner would say, "Ninety-nine. Ship." This acts as a clue to the student, who can thus get set for the test word, *ship*, and it helps the class feel sure that they have not skipped or miscounted an item. If the examiner by mistake repeats or skips an item, the class immediately tells him, and the error is corrected. Thus, numbering the items and reading the numbers to the students is advisable even for dictation.

5. Giving the test. In giving informal as well as formal tests, try to set the students at ease. The tendency of the students is to get worked up and to make mistakes they would not have made if they were more relaxed. Hearing the sounds of language is not a highly intellectual affair, and the scores obtained while the students are not under pressure are if anything more valid than others. It is advisable even to avoid using the word *test* and merely to say that you are going to have an exercise.

Give the instructions informally, as much as possible like everyday lesson instructions, while a student distributes the students' booklets if they are required. Tell the class to prepare a sheet of paper, to write vertically numbers one to ten or to whatever the number of items of the test is going to be, give them an example or two illustrating the test, and begin. Do not *explain* the items; merely *illustrate* how they are to be taken by means of examples. It takes a long time to explain even a simple testing technique, especially since some students will want to ask more questions than necessary because of the fear of the test. If they do not seem to understand the example, give other examples or repeat the same ones rather than be caught in endless explanations. The students will actually ask for explanations, but examples will work much more effectively.

Read the items in a clear natural style, without being over precise and over clear or deliberately obscuring the sounds to make the test "more challenging." The ideal is to test the students on their hearing the sounds in natural communication situations. When addressing a group one must speak clearly but naturally; the same holds when giving a sound recognition test.

6. Scoring informal tests. Informal tests can be scored by the students. If the answers are in the form of numbers, a good way to score them is to read aloud the numbers of the right answers. The students cross out their mistakes and count them up at the end. They may also write the correct answer beside the wrong one they chose, but this has no value in the number techniques since they cannot remember what the item was. In reading the numbers of the right answers it is helpful to read them in groups of three or so with brief pauses between groups. This helps the student retain the numbers a little longer and correct the paper more comfortably and accurately.

It is not practical to read out the correct sound or the correct choice in scoring the tests, because the sounds are not heard well precisely by the students who miss items and precisely in the items missed. The names of the letters or of the phonetic symbols may be used in those cases in which they do not depend on the sound contrast being tested, otherwise we are back trying to correct items through the very sounds that are not heard correctly by the students.

With items that require the student to write what he hears in ordinary writing or in phonemic symbols it is convenient to have a movable blackboard and to ask one of the students to write his answers on this blackboard rather than on a piece of paper. The blackboard is turned away from the class while the test is given. When correcting it, the blackboard is turned round so that the class can see it clearly. The teacher then corrects the answers on the board, and the class correct their papers from the corrected answers on the board. The teacher takes care not to cover the answers with his body while correcting them so that the class can be correcting their own papers at the same time the teacher is correcting the answers on the board. Perfectly good variations of this procedure are possible. The teacher may tell the student at the board to correct the items he has missed by giving him the right answers. The class still correct their papers from the corrected answers on the board.

When there is ample blackboard space in a room and when the teacher can enter the room before class, the answers can be written on the board before class and covered with a paper or curtain. After the test is given, the paper or curtain is removed and the answers become visible to the class for the correction of their papers.

Even without consideration of honesty in correcting the papers it is more varied and usually more interesting to have the students exchange papers for correction. This is done by simply telling the class to pass their papers to the student at their right. The student at the right end of each row must pass his paper to the first student of the row. Thus each student corrects the paper of his neighbor to the left and has his own corrected by his neighbor to the right, except of course the students at both ends of each row. When the tests have been scored they are returned to their owners who check the corrections and the mistakes. With young children who may be tempted to make special arrangements with their neighbors for overlooking their errors, the class can be asked to pass the papers to their neighbors to the right, and when this is done, they are asked to pass the papers once more. The papers are thus corrected by the student beyond the immediate neighbor.

It is usually effective to ask for the papers and to record the scores and take stock of the problems of the students. Students may at first claim that they will work as hard if the scores are not reported to the teacher, but in most school situations the students will work better for the teacher than for themselves. This is understandable as it concerns learning a foreign language when we consider that working for themselves the students will tend to go at their own speed, which in this case would be to use their native language sound system, while working for the teacher means forcing themselves to use the foreign sounds. The interesting thing, however, is that probably most students enjoy working for the teacher more than working for their own edification.

The tests described in this chapter permit us to obtain both a numerical score indicating the number of items missed or their proportion to the number of items answered correctly, and a diagnostic score for each of the problems tested. The numerical score gives us the relative standing of the student in relation to the other students and the absolute number of items that the student would have to get right in order to make a "perfect" score. These scores can be used to stimulate the students to greater effort in the right direction and to arrive at the final grades that teachers have to give their students in most teaching systems.

The diagnostic scores for each problem permit the teacher to know the specific weaknesses and strengths of each of his students and the weaknesses of the class as a whole. When he discovers that a class does not yet hear accurately a sound contrast, he teaches it again, or gives additional drill to help the class as a whole.

More elaborate devices for scoring will be described in connection with the discussion of formal tests of sound recognition.

7.6 FORMAL TESTS OF RECOGNITION

Although basically the testing of sound perception and recognition is the same in informal classroom tests and in formal testing situations, the formal tests will require certain standards of form, validation, etc., that call for additional considerations. Preparing a more formal type of test will require a list of problems to be tested, the words and phrases containing the problems, and the writing of items. A formal test requires initially from 20 per cent to 100 per cent more items than are finally used. In addition this experimental test must be edited with greater severity than an informal test. It also needs instructions for the examiner and the students who will take the test, since one of the characteristics of a formal test is that it is to be given by teachers and examiners other than those who prepare it.

The next step is to administer this form of the test, which we may call X–1, to native speakers of the foreign language for validation. If native speakers are not easily available, non-native speakers who make the phonemic distinctions in their speech may be used as a validating sample, since they will hear phonemic contrasts if they use them. Form X–1 is edited on the basis of these scores to produce form X–2. The test is then tried on a sample of the students for whom it is intended, an item count of the papers of these students is made, the items are rearranged so that they go from easy to difficult, the test is reproduced, and a manual is prepared giving its reliability, validity, instructions, scoring, etc. Each of these processes requires further comments which appear below.

1. Listing the problems and choosing the words. These first two steps are the same as for informal tests. The only possible difference is that completeness and accuracy must be greater in a formal test because it will be used by others.

2. Preparing the items. The process of preparing items is the same as for informal tests. We must, however, prepare more items than will actually be used in the final form of the test. This is necessary, because no matter how carefully the items are edited, some of them invariably turn out to be defective when administered first to native speakers of the language and then to a sample group of the students for whom the test is intended. Pronunciation items prepared according to the instructions given and based on an accurate and complete description of the problems to be tested are already highly selected. With these, it is usually enough to prepare approximately 20 per cent more items than will be used in the final test.

We must also consider the fact that with techniques using phonemic symbols, not all the students may be familiar with the symbols ordinarily used by the examiner or test maker. It must also be remembered that familiarity with the symbols is distinct from the ability to hear the sounds.

Often in writing items one senses that a particular item is not as strong as we would like it to be. Rather than discarding it at this stage it is better to keep it and to write another item for the same problem. Later when all the items are finished, we may succeed in improving the weak one, or on second reading, it may not appear as weak as we thought when working so close to the problems.

In preparing the test items it is usually convenient to write them on separate cards. This permits rearrangements, rewriting of undesirable items and addition of new ones. Standard 5×8 cards have the advantage of providing space for writing considerable information on the performance of the item.

3. Editing of form X-1. No matter how carefully we write each item, things will be missed on first writing. When the items have been written, we must go back and re-read them carefully again. Items that are unnatural, items that are ambiguous, that are too elaborate, that give away the answer, that are humorous and will produce a disturbing laugh by the class, that use words that may offend a particular cultural group, that contain problems other than pronunciation which may actually invalidate the result, and any others that in the judgment of the writer-editor will introduce factors that reduce or cancel the value of the test must be edited or eliminated. At this stage, a careful reading of the items by a colleague or several colleagues is highly recommended. To save time, the colleague can be asked to write question marks, checks, or brief comments at the points where he has some doubt regarding the test items. If no one is able to give the test maker this kind of assistance, he will have to rely on his own editing without the benefit of having the test looked at by one who has not been as close to it as the test maker.

4. Instructions to the examiner. The instructions to the examiner must be as clear, precise, and brief as possible. Probably the most effective style is that of request sentences, for example: " Count the exact number of tests for the exact number of students. Distribute the tests by rows, giving each row the exact number for the number of students in it. Say, 'KEEP THE BOOKLETS CLOSED. WRITE YOUR NAME AT THE TOP OF THE PAGE.' Hold up your copy of the test with the front part to the class. Point to the place for their name."

As illustrated in this example, which is incomplete, the parts that the examiner must say to the class should be set in different and very clear type to set them apart from the rest of the instructions. Bold face or capital letters will do.

Following is an example from a test of aural perception:

ADMINISTRATION OF THE TEST

This test should be administered by a native speaker of standard American English or by one who can speak English with all the pronunciation contrasts of a native speaker. It should be read in a *clear natural style*. Differences should not be exaggerated or minimized in any way. The items should be read *only once*. Each word or sentence must be read with the *same intonation*, preferably a falling, high-low type.

The test should be given to small groups of up to twenty students. It should not be given to larger groups unless the room has exceptionally good acoustics.

Proceed as follows:

1. Seat the students not closer than in every other seat.
2. Distribute the answer sheet to the students.
3. Ask the students to write their name and the date on the answer sheet.
4. Read them the following instructions and examples:

THIS EXERCISE IS TO DISCOVER WHAT ENGLISH SOUNDS YOU CAN HEAR CLEARLY. ANSWER EVERY QUESTION.

PART I—A. I AM GOING TO READ THREE WORDS. CHECK THE NUMBERS OF THE WORDS THAT ARE THE SAME. WHEN NO TWO WORDS ARE THE SAME, CHECK THE ZERO.

EXAMPLE A: CAT. CAT. COT. (Brief pause)
NUMBERS I AND 2 ARE THE SAME. CHECK I 2.

EXAMPLE B: RUN. SUN. RUN. (Pause)
NUMBERS I AND 3 ARE THE SAME. CHECK I 3.

EXAMPLE C: LAST. LAST. LAST. (Pause)
THE THREE ARE THE SAME. CHECK I 2 3.

EXAMPLE D: BEAST. BEST. BEST. (Pause)
NUMBERS 2 AND 3 ARE THE SAME. CHECK 2 3.

EXAMPLE E: PAIR. FAIR. CHAIR. (Pause)
NO TWO ARE THE SAME. CHECK O.

Repeat the examples if the students still do not understand the procedure.[1]

5. Instructions to the student. If the instructions to the examiner must be clear, precise, and concise, the instructions to the student must be doubly so on all counts. In general there should be a brief statement of the material of the item and another of what the student must do with the material. For example, with items that identify sounds through numbers, the instructions to the student might be: "The examiner will read a word or phrase. It contains the vowel /iy/ or /i/. Identify the vowel by number, 1 for /iy/ and 2 for /i/."

With items that identify sounds with letters or phonemic symbols, an example might be: "The examiner will read a word from each group. Circle the word you hear." With items that compare sound with sound you can begin: "The examiner will read two (or three) words (or sentences). Check the numbers of the words (or sentences) that are the same. If no two are the same, check the zero."

Then give as many examples as there are variations of the item. In the example from a perception test above, five examples were necessary because there were five different variants depending on the number and the order of the three choices of the item. Notice that item A has 1 2 as the answer, item B has 1 3,

---

[1] *Test of Aural Perception in English for Latin-American Students. Examiners Booklet.* (Robert Lado, English Language Institute, 1957.)

item C has 1 2 3, item D has 2 3, and item E has 0, all the possibilities. In addition the examples illustrate minimal pairs of vowels and of consonants.

Add also other information that is important. For example, "The words will be read only once." "Answer every item." "Blank items are counted as wrong items."

Since the purpose of the test is to see if the student hears the sounds of the language rather than to baffle and fail him, there is no harm in giving the instructions in writing in his native language, although this is not absolutely necessary.

Recorded tests do not change essentially the instructions to be given to the student or to the examiner. Information on the speed of the disc, on the quality of the machine employed, etc., should be added. The instructions on giving or taking the test can be recorded on the disc or tape along with the test proper and will therefore not differ from instructions given with a live voice test.

6. Using native speakers and non-native speakers in the validation of a test.

(a) *Native speakers.* Giving the experimental form of a test to native speakers of the language tested permits a partial validation of the test. Since native speakers of the foreign language know their language functionally at least, when they fail an item in substantial numbers, we reason that some extraneous factor must be responsible for the failure.

Once a heavy extraneous factor is detected in the test its nature should be determined. The test may require special training in addition to mastery of the language, or the items may be too complicated mechanically, or they may require a memory span that the average person does not possess, etc. Would this extraneous factor also vitiate the results with the students for whom the test is intended? If so, items that require special training over and above mastery of the language, that are too complicated mechanically for native speakers, or require an unusually long memory span, will in general not be valid and should be eliminated or edited accordingly.

In other cases, however, the extraneous factor that results in failure by the native speakers may not disturb the foreign learners.

75

For example, if the responses are in the language of the learners, it is obvious that native speakers would fail, yet the test might be valid for the foreign learners. If the native speakers have never studied a foreign language, they may be confused by an item that might still be valid for students who have studied a foreign language. If native speakers have been taught some artificial rule of correctness that does not agree with their normal use of the language, they may fail an item that would be quite valid for the students for whom the test is intended. Finally, if native speakers do not take the experimental test with the proper seriousness and desire to make a high score, the results cannot be used in validation.

The above are intended as proper limitations on the interpretation of results with native speakers in validating a test. We assumed that representative native speakers were readily available. In the overwhelming majority of cases, however, foreign language testing is done where native speakers are not easily available.

(b) *Non-native speakers.* If native speakers are not easily available, we can use non-native speakers as a validating sample provided we determine beforehand that they know the language functionally in the area tested. In other words, with representative native speakers we could safely assume that they knew the language functionally, whereas with non-natives we cannot assume this but must determine it empirically by screening them before they are used for the validating sample.

Screening non-native speakers for a validating sample is a delicate process that will require considerable labor. It is justified only on the grounds that in preparing a good formal test of language the labor that goes into it is repaid by the accuracy of the results obtained with the test when finished and by the great saving in time and labor that will be reaped from the final form. In any event, this step in validation should be used only when some less elaborate method is not possible.

For perception or comprehension as opposed to production, it is difficult to determine directly if a non-native speaker has or has not mastered a language problem. If he misses a contrast or the meaning of a pattern, is it because he does not know it or because an extraneous factor is involved? If he grasps the contrast or the meaning of the pattern, is it because he has mastered the problem or because there is some additional clue in the item? It is difficult to determine.

We assume, on the other hand, that if a non-native has overcome the problem in his speech and/or writing, he also perceives or understands it. Consequently, in screening non-natives for a validating sample in perception or comprehension we determine by systematic inspection if the non-native handles the problem satisfactorily. This systematic inspection may have to be elaborate and time-consuming; for example, the inspection of free oral production by the non-native.

For production, this initial step in validation might be omitted altogether if we have as our starting point an accurate linguistic description of the problem.

We reason as follows: the production test has to elicit from the student the words or sentences that contain the problem. If the items do in fact elicit these words or sentences without giving away the problem in the stimulus, we can score the response as representing a sample of the student's production. Care should be exercised not to consider wrong the variations that native speakers would normally show through dialect differences and permitted free variation. A good description of the language should include this information.

Henceforth, whenever we say that a test is to be tried with native speakers, the above discussion of the use of non-native speakers also applies.

Chapter 8

TESTING PRODUCTION OF THE SOUND SEGMENTS

8.1   **INTRODUCTION AND GENERAL CONSIDERATIONS**

Testing the production of the sound segments of a foreign language presents more problems for the examiner than testing recognition of the sound segments. Probably as a result, the testing of speaking is less advanced than the testing of listening, and although we talk a great deal about the pronunciation of students of foreign language we do relatively little about testing it.

1. Recognition usually runs ahead of production. If a student pronounces a sound contrast in a foreign language he will also hear it. Thus if we were able to test the student's production of the sound segments we would be assured of having tested his recognition also. The difficulties of testing production make this approach impractical in ordinary circumstances. At the same time, students learn to hear sound contrasts usually before they are able to pronounce them, and so in testing production we would not discover everything the student has learned to hear. And what is more to the point in this chapter, by testing recognition of the sound segments we will not have tested what the student has learned to pronounce. Finally, the distance between recognition and pronunciation is not the same for every student. Some students who learn to hear reasonably well still have very poor pronunciation, whereas others learn to pronounce almost as well as they can hear.

2. Production of the sound segments for communication. To be understood like a native in a foreign language it is not necessary to sound entirely like a native; it is necessary to use the phonemic sound contrasts and units of the foreign language. These include of course intonation, stress and rhythm, and the sound segments. Tests of pronunciation for general use by teachers should use communication as the ultimate criterion, judged systematically by means of the phonemic contrasts, units, and features of the sound system of the language.

To test the ability to pronounce a foreign language like a native in the sense of having conquered all the subphonemic variants, one needs to be an expert phonetician, and this is a career in itself. One can insist that teachers of foreign languages should have some basic phonetic training, but it would be another matter to expect them to be expert phoneticians. In any case, at the present stage in the professional preparation of language teachers it is safe to say that the great majority of them are not highly skilled in phonetics.

3. Vagueness of the testing of pronunciation in production tests. Because of the problems involved in testing production of the sound segments and because until recently we did not have the aid of phonemics to define the units of pronunciation, it is the rule to find vague references to and treatment of pronunciation in production tests. In one report we see "intelligibility" given as the major criterion. This is the same as communication, of course. Yet the tests failed because intelligibility was not defined formally and specifically beyond the idea that the students should be understandable to natives. This idea though correct still leaves us with such insoluble problems as what natives are to be used as touchstones since different natives have different skill in understanding foreign speakers. Another production scale in a foreign language uses a vague concept of oral readiness as the basis of fluency, which itself remains undefined. Pronunciation is included in these concepts, but no specific provision is made to elicit particular utterances to sample pronunciation.

References to pronunciation in the scoring scale are similarly vague and ineffective. Examiners are not able to decide objectively whether a response by a student falls into one of even a rough three-point scale with instructions like these: 1. Sufficiently approaches native speech to be completely understandable. 2. Can be understood, though with difficulty, because there are sounds which he does not utter correctly. 3. Would not be understood by natives because his pronunciation is so different from theirs. Or another scale: 1. Partially intelligible: . . . The response is either incomplete, or exceedingly hard to understand because of poor pronunciation or usage. 2. Intelligible but labored: . . . The delivery is hesitating, or regressive, but does not contain amusing or misleading errors in pronunciation or usage.

When is pronunciation so different from that of natives that the speaker would not be understood by them? What natives are we to take as guides? How can we tell if those particular natives would or would not understand? What is poor pronunciation? What is regressive delivery that does not contain amusing errors in pronunciation? These are not theoretical questions. They need to be answered by the conscientious examiner and they should be answered the same way by all examiners.

4. Informal unsystematic listening is ineffective. Informal contact with students, even the extended contact of the language classroom, is not very effective as a way to test a student's pronunciation. From this extended contact one can say that one student has better pronunciation than another in rough terms, but when asked to list the specific pronunciation problems of a particular student of ours we will remember only the very salient mispronunciations and will not as a rule be able to come anywhere near completeness. One feels the need to interview the student formally to check the list of problems and see which ones he has mastered and which ones he has not.

5. Need to test production problems specifically. Even if we do interview the students formally to determine how well they pronounce the foreign language we still feel the vagueness and inadequacy of trying to test pronunciation as an undifferentiated mass. We need to seek out the pronunciation problems and test them individually because they are specific and require systematic treatment.

8.2 TECHNIQUES TO TEST PRODUCTION OF THE SOUND SEGMENTS

The general procedure to test production of the sound segments is to stimulate the student to produce utterances that contain the pronunciation problems and to score the responses. This general procedure involves a number of variables which result in a variety of techniques. These variables are in the type of stimulus used, in the form and conditions of the response, and in the scoring.

1. Stimuli for production of the problems. Although free conversation in an interview is a highly valid way to observe the pronunciation of a student it is impractical because the student will not use all the sounds when we are ready for them and he will use some sounds with more frequency than we need or can handle effectively. Bloch reports that in a test of 2,000 running phonemes in colloquial Japanese two of the phonemes, /p/ and /z/, did not occur at all, while another one, /a/, occurred 296 times.[1] We therefore find it more practical to elicit certain utterances that we know contain the problem we wish to test. The stimuli for eliciting the desired utterances can be verbal, pictures, or written material.

PRONUNCIATION TECHNIQUE 8.1. **Verbal stimuli.** Verbal stimuli are questions, requests, or statements which elicit from the student utterances that will show his handling of the pronunciation problems. If possible the student should not be aware that pronunciation specifically is being tested. These verbal stimuli are particularly good because they represent a normal use of the language. They can be presented orally so that the student is placed in a conversational situation, or they can be put to the student in writing. Having the stimulus in writing gives him time to collect himself in responding.

Whether presented orally or in writing, these verbal stimuli can be used with individual students in an interview type of test or with a group. If oral stimuli are used for a group they can be piped to the group through individual earphones in order to

---

[1] Bernard Bloch. "Studies in Colloquial Japanese IV. Phonemics," *Language,* Vol. 26, No. 1, 1950, p. 115.

preserve the isolation of the response of the students, who would otherwise hear the responses of their classmates.

Since these verbal stimuli do not provide the content of what is to be answered, they must deal with common everyday experiences in order to prevent the content of the response from becoming a more important factor than the pronunciation we want to test.

To provide a uniform content for the responses it is possible to have the students read a brief passage from which they will be able to answer the questions or otherwise respond to the verbal stimuli. This use of a written passage for content has, however, the serious limitation of introducing differences in reading efficiency and in the power to memorize the content of a paragraph.

In testing pronunciation of beginning students, the questions, requests, or instructions may constitute comprehension problems themselves. It is possible then to translate these verbal stimuli to the native language. This increases the influence of the native language pronunciation somewhat, but it insures communication.

With all the advantages of using specific verbal stimuli to test pronunciation, this method does not always elicit either all the responses one wants or sufficiently uniform responses in many cases.

PRONUNCIATION TECHNIQUE 8.2. **Picture stimuli.** Pictures of various kinds are used extensively as stimuli for verbal responses by students. They constitute a very valid medium for pronunciation tests. Line drawings sometimes convey an idea simply and quickly. A line drawing of a man reading a newspaper elicits rather uniformly the utterance "He's reading the paper" with minor variations such as "The man is reading the paper," "The man is reading," "He's reading." In every case the students attempt to say, "reading," which is the test word.

If the pictures are classified into actions, things, and qualities, for example, the student tends to think he is being tested for grammar or for vocabulary and uses a pronunciation that is more his usual one.

A single composite picture is sometimes preferred as the stimulus. It has the advantage of requiring only one inspection for several responses. It has the disadvantage that not too many problems can be systematically elicited with any one picture.

No matter how clear and how well-planned pictures may be, if they are merely presented to the student without telling him what he has to do with them, he will merely look at them and wonder what to do. Pictures alone are not practical. We must give some verbal instructions with them. Sample instructions are, "What do you see?" "What is he doing?" "What is going to happen?" "Tell the story." These verbal instructions can be given orally or in writing. One simple way to give the instructions is to write them on the picture itself.

PRONUNCIATION TECHNIQUE 8.3. **Reading.** The most uniform, precise, and simple method for testing production of the sound segments of a language is to have the student read out loud the material you prepare for the test. The written material can be words, sentences, or connected paragraphs. Every student produces the same sample of the sounds of the language.

Since the ability to read is distinct from the ability to speak, the reading stimulus has the disadvantage of introducing the factor of reading ability. A person who has learned a foreign language as a child and has never had the opportunity to learn to read it will not be able to take a reading test, even though his pronunciation may be quite good. The factor of reading is less important among students who have all learned to read as they studied the foreign language, but differences in the ability to read aloud will remain and will affect the results of the pronunciation test. These differences in the ability to read aloud are present in the native language as well.

In English and other languages that are not spelled regularly, the effect of multiple spellings for one sound, and multiple sounds for one spelling, contribute an additional extraneous factor. The letters *o u g h* can represent the sounds /əf/ as in *enough*, /uw/ as in *through*, /ow/ as in *dough*, /ɔ/ as in *thought*, and in combination with other letters they can represent many more sounds. From a well-known example the letters *g h o t* could presumably represent *fish* to the unwary foreign speaker with /f/ as the sound of *gh* in *enough*, /i/ as the sound of *o* in *women*, and /š/ as the sound of *t* in *nation*. The interference of these spelling irregularities is not equal for every student or for every problem.

Chinese writing, which is logographic rather than phonetic, is a good stimulus because it does not give clues to the phonemes nor does it interfere with pronunciation through irregular representation of sounds. Knowledge of the Chinese characters is, however, a difficult matter, and the reading factor becomes heavy as a result.

A further limitation of reading as a pronunciation stimulus is that pronunciation in reading does not parallel entirely pronunciation in speaking. Certain reductions permitted in speaking are not permitted in reading, and certain leveling of transitions and of emphases are normal in reading but not permitted in speaking. This is not a serious limitation in testing the sound segments, however. Perhaps more important is the fact that in reading, the student's attention is on different things than in speaking. In reading his attention is on the graphic symbols which give him the words, the word order, the thread of the story. In speaking, on the other hand, he must operate the thread of his story, the sentences he must use, the word order, the words, etc.

These limitations do not eliminate reading as a testing device, of course, but they do show that there is as yet no ideal stimulus to test pronunciation on a production level.

PRONUNCIATION TECHNIQUE 8.4. **Translation.** Translation from the native to the foreign language is a valid and useful device to elicit the utterances we need in order to test pronunciation. Translation is limited by the fact that it is one of the most difficult things to do in a foreign language. There are multiple ways of translating things, and students who might be able to pronounce a sound might fail because they do not know how to translate something. With proper precautions so that the translation items used are not difficult to translate, translation can be a helpful testing device in pronunciation.

PRONUNCIATION TECHNIQUE 8.5. **Completion items.** Test items that give a sentence or phrase with some part omitted so that the student supplies the missing word from the clues in the context can be used effectively to test pronunciation. An example to elicit the vowel /iy/ might be, "There are seven days in a ——." The student reads aloud the sentence and should say *week* to complete it. Part of the spelling of the word can be given, for example, "Here is another stamp for his beautiful stamp co--ection." The student is to pronounce the whole sentence including the incomplete word.

When the entire word is omitted, the student might not be fully aware that he is being tested on pronunciation. These items, however, are difficult to write because there is always some possibility that a different word can be used in the blank spot. When part of the spelling of the word is given, the student soon realizes that he is being tested on his pronunciation.

Form and conditions of the oral response. The student's response is an oral one in pronunciation. We can, however, deal with it as it is uttered or we can have it recorded or taped for scoring and checking. Tape recorders are well suited for this work because the responses recorded on magnetic tape can be played as many times as the examiner wishes, they can be preserved as long as needed, and they can be erased at will. Magnetic discs now in limited use are also helpful for this type of work.

A person's pronunciation of a foreign language varies in accuracy depending on the tension under which he speaks. The same student who has conquered a problem when reciting in class will make elementary mistakes in front of a strange audience or facing a microphone. No test can hope to predict the mistakes a student will make under any and all conditions. All we can do is to devise a test that will be reasonably representative of language in use. We then test all the students under the same conditions, or as nearly the same conditions as possible, and make judgments on the basis of the performance of each student on the test under these conditions.

2. Scoring the production test. Objective scoring of pronunciation is one of the most difficult problems in this type of test. By objective scoring is meant assigning scores that are reliable, valid, and easy to arrive at so that average skill is enough to use them. Fully objective scoring is not yet possible in direct testing of pronunciation. Three considerations, however, will substantially increase the objectivity of scoring pronunciation: (1) Score only phonemic units, contrasts, and problems. Phonemic contrasts are easier to hear by untrained examiners if they speak the language well than subphonemic sound distortions. In other words, a speaker of English can tell if a person said *kill* or *hill*, illustrating a phonemic contrast, even if he is unable to describe the difference involved and even if he cannot detect the subphonemic difference between the front /k/ of *kill* and the back /k/ of *call* for example.

(2) To increase the accuracy of scoring, the examiner's attention must be focused preferably on one thing and one thing only. Judges in swimming races and in other athletic contests do just that. They do not look at the swimmers or at the pool; they look at the finish line only and are thus better able to see the first contestant who touches it. In scoring a response in a language test the attention of the examiner can be focused on the /d/–/ð/ contrast in English for example. The examiner may further limit his attention to the phonemic features "stop" versus "fricative" that are decisive in this case, or to the difference between *they* and *day* or whatever the minimal pair might be if he is not trained in phonetics. When the student's response has been taped it is of course possible to recheck it as many times as necessary, but it is not a saving to cluster the problems in an item if we then have to repeat it many times to score it.

(3) All the students should be tested on the same problems the same number of times in order to obtain scores that are easily comparable.

Since mastery of a sound problem does not proceed from absolute ignorance to full control at once but advances in gradual and fluctuating fashion, we are faced with a situation in which a student will pronounce a sound satisfactorily in a word but not in another which seems no more difficult, and in fact he may pronounce a sound well in a word and miss it on another occurrence of the same word. It would be more accurate to speak of the percentage of times that the student now handles the problem satisfactorily. As a result it is advisable to have several items testing the same problem in a test, and to have the same number of items for each problem.

3. Group tests versus individual tests of production. Any teacher having access to a language laboratory with a number of recording machines can administer production tests to as many students in a group as there are machines available in the laboratory. Group testing of production is now possible in many schools because such language laboratories are increasingly common.

To give a production test to a group of students in a language laboratory the stimulus is given in a booklet or through earphones, or both, to each of the students. Picture stimuli can appear in individual booklets or in a large poster visible to everyone, or by means of some projection machine on a large screen visible to the group.

Under these conditions, administering a production test will take no more time than administering any other group test. Scoring production tests has to be done individually, however, at the slow speed at which they were recorded regardless of whether they are given individually or in groups. Threading each individual spool of tape, and listening and scoring the responses takes considerable patience with any substantial number of students. Magnetic discs are easier to manipulate for this purpose. They are stacked on the same turn-table, and as each one is finished it is peeled off leaving the next one ready underneath. The difference, however, is not very great, considering the time it takes to listen to and score the responses. Playing back the response at double the speed at which it was recorded does not permit accurate scoring by the average teacher.

Individual tests take a great deal of time to administer, yet they can be scored as they are given. The total time it takes to give and score a production test thus takes approximately the same whether it is given as a group test or individually.

8.3   INFORMAL TESTS OF PRODUCTION

Preparing an informal classroom test of production involves the preparation of a list of problems, selection of words and phrases that contain the problems, preparation of items, giving the test to individuals or to groups and scoring it.

1. List of production problems. Before beginning any test the total list of production problems is prepared. This list is different from the list of recognition problems though closely related to it. The list is prepared by comparing the phonological analysis of the language to be learned with that of the native language of the students. When the sound system of the foreign language differs from that of the native language at any point so that when the native language system is transferred to the foreign language it results in less units or in differently structured units, or in differently distributed units, there will be a problem of production. For a discussion of the analysis of pronunciation problems see *Linguistics Across Cultures* by Robert Lado.

The list of problems should thus give each phoneme in the language to be learned, with the features that the students will distort because of their native language, the resulting different phonemes, and the environments in which they will be distorted. For example:

Production Problems of a Spanish Speaker Learning English

	English Phoneme	Distortion by Spanish Speaker	In this Environment	Result
1.	/d/	fricative	between vowels, after /r/, after /s/.	/ð/
2.	/ð/	stop	after silence or pause, after /l/, after /n/, sometimes in final position after a vowel.	/d/

2. Choosing words and phrases that contain the problems.
Working from the list of problems we choose words and phrases that contain the problems in the environments described. Some selection of these environments is desirable. If one environment seems more difficult than others and just as common we might prefer it, since pronouncing the sound in this environment would indicate that the others, which are presumed to be easier, would also be known. If on the other hand a sound may be subject to greater leveling in a particular position than in others, for example /ð/ after /z/ in *is there a hat there*, we might avoid this environment.

The words and phrases chosen for a pronunciation test must be within the active vocabulary of the students or the students will not be able to use them. Even if the students read the words in the test, if the words are not part of the active vocabulary of the students, the result will not be as representative as it would be if they were known to the students on a production level. In informal classroom tests, the teacher usually knows which words are familiar to the students without having to appeal to word counts or other inventories. With formal tests some objective criterion may be necessary.

Minimal pairs are not necessary for production tests ordinarily. The word *key* is a good one to test production of the vowel /iy/ even though a minimal pair with /i/ is not available. When there is a choice between two equally satisfactory words and a minimal pair can be found for one of them, this word might be favored, because scoring by untrained examiners will be slightly easier.

Words that have more than one current pronunciation are less satisfactory than those having a uniform pronunciation even when the variation is not in the sound being tested. The effect of variant pronunciations is distracting to the examiner. When the variation is in the sound being tested, the word is unacceptable.

If the test makes use of pictures as the stimulus, the words chosen must be picturable. Many words of actions, things, and qualities are easily picturable but not all are, and many words require such elaborate pictures that it becomes impractical to use them. Therefore, more words must be found than are actually used.

Once a picture has been given a name, however, it is remarkable how well the students will remember what it is. For informal tests, then, it is possible to use pictures that are not very clear or accurate if we once tell the students what they are. The pictures can then be used as a stimulus with these students.

3. Writing the test. With the list of problems and the words that contain the problems ready, the test proper can now be written. The technique must be chosen. If the test is long, an alternate technique is required. When the number of items that can be given in the time planned for the test has been determined, the problems are then distributed over this number of items.

The important thing in writing production items is to give the maximum context in a short item. In other words, in order to make sure that the student will produce the words that contain the problems, he is given as clear a set of clues as can be packed into the item. If we use verbal stimuli, these should be clear and simple. If pictures are used, they also must be as clear and simple as possible. In a reading technique, the sentences must be natural and clear. Common, everyday situations are usually preferable because they are more likely to be within the experience of all the students. Cultural differences that will interfere with the responses should be avoided.

The verbal instructions, if they are to be given orally, should not contain the test words, otherwise the student will have a chance to hear the word immediately before he attempts to produce it. This reduces the production test to a test of mimicry, which is only a rudimentary check on pronunciation.

When we fail to produce an item with the one technique the alternate technique should be tried. A third technique may have to be added if the first two fail. A reading technique will always permit the testing of any problem not tested otherwise. After the problems have been built into items, the items are separated according to technique and presented as separate parts of the test.

Following are some sample items:

Problem: Initial /ǰ/ voiced affricate rendered as /č/ voiceless affricate or /š/ voiceless fricative. Test word: *January*. Verbal stimulus: "Tell me the first month of the year."

Problem: /d/ between vowels, a stop, rendered as /ð/, a fricative. Test word: *reading*. Picture stimulus with verbal instructions (Fig. 8.1).

Problem: /uw/, high close tense, rendered as /u/, high open lax. Test word: *true*. Reading matter: "The story is true."

Problem: /θ/, voiceless dental fricative, rendered as /s/, voiceless alveolar sibilant. Test word: *thousand*. Completion stimulus: "Ten hundred is one ——."

Fig. 8.1

4. Giving the production test to the members of a class.
Giving the same test to a class individually by one teacher poses
some difficult problems. With a large class a lengthy test may
not be feasible. Even with a short test, if some students hear
others taking the test, they will have some unfair advantage. If
they have a chance to ask a student who has just taken the test
what the questions were they will also have an undue advantage.
Give the class an assignment that will force them to concentrate,
and call each student to the teacher's desk for the test. Having
the students study in a study room or in the library and calling
them in individually for the test is possible if the facilities are
available. Group testing solves these problems, but the facilities
necessary for recording an entire class together are not generally
available.

5. Scoring the test. The examiner concentrates on the one
problem that the item is designed to test and disregards all others.
This restriction is necessary to achieve objectivity in scoring and
to obtain comparable scores. If possible, the examiner should
have before him the list of test words with the problems underlined or otherwise indicated so that when the student produces
his response the examiner is ready to hear the particular sound
being tested.

Sample scoring aid: 1, k*ey*. 2, spoo*n*. 3, h*a*t. 4, *th*ink.

Instructions to examiner: Check through the italicized letters
if the pronunciation is wrong. Check beside the word if it is
right.

A refinement of this procedure is to have not only the test word with the problem sound underlined but to have also a symbol representing the distortion that will be produced by the students who have not mastered the problem. This further helps the examiner to be ready for the response and it permits him to make a mark for every response whether right or wrong. When the response is wrong, the mark is made beside the symbol representing the distortion. When the response is right, the mark is made beside the letters or symbols representing the right sound.

/iy/ /n/ /æ/ /θ/
1, ke*y* /i/. 2, spoo*n* /ŋ/. 3, h*a*t /a/ 4, *th*ink /s/.

Instructions: Check the pronunciation rendered by the student.

8.4.   FORMAL TESTS OF PRODUCTION

The description and listing of problems, the selection of the test words, and the writing of items are the same for informal tests as for formal ones. One should be stricter in preparing items for formal tests, of course.

1. Instructions. The instructions to the examiner and to the student have to be carefully prepared and edited for formal tests. They must give all the essential information and tell the examiner as precisely as possible what he is to do in administering and scoring the test. If any discretion is left to the examiner on what to do, individual differences may be introduced by different examiners and the scores on the test may cease to be comparable. The examiner has to be instructed not to help the student or to hinder him. If the response is not entirely wrong, but it is not right either, the instructions should tell the examiner what course to take. One way is to say, "Any response that is not the phoneme expected will be counted wrong." The instructions should say whether second tries will be permitted. In general they should not. The examiner should not let the student know if he has made a mistake, because the effect may be inhibiting in the responses that follow it. For this reason, the examiner may not tell the student when he has given the right answer either. Special words of encouragement are probably desirable in an oral test. They should be general and at specific points in the test for all students. They can be, "You are doing fine. Continue." All of these things should be given in writing, with the parts that the examiner will tell the student set off in quotation marks and printed in capitals or bold face.

The instructions to the student should be brief. They should be chiefly examples. A good rule is not to give two consecutive sentences of instructions to the student without an example. If several points have to be made, two short sentences can sometimes be given consecutively and then an example showing the student what to do. For example: "COMPLETE THE SENTENCES. 'THE SUN SHINES DURING THE ———.' YOU SAY, 'THE SUN SHINES DURING THE DAY.' 'THE MOON SHINES DURING THE ———.' YOU SAY, 'THE MOON SHINES DURING THE NIGHT.' SAY THE ENTIRE SENTENCE, NOT JUST 'NIGHT' AND 'DAY.' CONTINUE." Nothing needs to be told the student about it being a completion item or a pronunciation test.

2. Experimental administration to native speakers. When the items have been written and the instructions prepared the test is ready for an experimental administration to native speakers of the language. In this experimental administration the mortality of items of the verbal stimuli and picture stimuli types is extremely high. To be safe we should have twice as many experimental items of these two types as we will need for the finished test. Of the completion or translation types we will need 50 per cent more than the final form will have. Of the reading type, which have a low mortality, 5 per cent more than the final test will have is a safe margin.

If this experimental test is given to fifty native speakers individually, a number of the items will show more than one response, and some of these variations will be useless because they do not contain the test word. If no way suggests itself to correct this by editing, the item should be discarded before the experimental run is finished. Items that are edited and from then on show uniform responses as expected can be kept. Also to be discarded are those items that do not elicit the desired response even if they elicit a uniform answer.

Items eliciting the desired response from native speakers 95 per cent of the time or better should probably be kept.

When native speakers are not easily available to the test maker, it is possible to substitute a sample of students for whom the test is intended. The purpose of the items is merely to elicit the key words from the student so that we may score his production. If the items do in fact elicit the key words from the student, we can validly use the items.

The only advantage in giving the experimental test to native speakers is to find out if the problem sound is used by them in the particular items of the test. Obviously, if educated native speakers do not use a particular sound distinction in the key words as elicited by the experimental test, it is not valid to expect the student who is learning the language to do so.

3. Experimental administration to a representative sample of students. With the test pruned of items that did not elicit the test words from native speakers or that elicited varied instead of uniform responses, it is ready to be tried experimentally with a sample of 50 to 100 students representative of those for whom the test is being prepared. These students are given the test under actual test conditions. An item count is made of the times that each item is missed by the students in the sample, and the items are rearranged according to difficulty, that is, according to the times they are missed, putting the easy items first.

When too many items test the same thing or are bunched up in the middle range of difficulty we may decide to eliminate some of these.

It is not necessary to check if each item shows discrimination among levels of mastery as indicated by the score on the test as a whole. If the students at the top of the scale miss a particular item more than other students who are below them, the item should still be kept. It represents actual production by students, and is valid in itself. A re-inspection of such items is of course in order, to make sure that the cause for the failure is not an extraneous one such as a misprint, defective wording, or something equally irrelevant.

4. Administration of the production test, norms, etc. Reproduction of the test in booklet form is convenient because it permits both individual and group administration. The test is now given to an adequate sample of students and norms are computed from the test results.

It is important in giving the test individually to avoid consultation between the students who have already taken the test and those who are waiting to take it. Giving the students written appointments to come for the test, and spacing the appointments so that only one student needs to be present in the waiting-room minimizes this problem of consultation. Students, however, tend to come in groups and to ask the one who finishes what the test was about. If the students are busy in a study room, they can be let out for the test individually, thus eliminating the problem of leakage. Group testing eliminates this problem by the fact that all the students take the test together. The availability of recording machines in sufficient numbers is the problem in this case.

The use of recording machines permits the shipping of the oral responses to central locations where expert examiners may score them uniformly. The time and personnel necessary for this kind of administrative operation makes this impractical in most situations. For research purposes, however, this is entirely feasible.

8.5 PARTIAL PRODUCTION TECHNIQUES

In spite of the advances that are possible in tests of production, these techniques that test production by inspection of an actual sample of the student's pronunciation are still complex and time-consuming. Group testing is possible only when an elaborate and expensive recording laboratory is available exclusively for the test. Scoring remains only partially objective, with many cases in which the examiner feels unsure whether to score a response right or wrong. As a result, scores by different examiners and by the same examiner differ.

There was very real need to develop types of items that would be objective, easy to administer and to score if we hoped to test production of the sound system on a wide scale. Various techniques involving such items have been developed recently and offer very interesting possibilities in the testing of pronunciation.

1. Objective, pencil-and-paper techniques that approximate the testing of production. These objective, partial production techniques are based on the fact that the speakers of a language can as a rule say whether or not two sounds in their language are phonemically the same. The student is not asked to identify a phoneme by a phonemic symbol or by a number or even a letter. He is merely asked if a sound in a word that is given to him in writing is the same as the sound of another word which is also presented to him in writing. No special training is required other than elementary ability to read.

These partial production techniques are not thought of as full substitutes for direct production techniques, but they can be used effectively in all those cases in which direct production techniques are not possible or are impractical.

2. Validity of partial production techniques. In the silent comparison of sounds in written words the student rehearses to himself the pronunciation of the words. He then decides whether or not he pronounces a particular sound in one word the same as a particular sound of another word. This is considerably removed from his saying these words aloud and having an expert listen to his pronunciation to decide whether or not it is within the acceptable limits of the phonemes being tested. For this reason, it is necessary to validate the partial production techniques, that is, it is necessary to compare the scores made by students using each technique with the scores made when they actually read the test aloud and it is scored by an expert.

A good way to validate a test of this type is to administer it silently to 50 to 100 students under normal testing conditions; then put away the test papers without inspecting them; have the same students read the test items aloud to an expert examiner who will score them on the basis of the student's actual pronunciation; score the tests taken silently; and compute the correlation between the silent scores and the more valid speaking scores. A correlation of ·70 to ·79 would be acceptable; ·80 to ·89 would be good; and ·90 or better would be excellent.

A further check on the performance of each item should be made. Items missed in the silent test but pronounced correctly and items not missed silently but missed when reading aloud by a very large per cent of the students should be eliminated if other items testing the same problems remain. They should be edited in an effort to improve them and save them if no others remain for the same problem.

Items that are not missed silently or in speaking by any students should be eliminated. Items that are missed by all the students in speaking and silently should be kept.

Validation with native speakers of the foreign language is also necessary with these techniques. Administering the experimental test to fifty native speakers and preparing an item count of the papers will show if any items are missed by more than 10 per cent of the native speakers, in which case the items should be eliminated or heavily edited. If an item is missed by 5 per cent or less of the natives it should ordinarily be kept. If it is missed by from 6 to 9 per cent, it should be inspected carefully and edited or eliminated depending on need for the particular item and on the possibility of its improvement.

3. Techniques. Considerable variety is possible within the general type of item that measures partial production of sounds through objective, paper-and-pencil techniques. These various ways will be classified into four techniques that are distinct yet show possible variations under each.

PRONUNCIATION TECHNIQUE 8.6. **Full spelling.** In this general technique the words containing the sounds to be compared by the student are presented to him in full spelling with the letters representing the problem sounds clearly marked by underlining, bold face, capitals, parentheses, or any other device that unambiguously tells the student what letters he must consider. The number of words to be compared may be two, three, or more. In the two-word type, the student is asked if the sounds represented by the bold face letters (or underlining, etc.) are the same. In the three-word type, he is asked which of the sounds represented by the bold face letters are the same. In the four and more word type he is asked which of the sounds represented by the bold face letters are the same as the first. Other variations are also possible and may be desirable for variety especially in informal tests. Additional variations are left to the ingenuity of the teacher and test maker. The words may be in isolation or in sentences or in a single connected paragraph. Following are examples of various types:

Problem: /uw/ versus /u/ as in *food* and *wood*. Instructions to the student: "Compare the sounds represented by the bold face letters. Write 'S' for *same*, 'D' for *different*." Item: F**OO**D. W**OO**D. Answer: D. The same item with words in a sentence: WE NEED DRY W**OO**D TO PREPARE THE F**OO**D.

The same problem tested with a three-word item: Instructions: "Compare the sounds represented by the bold face letters. Write the number of the sounds that are the same." Item:

   1   2   3

F**OO**D. W**OO**D. UNDERST**OO**D. Answer: 2 3.

The same item with words in three sentences:
    (1) I told him and he underst**oo**d.
    (2) He brought the w**oo**d for the fire.
    (3) We ate cheese, bread, and the other f**oo**d.
The answer is now 1 2.

The same problem tested with a multiple-word item and touching on other vowel contrasts: Instructions: "Compare the sounds represented by the bold face letters. Write the numbers of the sounds that are the same as the first." Item: W**OO**D

                                                     1

  2   3   4   5   6   7

F**OO**D, L**OA**D, W**A**LK, UNDERST**OO**D, C**U**T, SH**OU**LD,

  8   9

G**OO**D, R**U**DE. Answer: 1 5 7 8. The same item with words in

               1   2   3

context: THE W**OO**D FOR THE F**OO**D WAS C**U**T AS IT

 4   5   6   7

SH**OU**LD. WE W**A**LKED WITH A G**OO**D L**OA**D AS

           8   9

UNDERST**OO**D AND WERE NOT R**U**DE. Answer: 4 6 8.

PRONUNCIATION TECHNIQUE 8.7. **Omitted letters.** This technique has been the most successful thus far in this series. It is essentially the same as the full spelling technique, that is, the student has to compare silently the sounds represented by parts of words given to him in writing. The basic difference is that the letters representing the sounds are actually omitted. The words are identified by the remaining letters and by written context that goes with the words.

The same /uw/ /u/ problem tested with the same three words and sentences: Instructions: "Compare the sounds represented by the letters omitted. Write the numbers of the sentences in which the sounds are the same." Item:

   (1) I told him and he underst - - d.
   (2) He brought the w - - d for the fire.
   (3) We ate cheese, bread and the other f - - d.

The answer is 1 2.

The advantage of this item over the full spelling item is that it can be used to test contrasts such as /l r/ in English which are regularly distinguished in spelling and would always be given away by the letters.

The same problem tested by the same words in one sentence: Instructions: "Compare the sounds represented by the letters omitted. Write the numbers of the sounds that are the same."

         1

Item: IT WAS UNDERST - - D THAT THE FIRE NEEDED

 2   3

W - - D TO WARM THE F - - D. The contexts are slightly harder to build in this type, but the student has less extraneous reading to do.

The same problem using definitions as context: Instructions, the same. Item:

   (1) UNDERST - - D (past tense of understand).
   (2) W - - D (fuel to build fires.)
   (3) F - - D (what we eat).

The answer is the same.

Two-word and four-word items of these types are easily derived and will not be discussed.

Technique 8.7 has been partially validated with Latin American students with correlations in the ·80's and occasionally in the low ·90's. It is in process of validation with students of other linguistic backgrounds with tentative correlations that justify the use of the technique when direct scoring of oral responses by experts is not practical. With refinements that are routine, such as selection of items after trial administrations, this technique is of great value to the teaching and testing of pronunciation on a large scale.

PRONUNCIATION TECHNIQUE 8.8. **Picture context.** This technique is essentially the same as the previous one except that the context is provided by a picture rather than by a sentence or paragraph. Words in isolation are preferable since the amount of reading is thus reduced to a minimum. The items may be of two, three or more choices as with the previous technique. An example of a three-choice item will be enough to show the technique clearly.

Problem: /f/ as in *fish* produced as /p/ as in *pick*. The native language has /p/ but does not have /f/. Test words: *telephone, football, envelope.* Instructions: "Compare the sounds represented by the missing letters. Write the numbers of the missing sounds that are the same." The pictures:

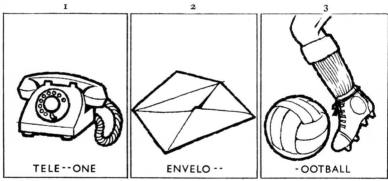

Fig. 8.2. Technique 8.8. Picture Context

The answer is 1 3.

This technique is better for children or for adults who have limited facility in reading than for highly literate adults. The pronunciation problems, however, are the same as with technique 8.7. Literate adults tend to think that these picture items are easier and feel that they are beneath their ability to pronounce. The test maker need not be disturbed by this bias of present views regarding pictures since pictures are time-consuming and difficult in their preparation and reproduction.

In this and in the previous technique the spellings representing the problem sounds can be chosen in such a way that they do not provide clues to the sounds. In the above example, a *ph* spelling for /f/ was chosen in the word *telephone* because it has the letter *p* which represents the phoneme /p/ in *envelope*. The other /f/ sound is represented by the letter *f* in *football*, an entirely different spelling from that of *telephone*. The irregularities of English spelling make it possible to use such devices to minimize the spelling clues to the sounds and thus force the student to rely primarily on his pronunciation of the words. Even in the contrast /l/ versus /r/ which is always distinct in English spelling we can compare a single *l* with a double *l* in the spelling, and a single *r* with a double *r* when the phonemes themselves are one /l/ and one /r/. The fact that the letters are omitted and that when the student remembers them they do not match as letters seems to be enough to have him fall back on his pronunciation of /l/ and /r/.

It will be noticed also that the words *telephone, envelope*, and *football* are long enough to be identified without the letters representing the problem sounds and without the aid of pictures. Often we must use shorter words which will not be identified without the picture context. The shorter words *foot, phone,* and *cope*, for example, become ambiguous if the key letters are omitted. — *oot* could represent *boot, hoot, shoot, root,* etc. — *one* could represent *tone, cone,* etc. *Co — e* could represent *cone, cole, code,* etc. With these shorter words the picture context would be decisive.

PRONUNCIATION TECHNIQUE 8.9. **Multiple choice with omission of key letters.** In this objective technique the student is given a word with the letters representing the problem sound omitted. The student compares this sound with those of five words given in full spelling as choices. The letters representing the sounds to be compared in the choices are printed in bold face, capitals or otherwise marked in clear fashion. Many variations are possible in the type of context used to identify the key word, the number of choices, the number of choices that are the same as the key sound, etc. Since this technique is an attempt to approach the format of conventional multiple-choice items, we might favor a variety in which the key word is identified by a short sentence context, and only one of the choices is correct.

Example: The problem is the phoneme /u/ as in *wood* in contrast with /uw/ as in *food*, /ə/ as in *cut*, /ow/ as in *load*, and /ɔ/ as in *walk*. The item:

Light the fire with dry w - - d.

   1   2   3   4   5

Food. Cut. Load. Walk. Understood.

The instructions: "Write the number of the sound that is the same as the sound represented by the letters omitted." The answer is 5.

This type of item is still experimental. If it proves effective it will offer certain distinct advantages. It permits the contrast of a problem sound with several others, thus making it easier to reach more than one language background in the same item. It is much like a conventional multiple-choice item, and students will tend to accept it more readily and manipulate it with a minimum of instructions. It seems easier to write and more flexible to edit. Any choice that does not contribute to the item can easily be changed without complicated rewriting.

PRONUNCIATION TECHNIQUE 8.10. **Rhymes.** In this technique the student is asked to identify the words which end in the same sounds, that is, the words that rhyme. For example, *state* rhymes with *weight* but not with *height* or *scat*. A sample item using these words might be presented as follows:

State rhymes with **height**
weight
scat

The assumption is that if the student pronounces the words properly he will match them properly as rhymes. Since there is more than one type of rhyme it is necessary to inform the student that both the consonants and the vowels must be the same in the endings to constitute the right answer.

This technique has the advantage that most cultures recognize rhymes in poetry and folklore. The student is thus familiar with the idea of rhymes. It may also be easier for most students to compare whole words rather than single phonemes.

Counterbalancing these advantages are some unresolved problems as well. Rhymes occur at the end of words so that pronunciation at the beginning or middle of words is not checked directly. Some languages have no final consonants, or have very few. The students may, therefore, not pronounce final consonants—and thus confuse them—yet pronounce well initial or medial consonants. Finally, the technique will work with some problems in English because of the variety of spellings for some sounds, yet in any of the well-spelled languages the spelling would always give away the answer, and even in English some problems such as /l/ and /r/, /b/ and /v/, etc., are always given away by the spelling.

4. General comments. The partial production techniques discussed and illustrated do not exhaust the possible variations by any means. With some thought and ingenuity, many other variations can be devised by the language teacher. Other varieties have been used already, but the ones presented above should be enough to make the partial production techniques fully clear.

In addition to the great saving in time and the fully objective scoring that these techniques afford, they also make it possible to range with considerable freedom over the entire area of problem sounds of a language in their various environments without regard to the existence of minimal pairs at any particular point. If they live up to their apparent promise, they should make it possible to include partial production of the sounds in all standard tests of language.

5. Preparing the partial production test. After the foregoing discussion the actual preparation of a partial production test should be reasonably clear. The list of problems is prepared, words that contain the problems are selected, the items written and edited, the experimental form is administered to 50 to 100 native speakers of education and maturity equivalent to those of the students for whom the test is intended. Items missed by more than 5 per cent of the native speakers are eliminated or edited and the test is administered silently to 50 to 100 of the students for whom it is intended. The students then read the same test aloud for direct scoring by the examiner.[1] Items that show wide

---

[1] See §23.2 for a discussion of this and other means of validation.

discrepancy between the performance of students on the silent administration and on reading out loud are eliminated or edited. The items preserved are rearranged in order of their difficulty. The test is then ready for reproduction in a quantity of 500 or 1,000 for further refinement and tentative norms.

The list of problems is the same as for a test of direct production. The list must give the phoneme that is mispronounced, the feature or features that are distorted at the phonemic level, the phoneme or nearest phoneme that results from the distortion, and the distribution of the problem. In choosing the words that contain the problems one takes into account the factor of spelling and whenever possible minimizes any spelling clues that might tend to give away the answer. If the same spelling can represent both the right phoneme and the one that results from the distortion, we favor this spelling. For example, the /uw/ and /u/ contrast can be given with the same spelling in such pairs of words as *food* and *wood*, *mood* and *good*, etc. Even if the student can reconstruct the spelling from visual memory, it helps him little and he must fall back on his pronunciation to answer the item.

What has been said above under *Validity of partial production techniques* applies here when administering the test to native speakers and to a sample of the foreign speakers for whom the test is intended. Other matters such as types and format of answer sheets, scoring systems, reliability, and norms are dealt with in Part V of this book.

Chapter 9

THE TESTING OF "STRESS"[1]

9.1 **IMPORTANCE OF STRESS FOR COMMUNICATION**

Languages use certain differences of pitch, duration and loudness to give prominence to some syllables and words over others. In this chapter we will discuss the testing of some of these differences in prominence, usually referred to as stress. We will call them *stress* even though they sometimes depend primarily on duration and pitch.

Stress is part of the communication system of many languages. It is used in the identification of words, their grammatical functions, and contextual prominence, and influences the form and selection of sounds and the form of morphemes.

1. Identification of words. In Spanish, the word *paso*, with greater prominence on the first syllable, can mean 'I pass' or '(a) step.' The word *pasó*, made up of the same segmental phonemes but with greater prominence on the last syllable, means 'he passed' or 'it happened.' Similarly, *peso*, with prominence on the first syllable, means among other things, 'weight,' and *pesó*, with the prominence on the last syllable,

---

[1] Recent research with the sound spectrograph and synthetic speech machines has contributed some evidence in support of the thesis that the physical correlates of English "stress" are primarily pitch and length, and only secondarily loudness. Consequently, some writers are adopting the term "accent" instead of stress. *Stress* will be retained in this book because accent would often be ambiguous. If the chapter heading were changed to "The Testing of Accent," it might be taken to mean, 'the testing of foreign accent.' "Prosodic accent" complicates the text unnecessarily at some points. *Accent* will be reserved for the over-all impression of the speech of a region or of a foreign language as in "a southern accent," "a German accent," "a Spanish accent," etc. The use of the word "stress" does not imply an exclusion of pitch and duration as physical correlates of prominence.

means 'he weighed'. In Spanish, then, stress is used to distinguish words. Stress is phonemic: it is employed to identify particular words and distinguish them from others. One who wishes to learn Spanish learns this matter of stress in order to understand and be understood, not merely to "sound Spanish."

English stress serves to identify words also. Not many minimal pairs such as Spanish *paso: pasó* can be found in English because when the stress shifts from one syllable to another the phonemes tend to change also. The noun *pérmit*, however, with the more prominent stress on the first syllable, and the verb *permít*, with the more prominent stress on the last syllable, constitute a minimal pair at least in some varieties of English. *Dígest*, the noun, with more prominence on the first syllable, and *digést*, the verb, with greater prominence on the second syllable constitute another minimal pair. They illustrate the fact that word stress is distinctive in English.

German, Portuguese, and many other languages have distinctive stress of the type illustrated for English and Spanish. Other languages such as French and Persian do not have a similar unit or units to distinguish words. Japanese has pitch prominence, that is, prominence is marked by relative pitch. Thai, Chinese and other languages known as tone languages have a system of contrasting pitch units to distinguish words that are otherwise the same in their sound segments.

The fact that the prominent syllable is distinct from the others shows that there are at least two degrees of stress that are distinctive, that of the most prominent syllable and that of the less prominent ones. In English most linguists recognize a third degree of stress which is intermediate between that of the most prominent and that of the least prominent syllables. These three degrees of stress can be observed in a single word such as *substitution*. The syllable *-tu-* exhibits the greatest prominence; the syllables *-ti-* and *-tion* are least prominent; and the first syllable, *subs-* shows intermediate prominence. We will use $/'/$ to mark the most prominent syllable, $/\backslash/$ for intermediate prominence, and no mark to indicate the least prominent ones.

2. Contextual prominence. In addition to the three degrees of stress illustrated for English and the two for Spanish, when words are used in context in larger units an additional degree of stress is observed. The highest degree of stress observed in single words turns out to be the stress center of the word and the center of a phrase as well. We were actually dealing with a phrase (or even an utterance) of one word. If a phrase has more than one word which would carry /′/ if pronounced in isolation, only the one at the center of the phrase remains as /′/, the others are usually reduced to less relative prominence than /′/ but more than /ˋ/. This additional degree of stress is represented by /ᐱ/.

The words "sign" and "here" would normally have /′/ if they are one-word phrases. If they are both in a single phrase, only one will retain /′/ and, depending on context, we may have

sígn hêre,

or   sîgn hére.

If they both keep /′/ they would constitute two phrases.

Similarly, the words "elevator" and "operator" would both have /′/ if pronounced in isolation. If combined into a single phrase, however, only one retains /′/ and we might have, depending on context,

élevàtor óperàtor,

or   élevàtor óperàtor.

/′/ usually occurs on a specific syllable of a word and on a specific word in a phrase, but it can occur in any syllable and any word under the proper context. The speakers of English grasp the special significance of /′/ when it occurs in other than the usual locations. In other languages the position of stress is not significant.

Although /′/ often occurs in the same syllable as the highest pitch in English, /′/ is not tied to a high pitch as it also occurs with low pitch. For example:

sígn ìt.

sígn ìt?

Similarly, although /′/ and other stresses correlate with grammatical structure in English, stress and grammatical structure are autonomous systems as illustrated by the variety of stress arrangements possible with most structures. For example:

sígn hêre,
sîgn hére,
sígn (pause) *hére* (two phrases).

/′/ functions primarily as the center of the intonation phrase.[1]

/′/ has been variously identified and called sentence stress, sense stress, contrastive stress (when placed in special locations), and primary stress. We will refer to it as *primary stress*, keeping in mind that it is an intonation-center stress and that it may be signaled by length and pitch change at least as much as by loudness.

/ʌ/ has been called word stress, secondary stress, lexical stress, etc. We will call it *secondary stress*, following majority usage among American linguists.

/ˋ/ will be called *tertiary*, and / / will be called *weak*.

3. Rhythm. Each language has certain permitted sequences of stresses and length units which, as they follow one another, give it a rhythm of its own. English tends to make uniform the length of time from primary stress to primary stress regardless of the number of intervening syllables. Thus the phrases separated by a vertical line in the following example are of approximately the same duration even though the first has only one syllable and the second has four. *Sign | the documents | in ink.* Because of this timing based on stress units, English rhythm has been called *stress-timed rhythm*.

Spanish, German, French, Japanese and many other languages have *syllable-timed rhythm*. The duration of each syllable tends to be uniform though not identical, and phrases and sentences tend to be proportionally as long as the number of syllables they contain.

4. Influence of stress and rhythm on segmental phonemes and morphemes. In many languages the segmental phonemes show variation in their phonetic form according to whether they are under prominent or weak stress or preceding or following a prominent stress. Thus English /p t k/ are rather heavily aspirated (with a puff of air released after the stop) preceding a vowel under primary stress as in *pin, tin, kin*, but lightly aspirated

---

[1] " Intonation phrase " is Hockett's (1) macrosegment.

or unaspirated before weak stressed vowels as in *pathetic, tomato,* and *collect.*

Of even more importance for communication in English are variations in morphemes and words that accompany changes in stress. Thus syllables that under primary stress in English have the vowel phonemes /a æ e/ as in *what, have,* and *where* may all be produced with /ə/ under weak stress as in the constructions /hwət iz it/, /wi həv dən it/, and /hwər iz it/. The vowel may disappear altogether and cease to constitute a syllable if the stress is eliminated.

9.2 STRESS PROBLEMS IN LEARNING A FOREIGN LANGUAGE

Since the operation of the stress system of the native language is largely a matter of habit the student tends to transfer the native language system to the foreign language. This means that the stress units, their distribution, and their function are transferred.

By comparing the stress system of the native language with that of the language to be learned we can locate and describe the learning problems. This comparison needs to be carried out systematically using linguistically sound descriptions that give the stress phonemes and their distribution in patterns of words, phrases and sentences. Between English and Spanish we see that English weak stress is not paralleled by any stress in Spanish. As a result we expect English speakers learning Spanish to transfer their weak stress phoneme and distort the stress pattern of Spanish and all the vowels that come under this transferred weak stress. The Spanish speaker learning English transfers his weak stress, which is phonetically similar to English tertiary stress, and substitutes it for English weak stress.

The stressed-timed rhythm of English and the syllable-timed rhythm of Spanish when transferred to the other language constitute a serious learning problem. Other problems result from the particular stress sequence observed in word patterns, for example those words ending in the suffix *-tion* in English which are similar to words ending in *-ción* in Spanish. In English the primary stress is on the syllable preceding *-tion*; in Spanish it is on the suffix *-ción* itself. Thus Spanish speakers will tend to stress the last syllable of English *nation* and English speakers may stress the first syllable of Spanish *nación*.

These matters in which the two systems differ constitute the learning problems. They should be listed and described accurately before the test items are prepared. For example, the Spanish speaker will not have difficulty hearing or producing primary stress as such, because he has something of the sort in Spanish. Thus he hears the difference between *pérmit* and *permit* without trouble, and he will produce it satisfactorily if he remembers which syllable to stress in each. English weak stress on the other hand will not be heard or produced distinctly from intermediate stress by him.

1. **Criteria for selecting words, phrases, and utterances that contain the stress problems to be tested.** Although the description of the stress problems to be tested is a technical matter involving abstract statements about the goal and native languages, the actual testing is done with specific words, phrases, and utterances containing the problems. There is ample support for this approach in the fact that native speakers, who actually use the stress system and therefore "know" it in this sense, are unable to describe the system unless they make a technical study of it. These native speakers can be tested on specific words, phrases and utterances but they cannot be tested on technical descriptions of stress.

When we select the words, phrases and utterances that contain and illustrate the problems, we must consider these words, etc. from two angles: (1) their importance as items and (2) the extent to which they represent the problem patterns we wish to test. If we think of the examples exclusively as items, we have to limit our selection to words and phrases that are known to the students or are within some arbitrary frequency range or selected list. The testing question is then whether or not the student stresses properly the items he knows or is expected to know lexically.

This limitation, though perhaps justified in testing elementary school children, is not justified if we wish to know whether or not the student has mastered the patterns of stress functionally, over and above specific knowledge of individual items, i.e., whether or not he has mastered the stress system of the goal language. To test this second dimension, each item selected must represent a problem pattern and may be chosen from a lexical range beyond that which the student may have mastered as items.

In selecting the examples containing the stress problems to be tested we choose at least one word, phrase or utterance that is presumed to fall within the lexical range known to the student and another word, phrase or utterance that has not been studied as an item in his lexical range but will be properly stressed by him if he has mastered the particular stress pattern involved. An example will further clarify this approach.

The English *-tion* pattern mentioned above, which shows word stress on the syllable preceding *-tion*, and the Spanish *-ción* pattern, which is stressed on *-ción* itself represent a learning problem for both English and Spanish speakers learning the other language. In selecting examples to test this problem in Spanish, we would choose a *-ción* word within the lexical range of the students, for example *constitución*, which is of high frequency.

We would also choose another word which might well fall beyond the lexical range of the students, for example, *excarceración, caseación, caseificación*.

9.3   **TESTING STRESS**

Testing auditory perception of stress problems in English is complicated by the fact that primary stress is often accompanied by an intonation peak, and this intonation peak is heard even by Japanese and French speakers, who might otherwise not hear the stress signal. Testing perception of weak stress in English is also difficult because there are no lexically different minimal pairs to be used in such a test. The general techniques of comparing sound with sound, which were successful in testing perception of the segmental phonemes, are not usable in testing stress. The techniques to test stress involve identification of stress by the student, who is asked to mark something on a printed representation of the word or utterance.

STRESS TECHNIQUE 9.1. **Perception of the syllable receiving a particular stress.** The examiner reads aloud a word, phrase or sentence, and the student marks on his paper the syllable or syllables which received the stress being tested. For example, in testing primary stress—if this is a problem—the examiner reads, "Impóssible?" The student, looking at the

$$1 \quad 2 \quad 3 \quad 4$$

numbered syllables of *Impossible* on his answer sheet, marks or writes the number of the most prominent syllable to indicate that he has heard it.

This same technique can be used to test perception of weak stress. The examiner says "The cònstitútion," for example, and the student writes or marks the number of the weak stressed

$$1 \quad 2 \quad 3 \quad 4 \quad 5$$

syllables in *The constitution*, which appears on his answer sheet. When read in a neutral context, the answer would be 1 3 5.

Variations in the particular way of representing the syllables that bear the stress we wish to test are possible, but it will be difficult to find a handier device than numbers. If we had enough minimal pairs such as *pérmit* : *permít* in English stress or *paso* : *pasó* in Spanish stress we could present the two words to the student with the stress distinction marked by means of capital letters, bold face type, a stress mark, or any other means. For example, the examiner might read "Pérmit," and the student would have to choose between *perMIT* and *PERmit*, or per**mit** and **per**mit, or *permít* and *pérmit*.

The number technique is more flexible, however, and can be used for sentences, with several possible answers, as well as for words. In the case of sentences we need only number those words or syllables which are pertinent to the test. For example, the examiner reads, "You can bûy thìs at the márket," with primary stress on the first syllable of *market*. The student has before him the sentence with numbered syllables as follows, YOU CAN

$$1 \quad 2 \quad 3 \quad 4 \quad 5$$

BUY THIS AT THE MARKET. He is asked to mark the most prominent syllable.

STRESS TECHNIQUE 9.2. **Production.** To test production of stress the general technique is merely to elicit from the student the words or sentences containing the stress problems we wish to test and to score his response by direct observation or by repeatable observation on a recording.

This technique can be varied in many ways, but the problems being tested remain the same. The stimulus can be a question or instructions addressed to the student so that he produces the desired word or sentence. This approach has the virtue of reproducing a conversational situation, but it is otherwise somewhat inflexible and restrictive.

Pictures accompanied by questions or instructions are more practical for eliciting a wider range of responses with greater certainty. Children who are not particularly advanced in reading can be tested better through pictures.

Written words or sentences in ordinary spelling without any graphic representation of stress are probably the best stimulus for testing the production of stress. English writing does not mark stress and is thus suited as a stimulus without change. Spanish writing, on the other hand, regularly represents stress. The stress marks should be deleted if Spanish writing is used to test stress. The ability to read is of course an important factor in this technique. Illiterates cannot use it. Only students who can read with some facility may be tested with this technique. To minimize the problems due to reading, the student can be permitted to read the material silently before reading it out loud for the test.

Scoring the spoken response of the student is quite easy and dependable if we are testing only the placement of primary stress. The average speaker of English or Spanish can score the placement of primary stress in spoken words or sentences with adequate objectivity. Ordinary speakers are often able to demonstrate improper placement of primary stress for humorous purposes. We thus see that in a three-stress system the stresses can be scored by the teacher of language, for if he can locate two of three stresses, he has in fact located the third as well.

Scoring of English secondary, tertiary, and weak stresses, on the other hand, is not always easy for the average language teacher unless he has received considerable training in practical phonetics. Scoring of these stresses will thus be limited to the phonetic training of the examiner.

STRESS TECHNIQUE 9.3. **Partial production.** Even when we succeed in preparing an effective production test to measure mastery of stress, we are faced with the same problems of the time required and of subjective scoring as were encountered previously in testing production of the sound segments. For extensive testing of stress objective group tests of production are needed or, lacking these, partial production tests that correlate highly with actual production.

The partial production techniques consist of written words or sentences which contain the stress problems, with numbers written under or above the syllables. The student is asked to mark or write the number of the syllable he pronounces with the primary stress or with a weak stress.

EXAMPLE:

Instructions: Circle the number of the stressed syllable.

 1   2   3
Item: CONVENIENT.

Comment: The student, presumably after rehearsing his pronunciation silently, circles the 2 if he does pronounce the word this way.

EXAMPLE:

Instructions: Write the numbers of the syllables that you pronounce with weak stress.

 1   2   3   4
Item: A MIRACLE.

Comment: The student who uses weak accent where he should will presumably write 1 3 4 as his answer to indicate that the first, third and fourth syllables are pronounced with weak stress by him.

EXAMPLE:

Instructions: Cross out the numbers of *four* syllables with weak stress.

           1   2   3   4   5   6
Item: THE GUIDE TOLD 'EM TO BE PATIENT.

Comment: The student should cross out numbers 2, 3, 4 and 6. Syllable 4, BE, could be rendered with intermediate stress as well. Asking for four weak syllables may not be enough to avoid a mistake here. This defect would probably be caught when the item is tried with native speakers of English.

EXAMPLE:

Instructions: Circle the numbers of the *two* syllables with heavy stress.

| | 1 | 2 | 3 | 4 | 5 | 6 |

Item: THE GUIDE TOLD 'EM TO BE PATIENT.

Comment: The student would presumably circle 1 and 5.

9.4   PREPARING A TEST OF STRESS

Nothing particularly different is involved in preparing a test of stress. We (1) begin with an accurate list of problems; (2) select words, phrases, and utterances that contain the stress problems to be tested; (3) write the items; (4) try the items in an experimental form of the test on native speakers of the language or qualified non-native speakers; (5) eliminate or edit the items that do not function satisfactorily; (6) give the test to fifty to one-hundred subjects representative of the population for whom the test is intended; (7) edit or eliminate the items that do not discriminate; (8) arrange the good items according to difficulty, and (9) reproduce for wider use in assembling norms. Refinements such as production of equivalent forms and checking the reliability of the test will be discussed in Part V of the book.

In each of these nine operations there are considerations that should not be forgotten. They have been discussed in some detail in the preceding chapters and do not require full elaboration at this time. We may indicate, however, that the list of problems will be different for production and for recognition. In writing the items, about 20 per cent more are needed than the final test will have. In items in which the context determines the particular placing of the primary stress a surplus of 50 per cent is required because the mortality of such items is high.

The native speakers employed in the validation of the items should match as closely as possible the type of student for whom the test is intended, i.e., they should be of the same educational level (elementary, secondary, university) as the students for whom the test is intended. Since these students have had experience in the study of the goal language, the native speakers used as a validating group should have had similar experience with a language other than their own to match the students properly.

Naive monolingual speakers of the target language might be confused by things that would be taken in stride by other native speakers who have had foreign language experience. Items that are missed by 10 per cent or more of the native speakers should, if possible, be eliminated. Items missed by fewer than 10 per cent might be edited if some obvious defect is apparent and can be corrected. Items missed by 5 per cent or less of the natives can usually be kept.

The discriminating power of each item can be computed in various ways discussed in Chapter 25. One way is to compare the number of times the item is missed by the top third, the middle third, and the bottom third of the students. The distribution of papers into thirds is determined by the score on the whole test. Items that show a clear difference in the number of times they are missed at each level are preferable to items that show very little difference. And, of course, those items that are missed more times by the top or middle third than by a lower third are eliminated or drastically revised and tried again.

The arrangement by difficulty offers no particular complication. The item count of the mistakes is the index of difficulty: the more the mistakes made on an item the more difficult it is assumed to be.

9.5   BIBLIOGRAPHICAL NOTES

Probably a majority of American linguists describe English as a four-stress system. Many had assumed that loudness or amplitude of the sound waves was the dominant feature of stress. Recent instrumental studies seem to indicate that length and pitch are more important in signaling accent than loudness or amplitude. D. B. Fry, "Experiments in the perception of stress," in *Language and Speech* (Vol. I, Part 2, April–June, 1958), pp. 126–52, is a case in point. (1) Charles F. Hockett, *A Course in Modern Linguistics*, Chapter 5, "English Accent," shows awareness of this view. (2) G. S. Trager and H. L. Smith in *Outline of English Structure* present the four-stress loudness description in detail.

Chapter 10

THE TESTING OF INTONATION

10.1   **INTONATION**

Pitch, the quality of sound usually described as high or low, as rising, level, or falling, is basic to communication through language. In English, the phrase *a pencil* spoken with a mid pitch on *a*, a high pitch on *pen-*, and a low pitch on *-cil* is different from the same phrase spoken with a mid pitch on *a pen-* and a high pitch on *-cil* even though the words are the same. The difference is signaled primarily by the sequence of pitches.

In a great many languages these differences in pitch are spread over phrases and sentences and constitute what is called *intonation*. In Chinese, Thai, and other languages there are also pitch units that form part of words as distinct from phrases and sentences. These pitch units are known as *tones*, and languages that have tones as part of their word forms are called *tone languages*.

These differences heard as high or low, rising or falling are primarily related to the frequency of the sound waves. The human hearing and speaking mechanism is highly sensitive to differences in pitch. Differences of five cycles per second are heard by average speakers of English. And persons with unusually fine hearing acuity can perceive differences of one cycle per second.

In spite of its importance in many languages, intonation signals such as those of our example have been the last to be analyzed linguistically, and still remain somewhat controversial in the few languages which have been analyzed. A possible explanation for this retardation may be the fact that intonation patterns seem to be learned at the earliest stages of language learning and are deeply embedded in the habit mechanism of our use of language. Be that as it may, we must deal with pitch patterns in foreign language learning and testing. We know enough about the importance of intonation to conclude that language teaching and testing that do not take intonation systematically into account are in this respect obsolete.

Pitch variations in the intonation of a language constitute a system of distinctive, contrastive units and patterns. For example, English, which has received a great deal of attention as regards intonation, has four distinctive pitch units. They may be called *low, mid, high,* and *extra high,* and are conveniently represented with small numbers above the line of print. Letting /1/ represent low, /2/ mid, /3/ high, and /4/ extra high, we represent the pitch phonemes of *a pencil* as

(1) ^2a $^3pencil^1$ (mid-high-low)
(2) ^2a $^2pencil^3$ (mid-mid-high)

These examples show three of the pitch units, /1/ low, /2/ mid, and /3/ high. The fourth unit, /4/ extra high, often appears when in context "pencil" must be pointed out as related to something said before. For example:

(3) ^2These are ^3three of the $units^1.$ ^2The ^4fourth $unit^2$ . . .

The absolute pitch of these units varies considerably for different speakers and even for the same speaker on different occasions or in different parts of the same conversation. All of the units are higher when speaking to someone at a distance, they are lower when speaking softly in a doctor's waiting-room, the intervals between units are greater when the speaker is emotionally excited, etc. But the four units remain in relative contrast to each other as phonemes of pitch.

Each intonation phrase has a *center,* which is marked by a primary stress. In both ^2a $^3pencil^1$ and ^2a $^2pencil^3$, the center is the syllable *pen-.* A convenient way to represent the center of an intonation phrase is to mark the primary stress. Indicating the center of the above examples we have

(4) ^2a $^3péncil^1$
(5) ^2a $^2péncil^3$
(6) ^2These are $^3thrée$ of the $units^1.$ ^2The ^4fóurth $unit^2$ . . .

These intonations, as we may call them for convenience, some-times have a *pre-center section* and a *terminal border*.[1] The pre-center section is the pitch of any syllable or syllables that precede the center, as ²*a* in ²*a* ³*péncil*¹. ²*These are* in ²*These are* ³*thrée of the units*¹. Many intonations do not have any syllables before the center and therefore do not have a pre-center section.

1. Intonation borders. The border of an intonation marks the end of the intonation phrase. There are three distinct borders in English. In one of them the vocal apparatus relaxes in anticipa-tion of silence and inaction: the muscular tension diminishes, and the voice glides downward into silence. This border can be symbolized by a period /./ with the warning that a period as used to denote an intonation border is not to be confused with a period as an ordinary punctuation mark, which does not correlate with intonation but with some grammatical units and rules.

In another, for example, in ²*a* ²*pencil*³, the rise on -*cil*³ con-tinues to the end of the phrase. This rise is observed also when the intonation drops from high to low as in

(7) ²*a* ³*péncil*¹?

The rise from /1/ does not reach the next higher pitch point /2/. The rise will be represented by a question mark /?/, again keeping in mind that the question mark used to mark an intonation rise as a terminal border is different from the question mark used in ordinary punctuation where it often does not represent a rise in pitch.

The third kind of intonation border is characterized by sus-tained pitch and therefore by the absence of a drop to silence as in /./ or a rise as in /?/. We will represent it with a comma /,/ not as a grammatical signal as the comma is used in punctuation but indicating an intonation border.

2. Form, meaning, distribution. The intonation phrases of a language, distinct sequences of pitches ending in a border, have different *meanings* expressing the attitude of the speaker, the type of question, the sequence relation between a phrase and the context, the span of a grammatical structure, etc. The parti-cular intonation phrases that are associated with these and other

---

[1] "Pre-center section" is Pike's (1) "precontour" also labeled "pendant" by Hockett (2). "Terminal border" is Trager and Smith's (3) "terminal juncture," called by Hockett (2) "terminal contour."

meanings are characteristic of each language and are therefore different from language to language. The specific sequence of pitches with a center and a border that constitute an intonation phrase we call its *form*. Thus the sequence symbolized /2 3′ 1./ is the form of the most common intonation phrase in English. The pre-center section is not as essential a part of the form as the center and border since the presence of the pre-center is determined mechanically by the occurrence of syllables before the center. Thus we will say that /2 3′ 1./ and /3′ 1./ are the same intonation pattern even though they are different intonation phrases. Similarly the sequence symbolized /2 2′ 3?/ is the same pattern as /2′ 3?/. The fact that particular intonation patterns will have particular meanings in one environment and a different meaning in another environment constitutes a third matter that must be considered in describing and using intonation. This matter of environments we call *distribution.*

3. Dialect differences. Just as there are wide geographic and social differences in the segmental phonemes of a language there are also wide differences in intonation. The intonation of the question "What are you doing?" which in Midwest American English would usually be rendered as

(8) *²What are you ³dóing¹.*

is more likely to be rendered as

(9) *³What are you ¹dóing²?*

in Received Pronunciation, as described by Daniel Jones.[1] These differences are observable among the various dialects of American English and even more markedly among the various dialects of the English of England and those of Scotland.

It is commonly assumed that these differences are limited to a few intonation patterns, but dialect information on intonation is not readily available yet. We must, meanwhile, expect such differences and allow for them in testing, either by accepting variant intonations that may be the pattern in different dialects or by clearly indicating that the test deals specifically with a particular dialect.

[1] *An Outline of English Phonetics*, Eighth Edition. (New York: E. P. Dutton and Co., Inc., 1956.)

10.2   INTONATION PROBLEMS

1. Knowing the intonation of a language. One "knows" the intonation of a language when he can produce and recognize functionally the intonation patterns of the language in the stream of speech. For our purposes we will further specify that producing and recognizing the intonation patterns is achieved when they include the distinctive pitch points and sequences of pitches, the center, the borders, the distribution and the meanings of the patterns for a particular dialect in use.

Knowing the intonation of English includes then the four pitch phonemes symbolized, /1/, /2/, /3/, /4/, the center /'/, the three borders, /./, /?/, /,/, sequences such as /2 3' 1./, /2 2' 3?/, and their meaning and distribution. Since what we call "knowing" is use of these things, it is neither necessary nor sufficient for the student to be able to define or describe them so long as he can produce them and perceive them in speech.

2. The learning problems. Under our theory we assume that the student transfers the habit system of his native language to the foreign language. This includes the intonation habits. Thus we assume that the student transfers the pitch phonemes, the center, the borders, and the intonation patterns including their meanings and distribution from the native language if these are functioning elements or units in it. Consequently he will have trouble producing and perceiving those patterns, phonemes, borders and centers that are structurally different in the foreign and the native languages. These differences may involve the form, the meaning, the distribution, or any combination of them. In general, when one form unit or pattern in the native language is transferred into an area where the foreign language requires two or more form units or patterns the students will have maximum difficulty in mastering the foreign language intonation.

Although it may seem simple to examine the distortions produced by students and thus arrive at the learning problems, if one hopes to achieve any degree of completeness it turns out to be an extremely laborious and uneconomical approach. It is much more rewarding and simple to compare the structural descriptions of the intonation system of the native and the goal languages. By comparing the form, meaning and distribution of each intonation pitch, center, border, and pattern we arrive at a nearly complete list that can more readily be checked against the performance of students. Examining the performance of students without a previous comparison of the two systems will fail particularly in the problem of perception.

EXAMPLE: Let's assume that in a variety of Portuguese of the south of Brazil there is a common pattern illustrated by the following utterance:

(10) $^2\hat{E}le$ $é$ um $^4a^3lúno^1$. ^1Não $é$ um $pro^3fe^1ssór^1$.*

This pattern is transferred in lieu of the English pattern illustrated by

(11) $^2He's$ a $^3stúdent^1$. ^1not a $pro^2féssor^1$.

If the analysis implied by the numbers is correct, the student will not have trouble in producing and hearing the pitch points (phonemes) of English because he has four pitch phonemes in his native dialect. Because of the occurrence of a higher pitch preceding the center, he will have trouble with the most frequent English patterns which have the highest or lowest pitch at the center of the intonation. And he will have trouble with the English pattern /2 3′ 1./ as a pattern.

3. List of problems: production and recognition. From a systematic comparison of the foreign language intonation system with that of the native language emerges a list of learning problems that constitute our index to mastery of the intonation of the foreign language. The comparison should be made with the help of a neat structural outline of the intonation systems of the two languages. The outlines should give the pitch phonemes, the center, and the borders with major allophones and their distinctive phonetic features as well as the major patterns, their distribution and their meanings.

Because at present we lack such descriptions for almost all languages, our comparisons and our lists of problems will be rather inadequate unless we analyze the intonation ourselves.

Nevertheless we must attempt to produce as complete and

* The ′ in *alúno* and *professór* marks the intonation centers. The ˆ and ′ in *Êle* and *é* are Portuguese spelling conventions.

accurate a list of problems as possible before we begin writing items to test intonation. The problems of production are not the same as those of recognition although they are closely related. The list must therefore specifically state what the production and the recognition problems are.

10.3 TECHNIQUES FOR THE TESTING OF INTONATION

1. Problems of indeterminacy and variation. Perhaps because intonation is learned so early in our childhood and is so completely submerged in our habit system, or because in our writing traditions we have not been required to learn to write intonation, or for whatever other reason or combination of reasons, the average speaker of a language is not able to introspect what he does in intonation as he can in the sound segments, and he cannot react as readily or as accurately to whether or not an intonation is the same as or different from another as he can with the segmental phonemes of a word. Furthermore, one cannot as readily elicit from one's own speech the variety of possible intonation patterns as one can the variety of segmental phonemes and their sequences. As a result of these limitations, testing intonation will not be as effective as some of the techniques that have proved successful in the testing of segmental phonemes.

2. Perception techniques. Within the limitations mentioned above it is possible to test intonation receptively on three major levels: (A) through comparison of intonation with intonation without recourse to any specific meaning, (B) through identification of an intonation by means of some written representation, and (C) through meaning. Following are annotated examples of some techniques.

A. *Comparison of intonation with intonation.* In all the techniques involving comparison of one intonation with others, the examiner's voice gives two or more short utterances and asks the students to state whether or not the utterances are the same as to intonation. In the instructions it is necessary to emphasize the comparison of the intonation as distinct and separate from the words and the segmental phonemes, otherwise the students will limit themselves to the sound segments and may actually disregard the very intonation differences we wish to test. Clear examples showing utterances that have different segmental phonemes yet are the same in intonation should be given. The examples should also include utterances that are the same as to segmental phonemes but different in intonation.

INTONATION TECHNIQUE 10.1. **Minimal intonation pairs.**

EXAMPLE:

Instructions: You are going to hear two short sentences. Write "S" if their intonations are the same. Write "D" if their intonations are different. Compare the intonations *only*, not the words.

Item: The examiner reads the following pair:

(1) ^{2}*The* ^{3}*cómpany*^{2}, ^{2}*is* ^{3}*fíne*^{1}.

(2) ^{2}*The* ^{4}*cómpany*^{2}, ^{2}*is* ^{3}*fíne*^{1}.

Response: "D."

Comments: The two utterances differ only in the pitch of the first center; one is /3'/, and the other /4'/. If the student does not have a /4/ unit in his native language or if he does not have it in this pattern, he may not hear the difference between (1) and (2).

This technique varies only the intonation, that is, the segmental phonemes are the same in both utterances.

The same technique using different segmental phonemes is illustrated in the next example.

EXAMPLE:

Instructions: Compare the intonation, not the words of the pairs of sentences. Write "S" if the intonation is the same even if the words are different. Write "D" if the intonation is different even if the words are the same.

Item: The examiner reads the following pair:

(1) ^{2}*The* ^{3}*fáctory*^{2}, ^{2}*is* ^{3}*lárge*^{1}.

(2) ^{2}*An* ^{3}*óctopus*^{2}, ^{2}*will* ^{3}*dó*^{1}.

Response: "S."

INTONATION TECHNIQUE 10.2. **Triplets.** The above technique is linguistically sound. It is, however, statistically limited to only two possible answers, with the result that wild guessing may affect the scores heavily. To overcome this statistical limitation we may use three short utterances instead of two. The student then writes the numbers of the sentences that are the same. This gives five possible answers instead of two, and effectively reduces the influence of wild guessing.

EXAMPLE:

Instructions: Compare the intonation, not the words of the three sentences you will hear. Write the numbers of the sentences—1, 2, 3—that have the same intonation regardless of the words.

Item: ^{2}*The* ^{3}*cómpany*^{2}, ^{2}*is* ^{3}*fíne*^{1}.
^{2}*The* ^{4}*fáctory*^{2}, ^{2}*is* ^{3}*lárge*^{1}.
^{2}*An* ^{3}*óctopus*^{2}, ^{2}*will* ^{3}*dó*^{1}.

Response: " 1 3."

Other variations are possible, of course, but these will suffice as illustration of the techniques that ask the student to compare intonation with intonation.

B. *Identification of an intonation through some written representation.* In these techniques the examiner speaks an utterance and the students identify it by checking its representation among others on their answer sheets or by writing its representation. When the student is given several possible answers and is told to indicate which one has been read we have essentially a multiple choice item. When the student is asked to write the representation we have a form of dictation.

Both the multiple-choice and the dictation techniques have some serious drawbacks. They require symbols for the representation of intonation which are not common knowledge but must be taught as a special skill. Hence, failure to answer an item correctly may in many cases be the result of interference from the symbolization rather than failure to hear the intonation of the item.

For informal classroom tests these techniques are fully adequate, however. And some of the techniques might also prove useful for more formal and wider testing of intonation. The following are examples of multiple-choice and of dictation techniques.

(*a*) *Multiple-choice techniques.* These techniques differ according to the written symbols chosen to represent intonation. These symbols might be lines, lines and dots, numbers, letters or other conventionalized figures. The lines and dots usually represent pitch height on a vertical scale and time on a horizontal scale. Once this convention is understood by the student he can interpret the lines and dots on his own.

INTONATION TECHNIQUE 10.3. **Intonation represented by lines.**

Example using lines to indicate intonation and a small circle to indicate the center of the intonation:

Instructions: Check the line that best represents the intonation of the sentence as read. The circle indicates the center of the intonation. When the line rises it represents a rise in pitch: when it drops, it represents a drop in pitch.

Item: The examiner reads,
[2]Good [3]mórning[1].

Choices: The student chooses from the following:

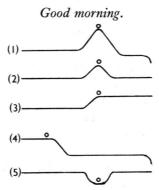

Good morning.

Response: (1).

Comments: The lines could be drawn differently or other symbols used instead. The aim is to make them as "readable" as possible for persons who have not used such a system to represent intonation or who have never even listened for intonation as such. The particular lines chosen are suggested by the kind of lines drawn by native speakers of English when they are asked to represent the intonation of sentences they hear on a tape recorder.

INTONATION TECHNIQUE 10.4. **Intonation represented by letters.** The same multiple-choice technique can be used with letters instead of lines representing the pitch points. Any letters would do. For mnemonic reasons it might be helpful to use L for low, M for mid, H for high, and X for extra high. To represent the terminal borders we might use /./ for fade out, /,/ for sustain, and /?/ for rise.

The same item used to illustrate the line technique would now appear as follows:

Instructions: Check the sequence of letters that best represents the intonation as read, L=low, M=mid, H= high, X=extra high, /./=final fade out, /,/= final sustain, /?/=final rise, /′/=intonation center.

Item: The examiner reads,
²*Good* ³*mórning*¹.

Choices: The student chooses from the following:
(1) M H′ L .
(2) M H′ M ,
(3) M H′ H ,
(4) H′ L L .
(5) M L′ M ,

Response: (1).

Comments: For purposes of a test, this letter representation seems less promising than the line representation used above.

INTONATION TECHNIQUE 10.5. **Intonation represented by numbers.** Letting 1 2 3 4 represent the four pitch phonemes from low to high, and letting ⌐ — ⌐, or . , ? represent the terminal borders the same item would then be as follows:

Instructions: Check the sequence of numbers that best represents the intonation as read. /1/=low, /2/=mid,
/3/=high, /4/=extra high, /⌐/=final fade out,
/—/=final sustain, /‿/=final rise, /′/=intona-
tion center.

Item: The examiner reads,
             ³*Good* ¹*mórning*¹.

Choices: The student chooses from the following:

          (1) 2 3′ 1⌐
          (2) 2 3′ 2—
          (3) 2 3′ 3—
          (4) 3 1′ 1‿
          (5) 3 1′ 1⌐

Response: (5).

Comments: Although numbers are a very convenient way to
             represent intonation for teaching, they require
             more preparation for testing than the lines used
             above.

(*b*) INTONATION TECHNIQUE 10.6. **Dictation.** The dictation techniques to test recognition of intonation consist of
reading an utterance to the students and having them write the
intonation they hear by means of lines, letters, or numbers.
The sentence read should be already written on the answer sheet
to save time and to permit the student to concentrate on writing
the symbols for the intonation itself.

In order to avoid unnecessary variation in the responses it
may be desirable to provide five horizontal lines (or four, three
or two depending on style) for line responses and to instruct the
students to go clearly above or below these lines to show pitch
differences.

EXAMPLE:

Instructions: Draw a line indicating the intonation height of the
sentence as read. To show a pitch change your
line must cross above or below one of the dotted
guide lines of the frame above the sentence.

Item: The examiner reads,
             ²*It's an* ³*ánimal*¹.

Response: The student draws a line in the frame above the sentence.

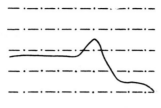

It's   an   animal.

Comments: The variety of possible ways of approaching a correct answer is a serious limitation of this technique as a formal testing device. It will, however, be useful as an informal classroom technique through some agreements between teacher and students on how to draw the answers.

Also, the final borders will not be regularly indicated unless additional instructions are given as to their presence and the manner in which they should be represented.

More uniform responses will be obtained by asking the students to represent their responses by means of letters or numbers. Parentheses indicate to the student the places where he must write a letter or number or other symbol representing the intonation phonemes and the terminal border.

EXAMPLE:

Instructions: Write in each parenthesis the letter representing the pitch or the symbol representing the terminal border that you hear at that point. Let L=low, M=mid, H=high, X=extra high. Let $/,/=$ sustain, $/./=$ fade out, $/?/=$ final rise, and $/'/=$ intonation center.

Item: ^2An $^3óctopus^2$, ^2will $^3dó^1$.

Response: (M) (H')   (M)   (M)   (H')   (L)
              An   *octopus*   (,)   *will*   *do*   (.)

The same technique may also be used with numbers.

129

EXAMPLE:

Instructions: Write in each parenthesis the number representing the pitches or the symbol representing the final border that you hear in the reading. $1 =$ low, $2 =$ mid, $3 =$ high, $4 =$ extra high, $/./=$ fade out, $/,/=$ sustain, $/?/=$ rise, and $/'/=$ intonation center.

Item: $^2An \ ^3óctopus^2, \ ^2will \ ^3dó^1.$

Response: (2) (3′)   (2)   (2)   (3′) (1)
         An   octopus   (,)   will   do   (.)

Comments: Both the letter and the number dictation techniques are highly serviceable as informal classroom techniques. They will have to be validated in various ways before we can use them for more formal tests.

C. *Comprehension techniques.* Testing intonation through meaning approaches more closely the use of intonation in speech and may therefore be more valid in this one sense. The testing of intonation through comparison with other intonations or through association with graphic symbols is more akin to the analyst's handling of language structure.

Testing intonation through meaning can be attempted in two ways: (1) through direct meaning of the particular intonation or some of its parts as distinct from the meanings of the words and grammatical structures of the same utterance, and (2) through the total meaning of an utterance which depends on a crucial intonation contrast. In both approaches we can use the multiple-choice type of item.

INTONATION TECHNIQUE 10.7. **Through direct meaning of the intonation.** This approach, though in theory a highly desirable one, suffers from the fact that intonation meanings are extremely vague and slippery. Some meanings, however, do appear regularly when native speakers are asked to indicate what an utterance means over and above the lexical meaning of the words and the meanings of the grammatical structures other than those signaled by intonation.

EXAMPLE:

Instructions: Listen to the intonation of the sentence you hear and check the choice that best represents its meaning.

Item: ^{2}*It's an* ^{3}*ánimal*^{1}.

Choices: The intonation indicates that
(1) the sentence is finished;
(2) the sentence is not finished;
(3) the speaker wants a verbal answer.

Response: (1).

By means of carefully written multiple-choice items we can force the student to show whether or not he perceives the intonation and terminal border phonemes. Another example will show how we can force a choice as to the center of the intonation. The multiple-choice approach permits us to ignore the final borders for a particular purpose.

EXAMPLE:

Instructions: Listen to the intonation and check the choice that best fits its meaning.

Item: ^{2}*The* ^{4}*fóod is all right*^{1}.

Choices: The intonation indicates that the speaker is probably making
(1) a matter-of-fact report;
(2) an emotional report;
(3) a comment that refers to something said by a previous speaker.

Responses: (3).

Comment: Items that attempt to get at the meaning of the intonation itself need to be tried on native speakers because of the vagueness of these meanings. This item may be ambiguous.

EXAMPLE:

Instructions: Listen to the intonation. Check the choice that best fits the meaning.

Item: ^{2}*Organize an export* ^{2}*búsiness*^{3}?

131

Choices: The speaker is probably

(1) making a report;

(2) making a request;

(3) asking for confirmation.

Response: (3).

Comments: The term "request" is not always understood readily by students learning English as a foreign language. "Giving instructions" might be a better wording for this choice.

INTONATION TECHNIQUE 10.8. Through total meaning that hinges on an intonation contrast. In some contexts the intonation will resolve ambiguities that appear on the basis of words and arrangements alone. In such cases we can test intonation receptively by asking the student to choose between the alternative meanings that are possible without the intonation signal. This does not mean that the intonation has that particular meaning; it means that under one intonation the words and arrangements have one meaning, and under another intonation they have a different meaning.

The following examples will demonstrate this approach to intonation.

EXAMPLE:

Instructions: Mark the choice that best fits the meaning of the utterance that you hear.

Item: $^3Bill^1$. $^1He's$ $^3h\acute{o}me^1$.

Choices: In this context, HE is

(1) the same person as BILL;

(2) another person, not BILL.

Response: (2).

Comment: Although HE could be the same person as BILL if the pause after BILL were particularly long, it is not likely that this is the case. In any case, trying the item out with native speakers of English will decide if the ambiguity has or has not been resolved.

Another example:

Instructions: Check the choice that best fits the meaning of the utterance you will hear.

Item: [2]*The* [4]*stúdents*[2], [1]*who are* [2]*hére*[1], [2]*want to* [3]*gó*[1].

Choices: Probably
(1) all of the students are "here;"
(2) not all of the students are "here."

Response: (1).

3. The use of recordings to test intonation. Because intonation is so easily changed by subtle attitude changes in the speaker, it takes a good deal of practice and self-control on the part of the examiner to render the test sentences with the intonation exactly as marked. Control of the intonation of the items is doubly difficult under test conditions, which require the examiner to address a group of people rather formally and to be on the alert for possible questions and other matters. Under these circumstances it is desirable to have the intonation test recorded beforehand on disc or tape. When a recorded test cannot be prepared or administered, the examiner should rehearse the reading of the test items carefully in advance.

4. Production techniques. To test intonation on a production level, that is, in speaking, the general technique is to elicit utterances from the student and to determine by observation where the intonation fails to contain the distinctive units of English.

There are various ways to elicit spoken utterances and of grading the responses. The major problems are (1) eliciting utterances that are representative of the student's speech and contain the problems we wish to test, and (2) scoring the responses uniformly so that comparable data are obtained. This uniformity of scoring we call objectivity. We are, of course, speaking of tests that can be given to substantial numbers of students by trained language teachers, not of the extended work of a linguist who is analyzing the intonation of a language not analyzed previously. Some of the techniques may be useful in both situations, but the sharpness and concentration of a student test requires that the problems be known beforehand.

We begin by preparing an accurate list of the intonation problems of the students to be tested. When the key phrases and sentences that illustrate these problems are found, it is then necessary to find ways to elicit these phrases and sentences from the subjects. The following are some of these ways.

Conversational stimuli. A natural way to elicit the key utterances is through directed conversation. This consists merely of asking questions, making requests, or initiating sentences that require the use of the key utterances by the student in responding to the stimulus or completing it. Below are some illustrative examples.

Example with a question stimulus:

The examiner asks, "What do we call a store that sells books?"

Key response: ^2A $^3b\acute{o}ok$ $store^1$.

Comment: The question can be of various types depending on the response desired. Compare for example, "What do you ask before entering a room?" "What are the days of the week?" "What would you do with a million dollars?"

Example with a request stimulus:

The examiner says, "Please ask a close friend of yours, whose name is John, if he is tired. Use his name in your question."

Key response: $^3\acute{A}re$ you $^2tired^2$, $^2J\acute{o}hn^2$?

Comment: A number of different intonations might legitimately be used in the response, but there should be two intonation phrases with a border after *tired* so that *tired John* does not become a modification structure. The border should be of the sustain type, to avoid making *John* a nonsense response to *Are you tired?*

Example with an incomplete sentence as stimulus:

The examiner says, "We drink water when . . ."

Key response: $^2we're$ $^3thirsty^1$.

Comment: If the student is not sure of the reponse he may say, $^3we're$ $^3thirsty^3$? The examiner then says, "Yes. Now let's repeat the item." The intonation should be right the second time, if the student knows it.

The above examples merely illustrate the technique. A good many variations are possible. It takes considerable ingenuity to prepare good questions and many that appear satisfactory at first glance turn out to have loopholes when they are tried with a number of students.

Picture stimuli with accompanying instructions. With young children and with adults who are not advanced in the foreign language the use of complicated questions or instructions can become a heavy factor in the responses. Pictures of various types can be used to supply the content of the response and permit the reduction of the verbal instructions to a minimum.

The use of pictures to test production of the sound segments can easily be extended to include the testing of intonation. The pictures and the instructions must be prepared and edited with the object of eliciting the key utterances that contain the intonation problems. No special discussion seems necessary here.

Retelling something just read. Reading a story or a report provides something of a unified content for all the students in answering the verbal stimuli of a production test. Using written material to provide the content has the advantage of greater precision and wider coverage than pictures, and it is easier to prepare and reproduce. It has the disadvantage of requiring more memory for the responses and of introducing the factor of reading, which does not necessarily parallel mastery of the intonation of a language.

This technique consists of having the student read silently a paragraph or story and then giving him verbal stimuli such as questions, requests, and incomplete sentences to elicit the key responses.

Reading aloud as an intonation test. Having the student read the key utterances aloud is the surest way to elicit the problems. Furthermore, since intonation is not marked in ordinary writing —punctuation does not indicate intonation but grammatical relationships—the responses are valid production utterances as to intonation.

The chief shortcomings of reading as a test of intonation are that reading intonation is different in style from speaking intonation, and reading skill is a heavy factor precisely in the matter of intonation. The intonation system is the same for both, but in reading we use intonations of greater length and we tend to suppress a number of the points of prominence. This problem, however, can be partially overcome by using dialogue material as found in plays. Skill in reading aloud remains an important factor, for even highly literate native speakers show wide differences in their ability to read a play aloud. Letting the student read the utterances silently once before reading them aloud reduces the effect of this factor but does not eliminate it altogether.

Dialogue material read aloud may well be our most satisfactory technique for testing production of intonation among literate students. Verbal stimuli and pictures will have to be used with illiterates and with very young children.

5. Scoring the production test of intonation. General impressions of the excellence of the intonation of a student are not dependable beyond the extreme cases of those who are excellent and those who are very poor indeed. To rank those in the middle ranges, where the largest number are usually found, we are at a loss as long as we depend on our over-all impression of the intonation of the students.

When a skill is too complex to be graded as a whole we revert to its elements. Specific scoring of specific intonation problems will give us more precise testing of intonation as a whole. This follows from the fact that in our theory of foreign language learning and testing, to know the problems is to know the language.

Since we cannot observe accurately too many variables simultaneously even if each is clearly described, we fall back on scoring one thing at a time. We can improve the objectivity of scoring intonation tests by directing the examiner to listen and score one pitch phoneme at a time, or one terminal border, or one intonation pattern versus another. For each item, then, the examiner listens for only one item and scores it with as much objectivity as he is capable of.

The examiner's accuracy is improved by having a scoring sheet containing the key utterances with the acceptable intonation and the problem spots clearly marked. It further helps the examiner to have above or below the correct response the usual distortions. The examiner then checks the right response or the unsatisfactory one depending on the performance of the student.

Sample scoring material:

Key response: ^2A ^3bóok $stòre^1$.

Distortion: ^2A $bòok$ $^3stóre^1$.

Another distortion: —————.

Instructions to the examiner: "Listen to the placing of the intonation center. Check the appropriate line according to the student's response.

With all the simplification of the problem of scoring and with all the aids we can prepare to improve the accuracy of the scoring, grading a production test is still open to wide variation due if nothing else to the personality of the examiner. One examiner may pride himself in being strict in his grading and will consider wrong everything that is not completely right, while another examiner may like to be helpful and will accept any approximation provided it does not sound like a different unit altogether.

6. Group tests of intonation on a production level. All the intonation techniques to test production discussed above are essentially individual test techniques, that is, they are designed to test one student at a time. With the advent of tape recorders and other recording machines it is possible to use all of these techniques to test the students in groups instead of individually. We need as many recording machines as the number of students we wish to test as a group. The stimulus matter is given to all the students in individual booklets or is projected on a screen visible to all. The instructions can be printed along with any other stimuli or given orally by the examiner or in a recording.

Group testing solves some problems such as the exchange of information from the student examined to the following ones in individual testing. It does not solve the problem of the time it takes to listen to all the responses of all the students at the same speed as they were recorded.

7. Partial production techniques. Because of the need for trained persons to score the production tests of intonation, and because of the time it takes to score such tests even when they are administered as group tests, the testing of intonation productively is destined to remain a restricted activity in language testing with the consequent drop of interest in teaching intonation when it is not tested. There is need then for objective, easily administered, easily scored techniques to test intonation at least partially on a production level.

These partial production techniques are based on silent reconstruction of the intonation by the student and his recording of it by means of written symbols.

These partial production techniques are considerably removed from the actual use of intonation in speech and are therefore open to question as to their validity. Furthermore, since our object is to test intonation in use, we wish to know not only if the student can, when he sets his attention to it, reconstruct the intonation but whether or not he does use it in his speech. We are therefore responsible for correlating the scores obtained by students on these partial production techniques and their actual use of intonation on the same material when they speak it or at least when they read it out loud.

Writing the intonation with letters or numbers. This technique consists of giving the student the key utterances written with enough context to determine the intonation of the key phrase or sentence. The student then writes the pitch points or borders in parentheses placed at crucial points in the text. The letters or numbers or any other symbols to be used are carefully listed and illustrated at the beginning of the test.

Sample instructions: "Write in the parentheses the number of the pitch that you use at those points. Use /1/ for low, /2/ for mid, /3/ for high, and /4/ for extra high as in the following example: (2)*The* (3)*péople* (2)(,) (2)*are* (4)*wónderful*(1) (.) Write /,/ for sustained border, /./ for final fade out, and /?/ for final rise not to the next level. The border marks go in the lower parentheses.

Sample item: *A store that sells books is* (2)*a* ( ) *bóok store* ( ) ( )

Comparing intonation with intonation. In this technique the student has before him two or three phrases or sentences and is asked to compare the pitch level or border type at numbered places in each of the phrases or sentences. The student rehearses to himself the way he pronounces the three and writes the numbers of those he thinks he pronounces the same. An example will clarify the technique.

Example using three intonations:

Instructions: "Write the numbers of the pitch points that you pronounce the same."

1	2	3

Item: *A stone house. A nice garden. A home.*

Response: 1 3.

Comment: The particular example needs to be validated with native speakers of English, but the technique may be useful even if the item is not a good one.

Example using two intonations:

Instructions: "Write 'S' if the intonation pitch at 1 and 2 is the same. Write 'D' if it is different."

1	2

Item: *My feet are cold, but my hands are all right.*

Response: D.

These partial production techniques have not been tried to my knowledge. If they can be perfected to a point where they become useful they may make intonation one of the widely tested elements of language.

10.4   PREPARING AN INTONATION TEST

The steps recommended in the preparation of an intonation test are the same as for the testing of the sound segments. Trying the items with native speakers of the language comparable to the foreign speakers for whom the test is being prepared is particularly important in these highly experimental tests of intonation.

10.5   BIBLIOGRAPHICAL NOTES

The most extensive description of American English intonation is (1) K. L. Pike's *The Intonation of American English.* One of the clearest summaries of the structural description of American English intonation including the terminal borders is (2) C. F. Hockett's chapter on "English Intonation" in *A Course in Modern Linguistics.* This includes and clarifies (3) G. L. Trager and H. L. Smith's contribution to the description of terminal contours in *An Outline of English Structure.*

(4) Daniel Jones' description in *An Outline of English Phonetics* is still used as representing R. P. (Received Pronunciation), which

is also the subject of Roger Kingdon's *The Groundwork of English Intonation*. Other descriptions are in preparation for the English of England and of Scotland.

(5) For Spanish, Tomás Navarro Tomás' *Manual de entonación española* has the most extensive information. (6) Stockwell, Bowen, and Silva-Fuenzalida's article, "Spanish Juncture and Intonation," in *Language* exemplifies Trager and Smith's approach to intonation as applied to Spanish.

Chapter 11

TESTING CONTROL OF GRAMMATICAL STRUCTURE OF A FOREIGN LANGUAGE

11.1   **INTRODUCTORY**

The term *grammar* means different things to different people. To the grammarian it has often meant the analysis of his own language, or one he has mastered, in order to discover its "rules" of propriety, that is, what may and may not be said in the particular language. Earlier, when Latin was the language of the learned throughout Europe, grammar was the study of Latin grammar for the purpose of learning Latin. For the general public, grammar has been the study of rules of correctness, that is, rules that claimed to tell the student what he should and should not say in order to speak the language of the socially educated class. It happened that many of the rules that passed as grammar had no currency outside of the textbooks and the classrooms where they were presented and studied. As a result, a curious attitude is often observed toward this type of grammar. People say that they do not know their "grammar" and they make protestations of inferiority because of this fact, but they go on happily using the forms and patterns that are current. They sense that the patterns they use are acceptable, yet they feel compelled to pay lip service to the artificial grammar they studied in school.

Modern grammarians—probably since Otto Jespersen's time for English—try to collect and analyze examples of actual usage. Linguists attempt to analyze and classify any and all languages including their own. Some linguists such as C. C. Fries and others have recently attempted to lay bare the basic grammatical structure of English, the central framework upon which hang the countless variations of usage.

From the modern linguistic point of view the native speakers of a language have mastered the basic structure of their language, that is, the basic underlying patterns on which they build sentences and sequences of sentences. Thus, when native speakers study grammar they usually become involved, not in the basic framework, which they "know", but in problems of variant usage, of dialect differences, of social differences, of style, of artistic effects, etc.

In contrast with this the non-native speaker who is learning the language does not know its structure. He needs to acquire this basic framework in order to master the production and comprehension of the typical sentences of the language. Yet he and those who teach him often forget this fact and proceed with the teaching and learning of the foreign language as if it were the native language: they take up matters of variant usage, etc., losing sight of the central structure of the language and ignoring its importance and its difficulties.

The point of view followed in this chapter is that of learning and testing the basic grammatical structure, the basic underlying patterns of the foreign language, the molds into which the sentences of the language are cast for communication.

Problems of propriety and impropriety are also important, but they are relegated to second place by the fact that the student studies an acceptable variety of the language in the classroom.

11.2 WHAT IS GRAMMATICAL STRUCTURE?

1. **Definition of grammatical structure.** The patterns of arrangement of words in sentences and the patterns of arrangement of parts of words into words are its grammatical structure. The minimum language unit that functions as a full communicative utterance is the sentence. We speak in sentences, not in words or in parts of words. Sentences are made up of patterns of arrangement of word groups, words, stress, intonation and terminal borders. These patterns of arrangement have meaning over and above that of the individual elements of the sentence.

Sentences occur in sequences, and each language has its system for the ordering of sentences in sequence. Sequences may occur in the same utterance, and therefore be produced by the same speaker, or they may occur in different utterances by consecutive speakers. The latter are frequent in all languages in the form of questions and answers.

Most words can occur as full sentences with a sentence intonation. Because of this possibility, words have been defined as minimum free forms not made up of any other free forms. In practice it is found that native speakers of a language can readily break up a sentence into words even if their language has never been written or they are not familiar with writing. In ordinary writing, in many languages words are separated by spaces. The conventions of writing produce a few instances in which forms written between spaces are not words. These can be solved by the test of free occurrence as a sentence or by having an informant produce the item in an utterance with instructions to divide the utterance up into units at every point where a pause is possible.

Words are made up of *morphemes*, not phonemes. A morpheme is the smallest meaningful unit of a language. The word *book* is made up of one morpheme; the word *books* is made up of two morphemes: *book+s*. Morphemes consist of a phoneme or sequence of phonemes and a meaning. If a sequence of phonemes has two separate and unrelated meanings it is probably two morphemes. For example, -s$\{$/-s/ $\sim$ /-z/ $\sim$ /ɪz/$\}$ has the same form when it is the plural of nouns and when it is the third person singular inflection of the present indicative of verbs. Since these meanings are clearly different and unrelated, we say that we have two morphemes, not just one. Checking the various places in which this form can appear shows that with nouns it means plural and with verbs it means third person singular. This confirms the fact that they are two different meaningful units in English, two morphemes.

On the other hand, if /-s/, /-z/, and -/ɪz/, which are different in form, turn out to have the same meaning of plural and if in those environments where one appears the others are not permitted, we conclude that all three forms are variants of the same morpheme.

2. Grammatical patterns. An arrangement of words that has a meaning over and above the separate meanings of the words that constitute it and is a model into whose parts other words can be substituted without changing the meaning of the arrangement itself constitutes a grammatical pattern. A grammatical pattern is in a sense less meaningful than an utterance, for an utterance has a total meaning that includes that of the pattern plus that of the words; a grammatical pattern is more important than any single utterance since it is the mold from which countless utterances can be produced.

If we have a set of sentences such as *I am here, You are here, He is here, I was here, You were here, He was here*, etc., we notice that although they are different in total meaning because the words change, the meaning of the arrangement itself remains the same, that is, they are all statements with a subject, a copula, and a predicate adverb. We say that all of these sentences are examples of one and the same pattern.

Furthermore, if the arrangement itself has two meanings, we may conclude that it represents two patterns. For example, the arrangement, *he feels,* in [2]*Hè fèels* [3]*fíne*[1]., and the same arrangement in [2]*Hè fèels the* [3]*léather*[1]. (e.g. *with his fingers*) are different. This is confirmed when we compare the range of environments where each may be used.

3. Levels of grammatical structure. One of the reasons why the analysis of grammar has been difficult and subject to many errors and controversies is the fact that the same forms operate simultaneously at several levels of structure. The short response utterance [3]*Thése*[1]. is a sentence, a part of speech, a word, three morphemes, and seven phonemes. Similar levels of structure are observed in other languages, though the formal devices and arrangements used in each language vary greatly.

The levels of structure that are important in outlining the structure of a language for testing purposes are *sequences of sentences, sentence patterns, parts of sentences, modification structures, parts of speech and function words, inflection, derivation, patterns of morphemes into words*, and *morphemes*. An example will serve to illustrate what is meant by these levels.

> "[2]*Whát did Mártin* [3]*dó*[1]."
> "[2]*Hè* [4]*tóld the stúdents*[1], [1]*a* [3]*stóry*[1], [1]*about* [3]*ánts*[1]."
> "[3]*Whŷ about* [3]*ánts*[1]."
> "[2]*Be* [2]*cáuse*[3]?"

The permitted sequences of sentences though not very clearly illustrated can be seen in the sequence of words, *What, He, Why, Because,* that begin the four sentences. The last two sentences, *Why about ants,* and *Because,* with intonation as indicated, could not occur at the beginning of a conversation, a fact that reveals distribution restrictions in sequences of sentences.

At the level of patterns of sentences the conversation has four sentences, showing four different patterns—two **statements** and two **questions.**

The parts of sentences are illustrated by **subjects**—*Martin, He*—; **verbal predicates**—*did . . . do, told*—; **objects**—*the students, a story about ants*—; **interrogative complements**—*what, why*—; and something that might be called **conjunctive complement**—*because.*

Modification structures are illustrated by *a story about ants* in which *story* is the head and *about ants* the modifier. Examples of other modification structures not illustrated in the conversation are *red ants, sugar ants, ants of stone,* etc., with *ants* as head.

Parts of speech are illustrated by **nouns**—*Martin, students, story, ants*—; **pronouns**—*he*—; **verbs**—*did, do, told*—; **adjectives** and **adverbs** are not illustrated. Function words are represented by *what, the, a, about, why, because.*

Inflection is shown by **tense**—*did, do, told* from *tell*; **number**—*student-s, ant-s*—; **gender**—*Martin-he.* Derivation is illustrated by *student* (compare *depend-ent, differ-ent*).

Patterns of morphemes into words are illustrated by words of one morpheme—*he, the*—; words of a stem and suffixes—*stud-ent-s*—, words of a stem and infix—*told* from *tell*—. Words and morphemes are well illustrated and need no further examples.

4. Grammatical categories. It is interesting and important from the point of view of testing that different languages show similar grammatical categories although the formal devices used to express them and the distribution of these formal devices differ widely from language to language. Some of the grammatical categories observed in one form or another in many languages are gender, number, person, case, voice, subject-object relation, head-modifier structure, and subject-predicate constructions. The users of these languages must cast their utterances in frames that require distinctions in these and other categories in addition to the particular message they wish to convey at any particular time.

5. Grammar as set of habits. Given the capabilities of human beings as we know them, we can understand that the use of a language is made possible by reducing much of the operation of these grammatical categories to sets of complex habits. The user of a language does not verbalize or define these grammatical distinctions before he uses them. He does not identify them by technical names, and he probably does not identify them as separate units at various levels of structure. He must, however, react to their functions with precision and speed through highly developed habits.

Notice the fact that, on one hand, many persons who can define the categories of a language and recite its grammatical rules are unable to use the language for communication, and, on the other, many efficient users of a language are unable to identify the parts of speech or the structures of an utterance either by technical terms or by definition. It follows that the teaching or testing of grammar as technical names and as the recitation of rules of correctness is not effective either in teaching or testing a foreign language or in teaching native speakers accepted forms of certain controversial usages.

11.3 STRUCTURE PROBLEMS AS DETERMINED BY THE NATIVE LANGUAGE

1. Transfer. With an accurate description of the grammatical structure of a language we can prepare good tests, but we know that the native language of the student is a major factor in determining which structure patterns will be troublesome and which will not. According to the theory the student transfers the set of habits of the grammatical structure of his native language to the foreign language. Thus when a given structure pattern has the same function, the same form, and the same distribution in the native and the foreign languages, the student will "learn" it easily and quickly by simple transfer. When the structural pattern is not paralleled in the native language, the student will have trouble learning it because of interference from the native language habit patterns.

2. Testing control of the problems is testing control of the language. We can safely assume that when a student has mastered the problem patterns of a foreign language he has also mastered those patterns that are not problems because they transfer satisfactorily from the native language. We can thus state as a working hypothesis that learning the problems is learning the language, and we can state that testing the problems is testing the language. The structure patterns of the foreign language that do not transfer satisfactorily from the native language because they are not parallel in meaning, form, or distribution are the ones we seek to discover in order to have the most effective testing materials. These problems are found and described effectively by a systematic comparison of the native and the foreign language grammatical structures. This procedure has the added advantage of making the tests independent of any particular textbooks since the tests are then based on the languages themselves.

3. Comparison of the structures of the native and the foreign languages. We begin by summarizing in outline form the description of the grammatical structures of the foreign and the native languages. The outline will contain the significant patterns at each of the levels of structure listed above, that is, *sequences of sentences*, *sentence patterns*, *parts of sentences*, etc. For each pattern the outline will give the *minimal essential features* that distinguish it from all others. Also included will be *permitted features* that are possible but not required, and *required features* that are not minimally distinctive.

An example will help to clarify this matter of distinctive, required, and permitted features. The question pattern illustrated by the sentence, *²Dòes he stùdy ³médicine¹?* has as minimally essential, distinctive features the verbal function word *does*, the pronoun subject *he*, and the word order *does he*. These are functioning as subject and verbal predicate. The sentence illustrates also the permitted features of the lexical verb *study*, the object *medicine*, the intonation phrase /2 3′ 1 ?/. These are not minimally essential since the sentence would remain a question if it had any of several possible intonation phrases, and if it did not have *study medicine*. The inflection of *does* is minimally essential at the level of the parts of sentences insofar as it identifies *he* as the subject by agreement, but it is not directly essential at the sentence type level since all that is required is a verbal predicate preceding a subject.

An example from Japanese will illustrate a required feature that is not minimally distinctive. The Japanese function word /ka/ occurs at the end of a favorite question pattern in Japanese. It parallels English *do* in that it signals question and does not have any clear lexical content of its own. This function word does not occur in any position that contrasts with the final position in questions, however. We say that the function word /ka/ itself is a minimally essential feature of this Japanese question, but its position at the end of the sentence is required but not minimally distinctive. In other words, in certain Japanese questions the presence or absence of /ka/ changes a question into a statement, but placing /ka/ in a position other than final does not change the question into some other pattern, it makes the result impossible in Japanese.

When we have the structural outlines of the two languages we proceed to compare the distinctive patterns at each level of structure. With each structure in the foreign language we need to know (1) if there is a functionally parallel pattern in the native language, (2) if it is signaled the same way, that is, by the same formal features and sequences of features, and (3) if it is similarly distributed in the larger structures of the language. An example will illustrate these points. Both English and German have the kind of sentences we call questions. Both English and German use word order as a minimally essential feature in some questions—a verbal predicate preceding the subject. Thus far we have not discovered any structure problem. English uses the function word *do* as the verbal predicate in many questions. German does not use any parallel word. We may then expect a German speaker to say for example, **Know you where the church is?* as a question instead of *Do you know where the church is?* He will simply be transferring the German pattern illustrated by *Wissen Sie wo die Kirche ist?* which would be similar to the pattern used with the verb *be* in English, but not with the verb *know*.

Another example with Spanish as the native language will further illustrate these cross language comparisons. Both English and Spanish have the type of sentences we call questions. But some questions which may be indicated in English by means of word order as a minimal essential feature are indicated in Spanish by intonation as the minimal essential feature. We can expect trouble here since the Spanish speaker has learned to react to the intonation signal and to disregard the order of the parts of the sentence, which in his language is not structurally significant in this case. He has to learn to react to a different formal feature —order of parts of the sentence—for the same structural meaning—question. The German speaker had less of a task since his problem was simply to use a new word, *do*, in a formal feature, order of parts of the sentence, which he already used in his native language to signal a question. In both cases, however, we have discovered points of difficulty of the kind that we need to locate for our tests.[1]

The list of problems resulting from the comparison of the foreign language with the native language is a most valuable tool for both teaching and testing purposes. It is nevertheless still a list of hypothetical problems which for final validation should be checked against the actual speech of students of the given language background who are learning that foreign language. This final check will show in some instances that a problem may not have been well analyzed and may be more of a problem or less of a problem than predicted. In this kind of validation we should keep in mind of course that not all the speakers of a language will have exactly the same amount of difficulty with each problem. Dialect and personal differences rule out such a possibility. The problems will nevertheless prove quite stable and predictable for each language background.

4. Production versus recognition. Although the structure problems met in learning to speak and to understand a foreign language are closely related, they are not identical. Learning to produce the question pattern illustrated by the sentence *Does*

---

[1] For a full discussion of the comparison of two grammatical structures by teachers of foreign languages, see Chapter 3 of *Linguistics Across Cultures* by Robert Lado.

he study medicine? includes among its problems the use of the inflected form *does* and the uninflected form *study*. Students tend to inflect the lexical verb *study* rather than the verbal function word *do*. Learning to understand this same pattern, on the other hand, does not present the problem of the non-inflection of *study*, because the sentence is not produced by the student but by a speaker of the language who will do it properly. In preparing the list of problems it is necessary therefore to indicate the production and the recognition problems for each pattern. It is good practice to use both labels in each pattern: "production problems," "recognition problems." If a pattern is not a recognition problem, it can be so stated after the label.

11.4   RECOGNITION TECHNIQUES TO TEST GRAMMATICAL STRUCTURE

1. General recognition technique. Testing structure at the recognition level is a relatively simple matter which can be solved satisfactorily under any of the usual conditions found in testing. In every case the general technique is to present to the student an utterance containing the structure problem and to check whether or not he understands. If we wish to test an actor-action sequence in English for example, we present the student with an utterance such as ^{2}*The bôy strúck the* ^{3}*cár*^{1}*.*, and then check to see if he understands who struck whom. To test control of this structure in listening we present the utterance orally to the student. To test it in reading we present the utterance on the printed page. The basic technique remains the same.

2. Controlling the context. The problem of how much context to provide is basically the same in listening and in reading. We must give enough linguistic and physical context to render the structure unambiguous, yet avoid giving away the answer and rendering the item useless. Careful inspection of each item usually reveals any defects of this kind. Those items that are given away by the context usually turn out to have no discriminating power or to be more difficult for the good students than for the less able ones. When discovered, they are either rewritten or eliminated altogether.

3. Speed of presentation. In ordinary tests of reading and of listening the matter of speed is controlled differently. In listening tests the examiner controls the speed by his rate of delivery and the length of the pauses between items. In reading, the examiner cannot control the speed of each phrase and sentence. He simply sets a time limit for the entire test or for each part of the test. As a result a student may reread leisurely some items and rush hurriedly through others. He goes at his own speed in reading while in a listening test he has to conform to the speed of the speaker.

For experimental purposes, however, the speed of reading can be controlled by flashing reading matter, phrase by phrase, on a screen at a given rate. When such a technique is used, the question of speed can be equalized with that of listening, and the length of the test utterances or written sentences becomes an important variable in determining difficulty.

4. Length of test utterances. The short conversational utterance is typical in spoken material and fully valid in a listening test. The longer narrative passage is more valid for reading. Published theatrical plays, which are used sometimes as reading material, might be considered an exception but they are not, since they are intended for oral presentation by the actors and they should contain the shorter utterances typical of conversation. Because of the difference in the length and style of reading material versus listening material the selection of problems for a reading test will differ from the selection of problems for a listening test even in the grammatical structures tested and especially in the complexity of the structures and sequences of structures. These matters will be taken up in the chapters on testing the integrated skills and therefore will not be discussed any further here.

STRUCTURE TECHNIQUE 11.1. **Action response.** There are various ways to check the comprehension of a structure. We can check comprehension by linguistic and by non-linguistic means. Among the non-linguistic means are actions and pictures. The action response is particularly useful in informal classroom testing, and it is better adapted to young students than to adults. This technique consists merely in having the student listen to the test utterance containing the structural problem and to perform some act that shows the examiner whether or not he understands.

EXAMPLE:

Instructions: Perform the actions you are told to perform. Remain still if no action is requested.

Item: *It's warm in the room.* (Pause)
The window is closed. (Pause)
Open the door. (Pause)

Response: The student does not move when he hears the first and the second sentences. When he hears the third he gets up and opens the door, provided he understands the request pattern in English.

Comments: Since this is a test, the examiner should use the same intonation for all three sentences, possibly /2 3′ 1./, to eliminate any extraneous clues to the answer.

If every sentence is a request, the items will stop testing the request pattern and become only a test of vocabulary.

The examiner avoids giving any gesture clues to the request sentence.

Example using French request sentences as the problem:

Instructions: Perform the actions requested. Remain still if no action is requested.

Item: *Levez-vous.* (Pause)
Montrez-moi le livre. (Pause)
L'élève est assis. (Pause)

Response: The student stands up after the first sentence, he points to a book after the second sentence, and remains standing after the third, which talks about sitting but is not a request.

Comments: This technique, which is often used in teaching by a direct method, varies essentially when used for testing. In teaching, the instructor uses gestures or demonstrates the actions in order to make the students understand and react accordingly. The instructor's purpose in teaching is to provide enough context to make the meaning of the pattern clear. Later he may include some sentences that are not requests in order to show the contrast. In testing, the examiner avoids any gestures or clues that would give away the meaning. His purpose is to force the student to decide his action exclusively on the basis of the linguistic pattern being tested.

The action identifying a particular object may be used as a more indirect way to check comprehension of a contrastive pattern.

EXAMPLE:

Instructions: The examiner places a watch on his desk away from him and unbuttons his coat so that a lower vest pocket or a watch pocket in his trousers is visible.

Item: The examiner then says, "Please point to the watch pocket."

Response: The student will point to the examiner's pocket if he understands that *watch pocket* is a pocket and not a watch.

Comments: In this English modification structure, the head is preceded by the modifier so that *watch pocket* is a pocket and *pocket watch* is a watch. In some languages the direction of modification in similar modification structures is the opposite so that the students understand *watch pocket* to mean a watch.

STRUCTURE TECHNIQUE 11.2. **Pictures.** Pictures of various kinds can be used as a valid non-language device to check comprehension of structure patterns. The technique is as follows: The examiner presents an utterance that contains the structure problem, and the student chooses from two or more pictures the one that best fits the utterance. The pictures are drawn in such a way that one of them fits the utterance and the others fit utterances that would differ from it by a minimal distinctive feature. The student thus has to distinguish between utterances whose difference constitutes the learning problem being tested.

EXAMPLE: The examiner presents the sentence, "The boy hit the car." The students are asked to choose between the two pictures of Figure 11.1. If the student understands that in this

A   B

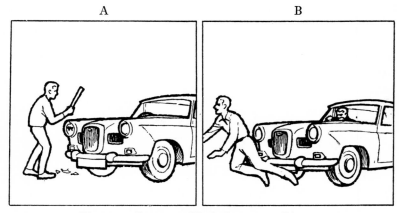

Fig. 11.1. Structure Technique 11.2. Pictures

pattern the boy did the hitting he will choose A. If the utterance were, "The car hit the boy," picture B would be the expected choice. Since the only difference between the two utterances, "The boy hit the car" and "The car hit the boy," is one of word order, comprehension of this word order signal is decisive in choosing one picture or the other.

As in technique 11.1, action response, the pictures may be used to depict objects whose identification depends on the recognition of a minimal distinctive structure clue.

EXAMPLE: For the contrast between *watch pocket* and *pocket watch* the student is told to choose one of the following two pictures after being asked "Which is the watch pocket?"

A   B

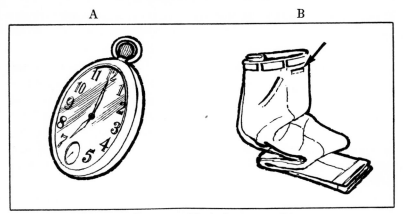

Fig. 11.2. Structure Technique 11.2. Pictures

Since a watch pocket is a pocket the expected choice is B. If the sentence were "Which is the pocket watch?" the expected choice would then be A.

With two-way contrasts such as these it is difficult to prepare a third picture that is effective. A combination of two structure signals, however, easily provides a three-way contrast and thus helps to reduce the effect of guessing.

EXAMPLE: The actor-action sequence of "The boy hit the car" may be combined with a singular-plural contrast in "boy-boys." When the student hears "The boy hit the car," and is asked to choose among the following three pictures he has to know not only who struck but how many—one or more than one.

A   B   C

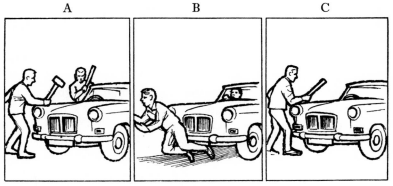

Fig. 11.3. Structure Technique 11.2. Pictures

Picture C is the expected answer because in addition to knowing that the boy is the actor, we also know that it is one boy only.

To provide a full range of choices a fourth picture depicting two cars striking a boy might be added to these three. A question of economy then comes in. The effect of wild guessing is more effectively reduced with four choices than with three. If the "reading" of four pictures does not become too complicated, there is an advantage in using the four pictures. If, however, the pictures are not easy to understand at a glance, the three pictures might remain the better test.

5. Observation of speech in real language situations is impractical and inaccurate. Theoretically the most valid way to test comprehension of structure patterns is the observation of real language situations. This approach is usually impractical, however, because it requires a good deal of time to test a single student, and what is more important, our results will often be incomplete and not fully reliable. It takes a considerable chunk of unselected speech to sample the entire structure of a language, and because of the uncontrolled context, we cannot always be sure that a structure has or has not been understood. The student will sometimes respond properly not because he understands the structure but because the context makes the meaning obvious. Furthermore, we all know that a polite "yes" does not always mean that the student understands.

In spite of these limitations as a practical test, whenever the problem is to check thoroughly a single structure or a limited number of them, direct observation of real language situations can be put to good use.

STRUCTURE TECHNIQUE 11.3. **Choices in the goal language.** Among the language media that can be used to test comprehension of structure are the goal language, that is, the foreign language for the student, and the student's native language. In the very special case of a field situation in which the examiner does not know the native language of the students and the students do not know much of the goal language they are learning, we might of course use a third or trade language understood by both the students and the examiner. This can hardly be considered a representative testing problem and will therefore not be discussed further.

The goal language can be used in the choices to verify comprehension of the test utterance in that language.

EXAMPLE: With the test utterance, "What is a watch pocket?" the choices might be

(A) A watch;

(B) A pocket.

This technique is desirable because it permits the good student to remain set in the foreign language instead of switching back and forth from it to his native language. A limitation, on the other hand, is the fact that since the choices are in the language being tested they must be easier to understand than the test utterance itself or there would be no test of the structure problem. Making the choices easier than the test utterance is not always simple or even possible, and in some instances it is difficult to determine whether the choices or the test utterance will be more difficult. The following example illustrates the technique in Spanish. It is a defective item because the choices are more difficult than the utterance whose comprehension is being checked.

DEFECTIVE ITEM:

Test utterance: *¿Quién es usted?*

Choices: (A) *El locutor quiere saber con quién habla.*

    (B) *El locutor quiere saber con quién quiere hablar usted.*

The test utterance means 'Who are you?' which has the same word order in English and in Spanish. To understand this sentence all the student has to learn are the three words *quién* 'who,' *es* 'are,' and *usted* 'you,' which are common everyday words. To understand the choices he has to learn more difficult words, more of them, and more difficult structures.

The choices need not describe the exact literal meaning of the test utterance; meanings that can easily be inferred from the utterance might be used to advantage to test some structures. We must take care that the inference is within the range of the

157

intelligence of the students being tested; otherwise we will be testing intelligence rather than language. The following item has proved satisfactory with adult students learning English.

EXAMPLE:

Test sentence: "If the windows were closed I would ask you to open them."

Choices: (A) The windows are closed.
(B) The student goes to the windows and opens them.
(C) The student remains seated.

Choice C is the one that can be inferred from the "if-were-would" pattern.

This type of item has been used to test reading comprehension, particularly in connection with vocabulary matters. It has also been used to test inferences from the total paragraph that is presented to the student for reading. The use of the technique to test structural comprehension requires a clear analysis of the problem being tested and strict control of the amount of context provided.

Five-choice items are more desirable in multiple-choice tests because the effect of wild guessing is then greatly reduced. One should avoid, however, introducing choices that are irrelevant to the structure being tested if the purpose is merely to have five choices.

The following example with five choices tests recognition of the head of a subject construction in English.

EXAMPLE:

Test sentence: The friend of the teacher that John met when he visited his mother and his aunt visited the library today.

Choices: A person visited the library. This person was
(1) the friend;
(2) the teacher;
(3) John;
(4) the mother;
(5) the aunt.

The expected reply is (1).

For the sake of variety and sometimes to accommodate a problem that is not easily tested with this technique as described, the structure problem can appear in the choices themselves, leaving the main test sentence only to provide the meaning and the context. In this case the main sentence or sentences must be easier than the choices, which are the real test material.

EXAMPLE:

Meaning and context: Mr. Martin visited the teacher. John saw them.
Choices containing the structure problem:
(1) Mr. Martin knows who visited John;
(2) John knows who visited Mr. Martin;
(3) The teacher knows whom John visited;
(4) John knows whom Mr. Martin visited;
(5) John knows whom the teacher visited.

The expected response is (4), and the problem pattern is *whom x visited* versus *who visited x*. This variant of technique 11.3 has the disadvantage of requiring a good deal of additional reading on the part of the student.

STRUCTURE TECHNIQUE 11.4. **Choices in the background language.** Using the native language of the student to check his understanding of the foreign language structure is a well-known technique. This technique has certain clear advantages. Since the student knows his native language, the choices are easy to write and to understand. Comprehension of the problem can be tested with precision in most instances.

A serious reservation toward extensive use of this technique has to do with the fact that it involves translation. We know that as students advance in their mastery of a foreign language they operate more and more in the language and make less and less reference to their native language. By using translation in tests we force the advanced student to revert to his native language. We thus complicate the task of the advanced student beyond what it normally is. Another serious reservation to the extensive use of translation in tests is the influence this practice will inevitably have on teaching. A widespread concern among teachers in many countries is the fact that official examinations and tests often deal chiefly with translation. The teachers feel they cannot spend class time teaching the students to use the language efficiently because they must concentrate on the type of restricted translation on which their teaching excellence and their students' progress will be judged exclusively. For these reasons it is probably wiser to limit the use of translation techniques in foreign language tests to those problems that cannot be tested efficiently by other techniques. Technique 11.3, choices in the goal language, is preferable in this important sense.

Following are examples of the use of the native language in structure recognition items.

EXAMPLE: English structure with Spanish as the background language.

> Test item: "What is a watch pocket?"
> Choices: (1) *Un reloj de bolsillo.*
> (2) *El bolsillo del reloj.*

The native language can be used to define the meaning.

EXAMPLE:

> Item: *¿Qué es el bolsillo del reloj?*
> Choices: (1) A watch pocket;
> (2) A pocket watch.

Many other styles are possible with this and other techniques. The number of choices can be increased to five, an introductory phrase can precede the choices, etc.

STRUCTURE TECHNIQUE 11.5. **Translation into the background language.** Another technique which has been used indiscriminately is one in which the student translates the key utterance into his native language. The same considerations for and against technique 11.4 above obtain also with technique 11.5. In addition, this full translation technique has the disadvantage of not being easily scored. Students will use variant translations that in some cases are equally valid and in others are not. A student who is advanced in his understanding of the foreign language may decide to use a free translation that to him interprets the feeling of the original better than a word-for-word translation. In so doing he may not have to show that he understands the problem structure specifically.

To reduce the possible variant translations and to save time in giving the test and in scoring it, part of the translation can be provided in the answer sheet, leaving blank only the crucial sections of the test utterance.

EXAMPLE: Spanish problem: Subject signaled by inflection.

Item: *Le quedamos muy agradecidos.*

Translation: "———remain(s) very grateful."

The student fills the blank with " We."

STRUCTURE TECHNIQUE 11.6. **Grammatical usage.** The kind of item that presents various alternate phrases in a context and asks the student to choose the one that best fits the context has been used for tests written from the usage point of view. In them are given the supposedly correct form, the form that has been branded as incorrect, and other less likely forms as distractors. These tests have been challenged by English language scholars who proved that the forms branded as incorrect were often in good standing and the forms submitted as correct were artificial creations without currency outside of the tests and textbooks that perpetuated the myth. The techniques are made useless when employed to test such artificially invented problems. If, however, they are carefully directed to test real structure problems, the techniques can be useful to measure control of the structure of a foreign language.

EXAMPLE:

Instructions: Circle the choice that best fits the sentence.

Item: The $\left\{ \begin{array}{l} \text{boy} \\ \text{boys} \end{array} \right\}$ strikes the car and runs.

The verb "strikes" requires a singular subject. The expected choice is then "boy," not "boys." If the student does not react to "strikes" as a singular, he will not be able to make a choice except by guessing. He must also recognize "boy" as singular and "boys" as plural. We are interested in structure signals in language rather than in non-significant matters of usage. The correlation "boy-strikes"; "boys strike" is an important structural signal in English.

The same item can be enlarged to include the contrast between the third person and first and second persons in the verb. This is accomplished by adding choices in the first and second persons, which cannot go with the third person singular "strikes."

EXAMPLE:

Item:
$$\left.\begin{array}{l} \text{I} \\ \text{We} \\ \text{You} \\ \text{The boy} \\ \text{The boys} \end{array}\right\}$$ strikes the car and runs.

To simplify the scoring process the choices are usually numbered or lettered so that the student may write the number or letter of the right answer on a separate answer sheet or at the margin of the paper.

EXAMPLE:

Instructions: Write the number of the best choice in the parentheses provided at the right.

Item:
$$\left.\begin{array}{l} (1)\ \text{I} \\ (2)\ \text{We} \\ (3)\ \text{You} \\ (4)\ \text{The boy} \\ (5)\ \text{The boys} \end{array}\right\}$$ strikes the car and runs. ( )

Other formats are used. The important thing to remember, however, is that this type of item can easily be wasted in forcing a choice based on phrases that are irrelevant to the structure of the language. Not everything that can be worked into an item of this kind may be worth testing.

6. Comparing structure with structure is unproductive. The technique of asking the student if two sounds are the same or different is not easily adaptable to the testing of grammatical structure. The complexity of structural levels and of patterns enclosed in patterns that are in operation even in short utterances, and the difficulty in making clear to the student which of these levels and which of these patterns he must consider for his decision of "same" or "different" make the technique impractical for ordinary testing purposes. It takes a highly trained and skilled grammarian or linguist to focus on one particular level of structure and disregard all others for a particular comparison.

11.5   BIBLIOGRAPHICAL NOTES

Important new contributions toward the analysis of English structure have appeared recently. (1) *The Structure of English. An Introduction to the Construction of English Sentences*, by C. C. Fries, is an original and revealing study in the old field of grammar viewed from the point of view of structure. Several books have appeared as a result of Fries' contribution. (2) A. A. Hill's *Introduction to Linguistic Structures: From Sound to Sentence in English* is a valiant attempt to analyze English structure from the phoneme up, following the lines suggested by Trager and Smith in their *Outline of English Structure*. Of the older work (3) Otto Jespersen's *Essentials of English Grammar* is still excellent reading. New attempts to go beyond the above studies and techniques are best represented in *Syntactic Structures* by Noam Chomsky who has other work in preparation.

Chapter 12

TESTING PRODUCTION OF
THE GRAMMATICAL STRUCTURE
OF A FOREIGN LANGUAGE

12.1   **COMPLEXITY OF THE PROBLEM**

The problem of testing control of the structure of a foreign language on a production level is more complicated than that of testing structure on a recognition level. Probably for this reason, if not for others, the testing of production has not been solved as completely or as neatly as the testing of recognition. When we attempt to test production we are faced with a number of thorny questions. Are we testing what the student can say or are we testing what he does say? Experience shows that a student who learns to use a certain structure under favorable classroom conditions may completely forget the same structure when facing a microphone or a formal audience. The only way we could be sure of what a student does say is to observe him in all his activities. One cannot afford to do this except if one is conducting a thorough investigation into a limited number of structures or in cases of basic linguistic research.

In general our tests of production should provide as far as possible the same essential stimuli as an ordinary conversational situation and no more. Testing techniques sometimes have to use means that are removed in greater or less degree from the essential conditions of a language communication situation. These techniques may, however, be valid for preliminary stages of control of the structure or may prove to be valid by showing statistically high correlations with more direct but less objective techniques.

12.2   PRODUCTION TECHNIQUES

The general technique to test production consists of eliciting from the student certain key structures which we wish to test. If we are interested in oral production we have the student speak; if we are interested in written production we have him write. Written production lends itself readily to group testing since each student writes his answers independently and the examiner later reads them at his own speed. Oral production presents difficulties for group testing which modern recording machines have solved only in part. We can administer an oral production test to as large a group as we can supply with individual recording machines, but in scoring the test the examiner must listen to the recorded answers at about the speed that they were uttered and not—as in the case of writing—at the examiner's own working speed.

1. The problem of objective scoring of production tests. Objective scoring can be approached by impartial examiners in structure tests if (1) we make sure that the stimulus will elicit the key structure, (2) the key structure has been accurately described in structural terms, and (3) the examiner's attention is undividedly focused on the minimal distinctive features of the structure. For example, the minimal distinctive feature between "watch pocket" and "pocket watch" is the position of the head and the modifier. If we can stimulate a student to try to use "pocket watch" the examiner can focus his attention on this one feature and will find it easy to score the response objectively.

2. Effective stimuli to elicit the key responses. We rejected the extensive observation of spontaneous speech as impractical and unreliable as a test of recognition of grammatical structures. We must also reject it for the testing of production because it is impractical and because it does not provide a comparable sample of the speech of every student. We must also reject for the same reasons actions and the physical environment even when deliberately chosen to elicit given structures. These devices require more time than can be assigned to testing and they do not elicit the key sentences with sufficient regularity to be of practical use.

3. Actions as stimuli. One can stage the entering into a room where the student is and hope to elicit a greeting. We can fake a fall and perhaps stimulate production of "Be careful." "Watch out," or "Did you hurt yourself?" One can appear to be angry and may elicit "What's the matter?" or "What happened?" An examiner could thus theoretically observe and score certain structures. But this approach is obviously not suited for ordinary testing purposes.

4. The physical environment as stimulus. One may take the student to a museum and get spontaneously such utterances as "This is very beautiful," "I like this," "I don't care for this," "What is this?" We may take him to visit a prison and stimulate such utterances as "I wonder why he is here," "What do you think he did?" or "He doesn't look like a criminal, does he?" The utterances would certainly be representative of the student's speech habits, but the device used to elicit them is not adapted to ordinary testing conditions.

5. Language stimuli. Language itself can be used effectively to elicit specific key structures for the testing of production. The language stimulus can be more or less natural—question and answer—or more or less artificial such as substitution of elements in a sentence, conversion of one pattern to another, completion of a sentence, etc. These stimuli can be given in the language being tested or in the native language of the student. Pictures can be used effectively with language instructions to provide a content for the responses. We will discuss first the use of language stimuli in the language being tested, second the use of pictures with language instructions, and third the use of the native language as the stimulus.

STRUCTURE TECHNIQUE 12.7. **The goal language as stimulus.** Several varieties of this technique are treated separately below.

a. Questions. Questions can be used in an interview type of test. The examiner simply asks a series of questions in order to elicit the key structures he wishes to test.

EXAMPLE: The examiner asks, "Where are you from?"
Desired response: "I'm from . . . "
Question: "When did you arrive?"
Response: "I arrived . . ."

166

> Question: "What are you going to study?"
> Response: "I'm going to study . . ."

The examiner is observing the use of *am* with first person, the *-ed* preterite in *arrived*, and the *going to* future in " I'm going to study . . ." The particular country, the date of arrival, and the subject of future study will vary from student to student, but these are not part of the key material of the test.

The use of questions to elicit certain key structures has two important limitations: (1) Short answers not containing the desired structures may be used quite naturally, and (2) the form of the question itself may give away the answer. In the above example the three questions could have been answered without using the key structure material: Where are you from? Colombia. When did you arrive? Last week. What are you going to study? Medicine. The third question, even if it elicits the full answer, in part gives away the form of the *going to* future which is being tested.

The first difficulty can be partly obviated by asking the student to use "complete" statements. If for example he answers the question, "Where are you from?" with a simple and natural "Colombia," we ask him to use a "complete" statement, and he will usually understand that we want him to say "I'm from Colombia." The moment we ask the student to use complete statements we are of course using an artificial technique in the test.

The second difficulty, that of giving away the answer with the form of the question, reduces the value of the question technique in those cases in which the structure being tested must be contained in the question. In many other cases in which the structure need not be part of the question, the technique is an excellent one.

The question technique is highly effective in testing preterite tense inflection in English.

EXAMPLE:

Examiner's question: "What did you *eat* today?"
Expected response: "I *ate* . . ."

In the question we supply the simple form of the verb *eat* to

167

elicit the preterite form *ate* in the answer. What we supply is a lexical item which we are not testing, and we elicit a preterite structure signal which we do wish to test. Since the question pattern with *did* can be used with all English verbs except *be* in present-day English, we have here a device to test practically all the preterite forms or any sample we may wish to select.

b. Requests. Another fairly natural way to elicit given structures for testing is that of describing a situation or thing and having the student name it or say what would be said in that situation.

EXAMPLE: To elicit the question pattern illustrated by the sentence, "How old is the baby?" the stimulus might be, "A friend of yours had a baby. You want to know its age. What do you ask?" The response should be an attempt to produce the question pattern you are testing. If the response takes another form such as "Tell me the age," you may ask the student to say it another way, or you may further limit the response by saying, "Begin with the word *how*."

A slight variation of this technique is particularly useful in eliciting question patterns, which are often neglected in testing and in teaching. The technique consists in setting the situation in short statements ending with something like "You want to know (his name). Ask (him)." or simply, "Ask him his name."

EXAMPLE: "You meet a student. You want to know his name. Ask him."
Expected response: "What's your name?"
This particular item could be simplified to "Ask me my name."

OTHER EXAMPLES:

Stimulus: "You meet another student. Ask him if he likes tennis."
Response: "Do you like tennis?"
Stimulus: "Ask him where he lives."
Response: "Where do you live?"
Stimulus: "Ask him who his teachers are."
Response: "Who are your teachers?"
Stimulus: "Ask him if you can study together."
Response: "Can we study (algebra) together?"

Several variants of this technique are used by linguistic geographers to study dialect differences in preparing linguistic maps. The technique is pretty much the same, but the linguistic geographer can range rather freely in the stimulus questions and still be understood by the informant. In foreign language tests, the structures and vocabulary of the stimulus must be simple enough to be understood by students who are not fully acquainted with English. To minimize this limitation we may present the stimulus in writing to literate students. Having a chance to read the stimulus simplifies its comprehension. In addition we know that recognition tends to run ahead of production, giving us a margin of structures and words that will be understood by the student before he is able to use them.

c. Conversion of one pattern to another. There are various more or less artificial ways to elicit given structures by the use of language stimuli. One of them is simply to supply a given utterance and have the student change it into another which is the key pattern.

EXAMPLE: To test the use of negative verbal phrases one can supply affirmative sentences and have the student change them to negative sentences.

Stimulus: "John was absent yesterday."
Response: "John wasn't absent yesterday."
Stimulus: "He went fishing."
Response: "He didn't go fishing."
Stimulus: "Why did he go?"
Response: "Why didn't he go?"

The instructions in this case might be simply, "Change the sentences to the negative form."

This technique could be used in Spanish to elicit preterite forms of verbs. The question technique is not productive in this case because unlike English the Spanish question requires the preterite form of the main verb and thus gives away the response.

EXAMPLE: "Change these sentences to indicate habitual process in the past (preterite imperfect)."

169

Stimulus: Juan estudia medicina.
Response: Juan estudiaba medicina.
Stimulus: Vive en la casa de su hermana.
Response: Vivía en la casa de su hermana.
Stimulus: Es un buen estudiante.
Response: Era un buen estudiante.

This technique is often used in teaching, in which case the teacher begins by giving examples to show the student what to do. As a testing device, to give an example might be to invalidate the item. We therefore fall back on instructions which may include common grammatical terms. The effect of such terms is minimized by using common words like *question, report, ask, tell,* or setting the time with *yesterday, usually,* etc.

d. Substitution. This technique involves providing a sentence and then supplying substitutions for parts of it. The student produces the entire sentence, incorporating the substitutions and making the necessary adjustments in other parts of the sentence.

EXAMPLE:

Stimulus: "Please repeat, 'Where does he study now?'"
Response: "Where does he study now?"
Stimulus: "Substitute 'last year.'"
Response: "Where did he study last year?"
Stimulus: "Next year."
Response: "Where will he (is he going to) study next year?"
Stimulus: "Does."
Response: "Where does he study?"
Stimulus: "Was."
Response: "Where was he studying?"
Stimulus: "They."
Response: "Where were they studying?"

This is an artificial technique, to be sure, but it has the advantage that it can range over a variety of structures in a short time.

e. Completion. A widely used technique for recall or production of part of a sentence is the completion type of item. It is remarkably flexible and can appear in many shapes. It consists essentially of providing a context leaving some part incomplete. The student supplies the missing part, which contains the problem pattern.

EXAMPLES:

> *Stimulus:* "Someone asks, 'What time is it?'
> You answer, 'I don't know what time . . .'"
> *Response:* ". . . **it is.**"
> *Stimulus:* "We drink water when . . ."
> *Response:* ". . . **we're thirsty.**"
> *Stimulus:* "I'm interested, but he . . ."
> *Response:* ". . . **isn't.**"
> *Stimulus:* "You want to go to the Post Office.
> You ask, 'Where . . .'"
> *Response:* ". . . **is the Post Office?**"

Notice that this last example requires that *Where* not be made part of the same intonation phrase as *You ask* to avoid the structure, "You ask where the Post Office is." One way to set off *Where* as the beginning of a direct question is to render it as follows: [1]*You* [1]*ásk*[1], [3]*Whére*[2],. The response would then be, [2]*is the* [3]*Póst Office*[1].

STRUCTURE TECHNIQUE 12.8. **Pictures with instructions or context.** Pictures of various kinds could theoretically be used alone to stimulate production of specific structures for testing purposes. Pictures alone, however, can be quite ambiguous and uneconomical. One can show a complete silent film to a student and not obtain much of a verbal reaction unless we accompany the showing of the film with verbal instructions of some kind.

A simple question or request lets the student know what he is expected to do with a picture or series of pictures that is put before him.

EXAMPLE: Description of the following two pictures can be elicited by any of the sentences, "What do you see?" "What is happening?" "Tell me what you see," "Tell me what is happening," "Describe the pictures."

A   B

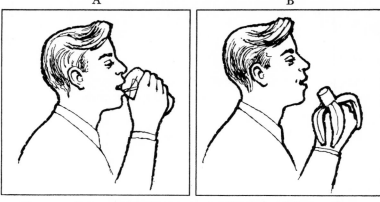

Fig. 12.1. Structure Technique 12.8. Pictures and Instructions

The usual response will be "He is drinking something." "He is eating something," or some variation of the same kind of sentence.

Variations of tense and aspect can be elicited with the same pictures by changing the verbal directions. One can say, "This happened yesterday. Tell me what happened," and the response will then be "He drank something," "He ate something." We can also say, "This was happening yesterday. Tell me what was happening," and the response will be "He was drinking," "He was eating."

We could also ask, "What happened to the water in the glass?" to elicit "It was drunk by the man," but another picture might be more likely to get this pattern as a response.

EXAMPLE: "What happened to the man?"

Fig. 12.2. Structure Technique 12.8. Pictures and Instructions

The expected response would be "He was bitten (or got bitten) by the dog."

To elicit *could* or *might* with a lexical verb we could use a picture like the following one.

EXAMPLE: "Describe all the possibilities for the rat if the cat were to jump the fence. Use complete statements."

Fig. 12.3. Structure Technique 12.8. Pictures and Instructions

The response would be something like, "If the cat jumped over the fence the rat would run away. The rat would run to the hole. It could run around the wall. Or it could climb up the tree." The examiner would listen only to the use of *could* or *might*.

The verbal context accompanying a picture might direct the student to reproduce the conversation that presumably takes place.

EXAMPLE: "What does she ask?"

Fig. 12.4. Structure Technique 12.8. Pictures and Instructions

This item elicits, "Is it raining outside?" from native speakers of English. From Spanish speakers learning English it often elicits, "It is raining outside?" or "Is raining outside?" with a rising intonation as the signal for question and without the word order signal of English. *Is raining* is not English in this case, and the statement order with the question intonation is a special type of question not intended by the Spanish speaker in this context. The examiner listens only for *is it* as contrasted with *it is* or *is*.

Since our object in using pictures is to elicit the key structures, not particular words, we are free to select any lexical content that is easily picturable.

The use of two or more pictures in a unified context of some kind also helps to define the responses that are expected.

EXAMPLE: "What does the man say?"

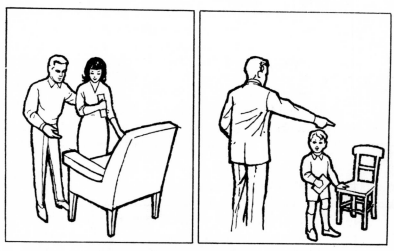

Fig. 12.5. Structure Technique 12.8. Pictures and Instructions

The response to A is likely to be a polite form such as "Please sit down" or "Won't you sit down?" The response to B is more likely to be "Sit down."

Story sequences such as the following have not been fully exploited for language testing, yet they seem to offer possibilities.

Fig. 12.6. Structure Technique 12.8. Pictures and Instructions

Single composite pictures seem less promising for the testing of specific key structures than the type of pictures discussed above.

6. Problem of misread items. Even with careful verbal directions and with painstaking editing of the pictures certain ambiguities are bound to arise for some of the students. We could choose to ignore these confusions and score the responses as if all the students had understood all the pictures and were clear on what utterances they were expected to produce. Since we know that this is not the case it is better to supplement the picture stimulus with additional verbal instructions in the student's native language when the picture and normal instructions have failed to elicit the key pattern. We can in some cases define the pictures verbally provided the definition does not reveal the right answer to the student. By using these additional props all the students will have tried every item and the scores will be more comparable as a result.

STRUCTURE TECHNIQUE 12.9. **Translation.** Translation from the native language of the student can be used effectively to test problem structures. A native language sentence or phrase is given as the stimulus. The student reads it to himself and produces the key pattern in the language being tested. The preparation of translation items is not as simple as it might seem on the surface. Problem patterns are precisely those that are not paralleled by patterns in the native language, and as a result we will find it difficult to give a stimulus in the native language that will force the use of the problem pattern in the foreign language. For example, the *'s* genitive inflection in the structure of modification in English is not found in Spanish or in many other languages. It is therefore a problem pattern for the speakers of Spanish and for others. If we use a Spanish phrase as the stimulus to elicit the English *'s* genitive it may be legitimately translated into a prepositional phrase in English. "A boy's hat" would be translated into Spanish as *Un sombrero de niño*, literally 'a hat of boy.' If a Spanish speaker is told to translate his phrase into English he might legitimately say, "A hat for boys," and we would not have elicited "A boy's hat."

Even when we can successfully elicit the desired pattern, the abuse of translation tends to hold back the most advanced students, who have learned to use the language without translating it, and it encourages the overuse of translation in teaching in order to prepare students to pass translation examinations.

7. Legitimate use of translation. Since our working procedure is first to prepare the list of problems to be tested and only then to prepare items to test these problems, an attempt should be made to test all the problems by the many techniques that deal directly with the foreign language and most nearly approach the essential elements of a communication situation. When the various practical techniques fail to test all the problems and a residue of untested patterns remains, a translation technique is legitimate and should be preferred to letting the items go untested.

To avoid introducing extraneous translation problems into translation items, the key sentence or phrase we wish to elicit should be translated into the native language of the student, and then checked with the retranslation to see if it produces the desired response. Additional explanations in the native language of the students may solve the problem of not getting the key response from the translation. In the case of the genitive inflection the student should be told to use the word for *niño* first.

12.3 PAPER-AND-PENCIL TECHNIQUES TO TEST PRODUCTION PARTIALLY

Oral production techniques, no matter how well used, have some limitations for wide use as formal tests. The time it takes to give and to score production tests limits their usefulness. We have seen that modern recording machines make it possible to give oral production tests to groups of students, but the scoring must be done at the slow pace at which they are recorded. Written tests of production can be scored at a faster pace, but legitimate variations in the responses must be judged individually. These variations introduce a subjective factor into the scores that reduces the reliability of the results.

To overcome these limitations some partial production, paper-and-pencil techniques have been developed that retain the essential element of production and are as completely objective as possible in scoring. Insofar as they succeed in retaining the elements of production and can be considered to represent production, they render a major service to testing by making it possible to measure production widely, objectively, and simply.

Essentially, these partial production techniques are production techniques with an objective way of recording the answers. This is accomplished by giving incomplete choices so that the student has to reconstruct the answer and then check it against the incomplete alternatives. Another way to accomplish the objective response type is by allowing more than one position in the lead material for the alternatives given in multiple-choice fashion. Practically all the production techniques described above can be turned into objective, partial production techniques. A few specially designed partial production types that have been used with some success are illustrated below.

STRUCTURE TECHNIQUE 12.10. **Objective type production items.**

a. More than one blank in the lead. The lead material containing the problem may define itself.

          1   2

EXAMPLE: " —— you —— understand English? "

      a. Do.

      b. Does.

      c. Have

      d. Has

The question mark defines the sentence as a question. *Do* in the first position is the only possible answer. The student who can produce this pattern easily produces the response silently by a quick inspection of the lead and the choices. He then writes the number of the blank and the letter of the choice that together constitute the right answer. In this example the right response is " 1*a.* "

Additional blanks could be left, and additional choices given, but this seems unnecessary, since the main contrasts of order and agreement are already built into the test and we already have eight alternative answers. As it is, the item can be used with an answer sheet that can be scored with a stencil key. The student may be asked to check one space in this format:

   ( )   ( )   ( )   ( )   ( )   ( )   ( )   ( )

   1a   2a   1b   2b   1c   2c   1d   2d

or two spaces in this other format:

   ( )   ( )   ( )   ( )   ( )   ( )

   1   2   a   b   c   d

b. Rearranging parts of a scrambled sentence. The parts of a sentence are listed in random order and the student is asked to construct a sensible sentence with them. The instructions may identify the kind of sentence desired.

EXAMPLE: Construct a question with all the following parts:

    1. English

    2. You

    3. Understand

    4. Do

A quick inspection of the parts gives the student enough context to try, "Do you understand English?" if he can produce such sentences with ease. Although the procedure seems highly artificial, it is not entirely unlike the process of speaking and writing. In the actual production of language we have in mind the message in more or less vague terms and put together the words in clusters from the stock we have available in our brain.

The student's response can be written out and scored objectively. The response can be recorded by writing the number alone. In this case the right answer is "4 2 3 1." It can be recorded by checking the proper sequence of numbers: ( )4231 ( )2431 ( )3214 ( )2314. Other combinations of the numbers are theoretically possible but they do not represent even remotely possible answers.

In order to simplify the mechanics of the item, part of the sentence may be given in proper order in the lead.

EXAMPLE: Complete the sentence by rearranging the alternatives:

"What—— —— ——?"

    1. You
    2. Understand
    3. Did

Again a quick inspection of the material provides enough context to produce "What did you understand?" if the student can produce such a pattern with ease. The various possibilities for recording and scoring the response are the same as above.

The lead and the instructions provide the context for the following item that tests word order in a modification structure.

EXAMPLE: Complete the sentence by rearranging the choices.

(The *friend* visited us.)

"—— —— —— —— —— visited us today."

    1. Teacher's
    2. That John met
    3. The
    4. When he went home
    5. Friend

This item may be more complicated than seems desirable, but in using language we handle much more complex material than this. If native speakers of English of the same intelligence range as the intended subjects of the test pass items like these without difficulty, we may find the items useful for testing complex modification structures.

c. Incomplete alternatives. The lead defines the context so that the student can complete the sentence without looking at the choices. He checks his answer against the incomplete choices to record it.

EXAMPLE: Complete the conversation silently. Then circle the choice that best fits your completion. Each line represents a single word.

"Does John speak French?"

"I don't know what . . ."

    1. does —— ——.

    2. speaks ——.

    3. he ——.

A quick inspection of the incomplete alternatives makes it possible to see that 3 matches the completion "he speaks" that suggests itself readily to one who has mastered this pattern. Alternative 1 would be chosen if this were a direct question, "What does he speak?" Alternative 2 might be chosen by a Spanish speaker translating word for word from Spanish.

12.4 SUMMARY OF STEPS IN THE PREPARATION OF STRUCTURE TESTS

Up to this point we have discussed (1) the kind of structure problems we need to test, (2) the list of structure items, describing separately the recognition and production problems, (3) various types of recognition, production, and partial production items. We should now (4) select sentences containing the structure problems to be tested, (5) write the items and the instructions, (6) administer the experimental test to native speakers of the language being tested, and edit the items on the basis of their performance, (7) administer the revised experimental test to a representative sample of the students for whom it is intended and edit and arrange the items on the basis of their performance, and (8) reproduce the test for wider use in collecting norms. The discussion of these steps in previous chapters is adequate for grammatical structure as well and will not be discussed further here.

Chapter 13

TESTING VOCABULARY

13.1   **INTRODUCTION**

Much work has been done on vocabulary counts and on vocabulary tests. The frequency of occurrence of words has been counted in large samples of up to five million words for English by E. L. Thorndike. The frequency of various meanings of words have been counted for English also by Lorge and Thorndike. Limited vocabularies have been prepared for students of English, Spanish, Russian, French, German, and Portuguese. Some of these vocabularies were selected on the basis of frequency, others on the basis of coverage of a maximum range of situations, and still others on the basis of power to define other meanings. Some have taken into account the age of the speakers and students, the subject matter of the sample, etc.

Vocabulary tests have been prepared for these same languages and for others. Vocabulary tests have also been prepared as measures of general ability or intelligence, and as measures of achievement in special subject fields.

Also pertinent to the testing of vocabulary is the monumental work of lexicographers who have compiled our dictionaries, the exhaustive ones using actual quotations of printed usage, the carefully edited abridged ones, the bilingual dictionaries, and the specialized glossaries and dictionaries.

It would be foolhardy to view this thoroughly tilled field as if it were virgin soil. Since we have a theory of language learning and of language testing to guide us, however, we will be able to treat the testing of vocabulary with a frame of reference that will help us understand problems not clearly understood previously.

13.2   WHAT IS VOCABULARY?

1. Lexical versus grammatical units. In the chapters on the testing of grammatical structure we dealt with words as units that were part of grammatical patterns. In that sense a word could be the subject of a sentence, the head of a modification structure, a structural signal in the form of a function word, etc. We will now deal with words as lexical units, that is, the linguistic form that we called *word* but considered now only as it attaches to the cultural meanings of a speech community and not from the point of view of grammatical function. For example, the word *dragon* as it represents a fierce looking creature which, as a matter of fact, does not exist in the physical world except for some culturally created pictures.

It is important to note that practically all words are both lexical units and grammatical units simultaneously in any utterance. For example, *dragon* in the sentence, "A very romantic *dragon* slept in the nearby woods," is the subject of the sentence and the head of the modification structure of the subject as a grammatical unit, while at the same time it is the fierce creature of cultural imagination known by young and old as a dragon.

This dual or even multiple function of words is not restricted to so-called content words. Even the function words, which often have crucial grammatical functions to perform are not as a rule completely devoid of a separate lexical meaning. The prepositions *into* and *through*, for example, have the same grammatical function in the sentences, "He went *into* the garden," and "He went *through* the garden," but they also have different lexical meanings.

In this chapter on vocabulary testing we are interested in lexical units and will assume that grammatical problems have been tested elsewhere. Thus, the noun *water* and the verb *to water* are grammatically two different words, but lexically they are closely related. They might in fact be considered the same lexical unit if *to water* were exclusively the lexical meaning of *water* plus the process or "action" meaning of verbs as a class. In actual fact neither *water* nor *to water* has a single meaning but a cluster of lexical meanings having to do with the common

liquid as used in the culture or properties of the common liquid
as abstracted and applied to various cultural meanings.

2. Lexical units versus words. Since languages use words
as the chief linguistic form for lexical units, it is sometimes
assumed that all lexical units are words. This is not the case of
course, and there are clearly identified cultural meanings that
attach to parts of words, to phrases and to whole sentences and
larger utterances. Most morphemes are lexical units even when
they are part of a word. *Book* is a lexical unit when it is a full
word as *book* and when it is only a part of word as in *bookish*.
There are often lexical units in the form of phrases: *Jack-in-the-
pulpit*, *red snapper*, *chick peas*, *call up* (to telephone). Sentences
are sometimes lexical units in this sense: *Merry-go-round, dog-
eat-dog, devil-may-care*. A word, phrase or sentence that acquires
a new denotation as a unit over and above the sum of its parts
becomes a lexical unit, or an idiom.[1]

3. Features of meaning and their relation to context.
Cultural meanings that are used in ordinary communication
usually become attached to specific linguistic forms and thus
form lexical units. These meanings have a number of abstract-
able features such as size, shape, instrument, agent, color, substance, etc., that distinguish one unit of meaning from another
in a culture. *Glass*, for example, is a transparent, brittle substance
used for windows, eye glasses, etc. The context in which a
lexical unit appears has the power to bring out some feature or
features of this meaning and produce a kind of metaphor or new
lexical unit. For example when we say that a prize fighter has a
"glass jaw," the substance of "jaw" is not 'glass' but bone.
The brittleness of 'glass' is abstracted and from this through
another metaphor, we get the meaning that he is knocked out
easily.

13.3   HOW MANY WORDS?

The question of vocabulary size has long been discussed and
cannot be escaped, much as one would wish to. How many
words does the student know? The answer is not a simple one
even after we have defined our word as a lexical unit. Many

---

[1] See Hockett's two chapters on "idioms" in *A Course in Modern Linguistics*
for some nice insights into idiom formation.

words can be inferred from others with which they have some-thing in common, e.g., *reason, reasonable, unreasonable, reason-ably, reasonableness.* Many words have multiple meanings. Metaphorical uses of words can produce new meanings.

1. Production vocabulary versus recognition vocabulary. All estimates indicate that the vocabulary needed for production in a foreign language, especially for speaking, is very different from that needed for recognition, particularly in reading. The difference is both in size and in the nature of the knowledge. There are 1,000-word vocabularies for speaking. Of these the most widely known is Basic English with 850 all-purpose words and 150 "international" words. There are 2,000-word vocabu-laries such as *A General Service List of English Words* by Michael West, who considers a vocabulary of 2,000 words "good enough for anything, and more than one needs for most things." West's list is a revision of *The Interim Report on Vocabulary Selection* prepared earlier by L. W. Faucett, M. West, H. E. Palmer, and E. L. Thorndike, representing a larger committee of most of the leading workers in the field of vocabulary selection. A 2,000-word vocabulary, therefore, represented the opinion of these leaders as to the size of a minimum vocabulary for speaking.

Vocabularies of 3,000 words for production have been pre-pared also, but they are not widely advocated. We should note, however, that the 1,000 and 2,000-word lists represented a con-siderably larger number of lexical units than these numbers would seem to indicate. It is also important to note that when-ever these vocabularies have been taught in their entirety, the students learn countless additional words and lexical units not found in the lists. Thus it may be closer to the facts to estimate that minimum production vocabularies are closer to 3,000 and 4,000 lexical units than to 1,000 and 2,000 words.

Reading vocabularies among native readers of English are much larger than once thought possible. R. Seashore reports vocabularies of from 16,900 basic words for Grade 1 up to 46,500 for Grade 12, and from 24,000 to 80,000 basic and derived words for the same grades.[1]

[1] "How Many Words do Children Know?" *The Packet*; Heath's Service Bulletin for Elementary Teachers, 2, No. 2 (1947): 3–17. Boston, Mass.: D. C. Heath and Company.

The size of the foreign language reading vocabulary of students doing successful university work in a foreign language environment has not been reported but it must certainly be closer to 10,000 than to the speaking vocabularies reported above as adequate.

"Knowing" words in reading is also a very different level of mastery than knowing words so as to speak them. An active speaking vocabulary means that a unit can be "recalled" almost instantaneously, put into sound through articulation of its phonemes, placed in its proper stress and intonation frame, into its proper structural position and functions, with its inflectional and derivational affixes in accord with the context. A passive reading vocabulary requires only grasping the meaning from the form in its partly redundant context.

13.4   SAMPLING A VOCABULARY

Even with the smallest speaking vocabularies it is not practical to test every single word in a vocabulary test. Instead, we select a representative sample of the total vocabulary we wish to test. A 50-word sample from a 1,000-word vocabulary means that only one out of every 20 words will be tested. A 50-word sample of a 10,000-word reading vocabulary represents one word out of every 200. We must select this one word with care if we are to make inferences regarding the other 199 that will not be tested.

The usual approach to this problem is to use a random sample of the entire "population," i.e., of the total vocabulary we have chosen. A random sample is obtained among other ways by alphabetizing the entire vocabulary into a single list and then counting the words in the order in which they appear, selecting every 200th word for a 50-word sample of a 10,000-word list. The assumption is that the student knows as many times 200 words of the total list as the number of individual words he knows out of this random sample.[1]

As an experiment to determine the vocabulary size of a student this might yield a valid approximation provided the test succeeded in testing the sample so that passing an item actually

---

[1] R. Seashore took a random sample of the words of an unabridged dictionary, checked his subjects on the sample, and made his vocabulary size estimates from the results.

meant knowing the word. In preparing an effective test, however, items that prove to be too easy or too difficult are eliminated. Items at an intermediate range of difficulty are also
eliminated   there are too many intermediate items. Thus the
final form of a test no longer represents a random sample of the
total vocabulary, and estimates of the size of a student's vocabulary from his score on the test are not very meaningful.

13.5   VOCABULARY PROBLEMS

According to the theory of language testing, the student will
tend to transfer his vocabulary habits to the foreign language.
He will transfer meanings, forms, and distribution of the lexical
units of his native language, and thus when these units operate
satisfactorily in the foreign language because they are functionally
and formally alike though never identical, there is facilitation
of learning and the units will not constitute learning problems.
On the other hand, when the lexical units and patterns of the
native language will not operate satisfactorily in the foreign
language because they are not functionally or formally alike,
there will be interference from the native language and the
student will have a learning problem to overcome.

Since in the theory, testing control of problems is the same as
testing control of the language, we will want to know which are
the problems and what their nature is.

Given a total vocabulary, say a production vocabulary of
2,000 words or a 10,000 word vocabulary for reading, we proceed to compare it item by item with the native language vocabulary. A possible short cut is to select a random sample from the
total vocabulary, say 200 or 300 words, and to compare this random sample rather than the total population.

The random sample should not be drawn directly from a raw
list such as Thorndike's or West's. Certain decisions regarding
the inclusion or exclusion of proper names, names of famous
places or persons applied in a figurative sense, numbers, days
of the week and months of the year, abbreviations, phrases as
lexical units, archaic forms, colloquialisms, children's words, etc.,
have to be made before selecting the sample for the comparison.
Once we have selected our total vocabulary, we may arrange

it alphabetically, select our random sample, and proceed to compare it with the native language vocabulary.

This comparison should probably be done from the spoken words for speaking and from the written words for reading problems. The comparison will yield:

A. Lexical units that are functionally the same in form, meaning and distribution in the two languages. These do not constitute learning problems and are therefore eliminated from the list and from the test.

B. Lexical units that are functionally different in meaning, form, distribution or a combination of these. These problems are of different types and require different strategy for testing. The chief problem types are:

(1) Units that are similar in form but different in meaning, distribution or both.

(2) Units that are different in form but similar in meaning and distribution.

(3) Units that are different in the pattern of form though similar in meaning and distribution.

(4) Units that represent a new meaning in the other language and culture.

(5) Units with widely different connotation.

These types of problems will be illustrated in connection with the writing of recognition items and later with production items.

1. Recognition problems versus production problems. The specific learning interference for a particular item differs according to whether the student has to recognize the unit or produce it. In recognition there are at least three potential sources of interference from the native language of the student. They are (1) the form of the lexical unit, (2) the context, and (3) the features of meaning of the unit. Let's take the English word *book* as an example of a recognition problem for a speaker of Spanish learning English.

(1) The English form *book* /buk/ could potentially, though not with certainty, be heard by a Spanish speaker as Spanish *boca*, /bóka/ "mouth," *bucal* /bukál/ 'of or pertaining to the mouth.'

(2) In the context, "Peter saw his friend, John, at the bank.

He said, 'Can you lend me some check *books* for my vacation? I haven't any,'" the words "bank," "lend," "check," "vacation," might make the idea of 'money' possible as the meaning of "book" for one who knows little English. This idea would then be interference from the context.

(3) Since *book* also means printed and bound material for reading, the student who has a vague notion of the meaning of *book* but not a clear enough understanding to see that "check book" is not likely to be a reading book, will have interference from the meaning features of the unit.

In the production problem, if the student wishes to say *book* in the sense of 'check book,' we assume that he begins from the meaning "check book" if it is found in his native culture. The interference may come from two sources.

(1) In attempting to say this meaning in English his Spanish word *libro* will exert some pressure. The form *libro* is more like English *liver* or *leave'er* than like *book*. This form *libro* which is now causing interference was not part of the interference in the recognition problem. This is interference from the native language form and may be called form-induced interference.

(2) If the student cannot recall or does not know *book*, and he rejects *liver* and *leave'er*, he may have interference through meaning synonyms of Spanish *libro*, e.g., *album*, *colección*. These synonyms or others may be translated directly into English and exert meaning interference exclusively, or they may interfere by transfer of their Spanish form, thus creating a meaning-form interference.

13.6   RECOGNITION TECHNIQUES

VOCABULARY TECHNIQUE 13.1. **Multiple-choice.**

a. Choices in the foreign language. The multiple-choice type of item has probably achieved its most spectacular success in vocabulary tests. Although there are variations of format and style, in general the item consists of a lead or stem containing the problem, one alternative representing the best response, and two to five alternatives representing distractors or decoys to lure the student who does not recognize the best answer.

EXAMPLE: What is the meaning of *integrity*?

1. intelligence
2. uprightness
3. intrigue
4. weakness

Since in this style the lead is the same in every item and does not contribute anything to the context, the test word is often presented alone as the lead.

EXAMPLE: **Integrity.**

1. intelligence
2. uprightness
3. intrigue
4. weakness

Opposites have often been used in testing vocabulary.

EXAMPLE: The opposite of **strong** is

1. short
2. poor
3. weak
4. good

Present-day understanding of the nature of vocabulary and of vocabulary problems does not sanction the use of words out of context in tests of vocabulary. A better type of item to test vocabulary as part of language is a multiple-choice item that provides an appropriate context for the lexical problem in the lead.

EXAMPLE: What we saw moving in the distance was a **seal.**

1. stamp
2. sentry
3. marine animal
4. wild pig

Some items have been prepared so that more than one alternative can be correct. This device increases the number of possible answers in a three-choice item from three to eight. Such items, however, are difficult to write, and they show a crippling proportion of loss of more than 50 per cent when they are given a trial run with native speakers of the language.

EXAMPLE: It isn't a poor yellow, it's a good **orange.**

    1. a fruit

    2. a color

    3. like an orange in one way

The same item would be better with only one best answer and three or four distractors.

EXAMPLE: It isn't a dirty yellow; it's a good **orange.**

    1. a fruit

    2. a color

    3. a drink made of oranges

    4. real courage

b. Pictures. Pictures are used as the alternatives especially to test children, adult beginners, and illiterates.

EXAMPLE: Item testing the lexical contrast *in, on, under.*

The apple is **in** the box.

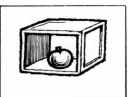

A single composite picture is sometimes used to test several words.

EXAMPLE: Make an " X " on the things that I ask about.

Where is the **clock**?

Where is the **table**?

Where is the little **boy**?

Where is the **cat**?

c. Choices in the native language of the student. This technique
has been used and perhaps abused in vocabulary tests. It is recommended when problems cannot be tested effectively without
recourse to the native language of the students.

EXAMPLE: English vocabulary item for a Spanish speaker.

Desk.

1. escritorio
2. mesa
3. muelle
4. descanso

EXAMPLE: The same but in context.

He stood on the **desk** to change a light bulb.

1. escritorio
2. escalera
3. puente
4. mesa
5. descanso

13.7   WRITING RECOGNITION ITEMS

1. General suggestions. Writing good multiple-choice items
is an art. Some people have greater facility than others in preparing them. A number of rules are usually given, however, to
improve the items produced by anyone and to edit these items
after they have been written. The following are some of these
rules which, as all general rules, may not apply in all cases.

(1) The problems must be valid ones for the field that the
test claims to measure.

(2) Each item must be independent of all others. Avoid using
related items in which the answer to one may unwittingly solve
another. Avoid interlocking items in which one cannot be
answered unless another is answered correctly.

(3) One alternative must be the right or best one. Others
must be distractors representing the factors that would normally
lead some students to incorrect solutions.

(4) The alternatives should be as brief as possible.

(5) The alternatives must be so prepared that the right one

cannot be selected except through understanding of the problem contained in the lead.

2. Specific suggestions for the writing of lexical items. In addition to the general rules there are some specific suggestions for the selection of effective distractors in writing vocabulary items. The suggestions are better illustrated in connection with the several types of vocabulary problems discussed earlier.

(1) The context of the lead must be enough to render unambiguous the meaning being tested and not so much that the answer becomes obvious without recourse to the lexical unit being tested.

Enough context:	He wears **glasses.**
	Something 1. for the rain
	2. to see with
	3. for ice
	4. to drink with

This illustrates a problem of normal difficulty—type 2, different form but similar meaning—for Spanish speakers. The context provided by the word "wear" makes the key word 'something to see with.' At the same time, since many things can be worn, we need the key word "glasses" to answer the item.

Too much context:	He wears **glasses** to read.

This lead no longer provides a test of "glasses." The right choice can be selected without understanding the key word.

Not enough context:	**Glasses.**

Without further information, "glasses" could mean 2, 'something to see with,' or 4, 'something to drink with.'

(2) One alternative should be a form-induced distractor, i.e., some word that resembles the form, not the meaning, of the key word in the native language. In the example above, the key word *glasses* vaguely resembles the Spanish forms *glacial* 'glacial,' or *glaciar* 'glacier,' hence alternative 3, "for ice."

In the case of problems of type 1, similar form but different meaning, this distractor representing the form is the most powerful one.

EXAMPLE: He seemed selfish then, but he is **actually** very generous.

1. in reality
2. at present

The English form "actually" is identified by Spanish speakers with Spanish *actualmente* which means 'at present' in most cases.

With problems of type 3, different pattern of form, there can be two distractors representing form if the key lexical unit in the item is made up of two words. English "two-word verbs," for example, lend themselves to this suggestion. *Run out of* in the sense of 'exhaust' permits one form distractor for *run* and another for *out*. A form distractor for "run" might be Spanish *ron* 'rum' (liquor from sugar cane). A form distractor for "out" might be Spanish *auto* 'automobile.'

EXAMPLE: It might be dangerous to **run out of** fuel there.

Right alternative:	1.	'exhaust'
Form distractor:	2.	'liquor'
Form distractor:	3.	'automobile'

Since the alternatives supposedly represent the lexical meaning of the key words of the stem there is no fundamental objection to the fact that none of the alternatives, not even the right one, can be actually substituted in the lead to replace the key words. Since "exhaust" is primarily a verb, it might be argued that students will derive from this an extraneous clue to the right answer. This possibility can easily be eliminated in this particular item by editing it to the following:

It might be dangerous to **run out of** fuel there.

1. exhaust the
2. have liquor
3. go by auto

(3) Another alternative should be a context-induced distractor. In the item "He wears *glasses*," the context-induced distractor is 1, 'something for the rain,' since it fits the context "He wears ——."

A context-induced distractor for "He seemed selfish then, but he's —— very generous," might be *never*. The item would now become,

He seemed selfish then, but he's **actually** very generous.

1. in reality
2. at present
3. never

(4) Another alternative should be a meaning-induced distractor. In "He wears *glasses*," the alternative "something to drink with" represents a different meaning of the key word "glasses."

In the case of *actually* there is no other major meaning we could use as a distractor. We then look for close synonyms, for example, "when you think of it," which comes close to being the right answer but is not. This item now becomes

He seemed selfish then, but he's **actually** very generous.

1. in reality
2. at present
3. never
4. when you think of it

With *run out of* the meaning distractor is a powerful one since students who do not have similar lexical combinations in their native language tend to take each word literally. We thus write a distractor representing the literal meaning of "run" plus "out," for example, *escape*. This item now appears as

It might be dangerous to **run out of** fuel there.

1. exhaust the
2. have liquor
3. go by auto
4. escape the

The context word "fuel" is exercising a restrictive pressure on "4. escape the." A more neutral substitute might be "containers," but this in turn restricts the value of "3. go by auto" as a distractor. Trial runs with native speakers of English and with speakers of Spanish will tell us if the item is satisfactory as it stands.

Let us now try these suggestions on a difficult item to write, one representing a problem of type 4, new meaning. The particular example chosen is a rather unusual one, but it illustrates the problem well. The Spanish word *zueco* [θuéko] 'shoe with a wooden sole,' which is different from *zueca* or *madreña* 'wooden shoe,' and from *zapato* 'shoe,' represents a cultural-linguistic meaning not in the vocabulary of English speakers. We write a lead in Spanish with *zueco* as the problem: *Quiero unos* **zuecos** *de buen cuero.* 'I want some shoes (with wooden soles) of good leather.' The right alternative would mean 'shoes with wooden sole,' (*zapatos con suela de madera*). The form *zueco* might suggest English "sweat," or "suède," so we select as a form-induced distractor, 'suède shoes' (*zapatos de ante*). The context word *cuero* 'leather' could suggest 'gloves.' 'Leather,' however, seems unusual if used alone for gloves. We can solve this by changing 'leather' to something more neutral, e.g., 'material.' As a context-induced distractor we select 'gloves' (*guantes*). Since the meaning of *zuecos*, 'leather shoes with wooden soles,' is culturally not known to the average English speaker, it will probably be lumped with wooden shoes. We thus choose 'wooden shoes' (*zuecas*) as a meaning-induced distractor.

We now have a likely item as follows:

Quiero unos **zuecos** *de buen material.*
1. zapatos con suela de madera
2. zapatos de ante
3. guantes
4. zuecas

But a general rule in multiple-choice items is that there should not be extraneous clues to the right answer, and the right answer is now suspiciously longer than the others. We do not seem to be able to shorten the right alternative, but we can lengthen at least one of the alternatives, number 3, to 'leather work gloves' (*guantes de trabajo de cuero*).

There are still some potential problems left in the item that should be edited out if possible, for example, the fact that *zuecas* is an unusual word and may not be understood by the students. We might write *zapatos de madera* 'wooden shoes' instead. And *ante* in *zapatos de ante* may also be outside the vocabulary range of the students. No simple way to solve this problem suggests itself, so the item should be tried without further revisions, with the idea that the trial runs may show whether or not any further editing is necessary.

3. Items that test live words. Knowing a word is more than merely knowing one of its meanings in isolation. The speakers of a language grasp its significance when a word is used in contexts that bring out apparently hidden features of its meaning, and, what is equally important, they grasp these features of meaning when the word is used in that sense for the first time in their experience. This is "knowing live words."

The use of words in special but clear extensions of their features of meaning is not restricted to literature; it is much more prevalent in everyday use of language than is commonly assumed. The following are some examples picked without effort:

Newspaper headline: "Navy *effort* circles globe." This lead at a time when earth satellites had first been orbited was crystal clear to daily newspaper readers. Yet no dictionary editor in his right mind would think of listing 'Earth satellite' as one of the meanings of "effort." By some sort of metonymy the "effort" of the Navy satellite team was applied to the satellite itself. In the linguistic context "circles globe," and the historical context of the moment, "effort" meant 'Earth satellite.'

Statement by a salesman: "This is a sincere effort to create an international exposition in which the dimensions of culture, art, drama, and history are used to *grease the wheels* of merchandise selling." (*Newsweek.*)

Statement by a reporter: "The shouting and tumult of the weeks-long political campaign *rolled* into silence across the harvest-rich land." (*Newsweek.*)

It would be pointless to list examples from daily conversation, friendly letters, radio broadcasts, etc., where these uses occur as a matter of course. Nor is it pertinent to attempt an exhaustive classification here. The figures of speech formerly taught in courses on rhetoric represent some of these uses. The point is that we have not made sufficient use of this fact of language in foreign language tests of vocabulary. Testing the advanced student on recognition of words in contexts which bring out these features of meaning offers considerable promise in the testing of vocabulary.

In short, (1) knowing a word implies grasping these differences brought out by context, and (2) we can test this type of vocabulary problem through multiple-choice items.

13.8   TECHNIQUES TO TEST PRODUCTION OF LEXICAL UNITS

VOCABULARY TECHNIQUE 13.2. **Production.** The testing of vocabulary on a production level consists essentially of giving the student the meaning of the key vocabulary item so that he may produce it if he knows it. When he fails to produce the key item or produces another one that does not fit the meaning, we assume that he does not know it.

There are various ways of providing the meaning without using the vocabulary item itself. We will classify these ways of providing the meaning into (1) foreign language context, (2) picture context, and (3) native language or translation context.

(1) *Foreign language context.* We can give the student the idea of the item through the language being tested, without giving him the key words themselves.

This determining context can be presented orally, in writing, or both. Oral presentation may be necessary or preferable with young children, illiterates, and for informal classroom purposes. Oral context has also been used in the study of dialects by trained field interviewers gathering data for linguistic geography.

Paper-and-pencil techniques to elicit production of vocabulary are the same as the oral ones except that the context is printed for the student to read instead. The student may respond orally in both cases.

The meaning of the key vocabulary item can be given in the lead in the form of a question.

"What do you call a man that makes bread?"
"A baker."
The lead can be a request.
"Tell me the name of a man that makes things of iron."
The lead can be an incomplete statement of several types.
"A man that makes clothes for men is called . . ."
"A tailor."

"My sister is my father's . . ."

"Daughter."

"When the teacher speaks you should . . ."

"Listen."

"I see three colors: one is blue, another is yellow, and —— other is red."

"The."

"We have a boy and a girl; he is five years old, and —— is three years old."

"She."

"The opposite of concave is . . ."

"Convex."

(2) *Picture context.* A combination of linguistic context with a clear picture or drawing can be an effective stimulus to elicit certain items of vocabulary.

Examples with complete linguistic context:

"A large animal with a trunk, ivory tusks, is . . ."

"An elephant."

 "A flower with white petals and yellow center is . . ."

"A daisy."

"An animal that gives milk and climbs rocks well is . . ."

"A goat."

 "A fruit from which we make wine is . . ."

"The grape."

Simpler instructions or context often suffice with pictures.

"What do you see in the picture?"

"A boat."

Series of pictures help to define each other.
"What do you see in the picture?"

"I see a **tall** man and a **short** man."
"What kinds of boats do you see?"

"A **sail boat**, a **row boat**, and a **canoe**."

(3) *Translation context.* Translation from the native language of the student to the foreign language can be used to elicit vocabulary items not otherwise readily accessible.

The entire lead, including the key words, can be in the native language.

Es un **manzano** *magnífico.*
"Apple tree."

The lead can be in the goal language but the key words are in the native language of the students.

"He is (**actualmente**) the best musician in the orchestra."
"At present."

199

13.9 OBJECTIVE, PARTIAL PRODUCTION TECHNIQUES

As in the case of production techniques to test pronunciation and grammatical structure, responses to production items in vocabulary always show a margin of variability that causes scoring problems with regard to objectivity and the time consumed in grading them. For general use of production tests of vocabulary we need objective items that test production.

VOCABULARY TECHNIQUE 13.3. **Objective partial production.** Following are two variants of an objective, partial production technique that has been used effectively for Spanish and English vocabulary tests. The technique involves essentially a completion type of item with the added feature that partial clues to several alternatives are given. The student produces the response silently, preferably without studying the alternatives, and then checks his response against the partial clues of the alternatives.

In one of the styles the alternatives are indicated by the initial and final letters and a hyphen for each of the letters omitted.

EXAMPLE: I admire him and wish to —— his banquet as a guest.

Form-induced distractor: 1. a----t (assist)
Right alternative: 2. a----d (attend)
Meaning-form distractor: 3. i-k (irk)

In the other style the number of letters of the right choice is given in parentheses, and only the initial letter of each alternative appears in the choices.

EXAMPLE: The cold air of winter transforms the clouds into
(4)
soft white —— .

Form-induced distractor: 1. N (needles)
Right alternative: 2. S (snow)
Meaning-induced alternative: 3. I (ice)

13.10   WRITING OBJECTIVE, PARTIAL PRODUCTION ITEMS

It should be noticed that this technique differs from a multiple-choice recognition technique not simply in the fact that the choices are incomplete in the partial production item. In this technique there is ordinarily no distractor induced by the context. The role of the context in production is to define the meaning of the key words. If any significant number of students grasp a different meaning, the context has failed, not the students.

The production item has one alternative representing the expected or best answer, and in addition alternatives representing the actual distractors that a student would have if he were using the language in a normal communication situation. According to the theory of language testing, the student tends to begin from his native language lexical unit. He transfers this to the foreign language, where the meaning may be satisfactory since it is given by the context, but the form of the native language vocabulary item may normally turn out to be a different word in the foreign language. This gives us a "form" distractor, a vocabulary item in the foreign language that resembles in form the native language item but does not have the proper meaning.

If there is another word of the same meaning in the native language that fits the context, the student might presumably start from this synonym and work from its form to the foreign language. This gives us a "meaning-form" distractor.

A fourth distractor can be prepared on the basis of form transfer. More than one form in the goal language will usually resemble the form of a native language word. For Spanish *asistir* there is "assist" but there is also "stir." "Stir" begins with "s" rather than with "a" as the Spanish word, but even elementary level students are familiar with Spanish words beginning with *est-*, *esp-*, *esc-*, which are related to English words beginning with *st-*, *sp-*, *sc-* or *sch-* and will therefore not be so far from correlating *st-* of "stir" with the beginning of *asistir*. The ending of "stir" is more like that of *asistir* than is that of "assist." So we may choose "stir" as another form-induced distractor.

The meaning-form distractor of this item, "irk," remotely

resembles Spanish *ir*, which can be used in place of *asistir* in this particular context. Another meaning-form distractor could be "hear" which also resembles ever so remotely *ir*. The item now stands as follows:

"I admire him and wish to —— his banquet as a guest."

    1. a - - - - t
    2. a - - - - d
    3. i - k
    4. s - - r
    5. h - - r.

For the item eliciting "snow" the Spanish word was *nieve* 'snow.' *Hielo* 'ice' is close enough in meaning for people without snow experience to have it constitute a meaning problem. "Needles" is a form-induced distractor because it resembles, even if remotely, the Spanish form *nieve*. Another form distractor might be "even." Because the choices give only the initial letter of the distractor we cannot add any other alternatives beginning with "n."

"Ice" is a meaning-induced distractor for *hielo* assuming that the student knows the translation. If he does not know the translation he may go fumbling into English forms that resemble *hielo* [yélo] in form. Thus "yellow" or even "yell" might be a meaning-form distractor for this item. The second item might now become

"The cold air of winter transforms the clouds into soft, white
    (4)
    ——."

    1. N
    2. S
    3. I
    4. E
    5. Y

Alternative 4 "E" may turn out to be undesirable because it may trap students who know the word "snow" but may mispronounce and misspell it as "esnow." Since we are not now testing the students on pronunciation, this problem is not legitimate for the item.

Although we reject context distractors in production techniques, a context distractor might be justified when the problem involves a new meaning in the foreign language and culture. The problem is precisely that the student is unable to think of the meaning because in his cultural experience it is not found or is very rare. With the Spanish word *zuecos*, for example, the English speaking student will not think of 'shoes with wooden soles,' because this meaning is not part of his cultural-linguistic inventory. In this case, one of the distractors might be suggested by the context and not by the meaning '*zuecos*,' or the synonym 'shoes.' We might again use 'gloves' as we did in the recognition item earlier.

Since the structure of a partial production item is different from that of a recognition item, it would be possible to give complete choices in a partial production item and still test something closer to production than to recognition even though outwardly both items would seem identical. The incomplete choices are more like full production and are therefore to be preferred.

Translation and pictures might be used to strengthen the defining context of the lead in partial production items, but these additional props seem unnecessary at this stage in the development of objective, production techniques.

13.11   BIBLIOGRAPHICAL NOTES

1. Eaton, H. S. *Semantic Frequency List of English, French, German and Spanish.*
2. Fries, C. C., and Traver, A. A. *English Word Lists, A Study of Their Adaptability for Instruction.*
3. Josselson, H. H. *Russian Word Count.*
4. Lorge, I. *The Semantic Count of the 570 Commonest English Words.*
5. Nunn, M. E., and Van Scroy, H. A. *Glossary of Related Spanish-English Words.*
6. Rinsland, H. D. *A Basic Vocabulary of Elementary School Children.*
7. Rodríguez Bou, I., *et al. Recuento de vocabulario español.*
8. Thorndike, E. L., and Lorge, I. *The Teacher's Word Book of 30,000 Words.*
9. West, Michael. *A General Service List of English Words.*

PART III

TESTING THE INTEGRATED SKILLS

Chapter 14

AUDITORY COMPREHENSION

14.1   **THE INTEGRATED SKILLS**

We have thus far dealt with the significant elements of language as distinct systems of pronunciation, stress, intonation, grammatical structure and vocabulary to be tested separately. In the actual use of a language the student is faced with all of these simultaneously in an integrated single stream of speech. Much attention has been given to teaching and testing language in integrated listening, reading, speaking, writing, and translation. Whether we test the elements of language separately or as part of one of these five skills we are still testing language. The decision between testing skills or testing elements, if a decision has to be made, will be made on the basis of what information we need concerning the student's knowledge of the goal language. Since our students already possess a native language, we know that they can perform the normal activities involved in using a language. What we do not know is whether or not they can use effectively the signaling system of the goal language in those functions in which they already perform satisfactorily in their native language.

In the integrated skills in addition to testing the elements of language which are pertinent for that skill we test them in alternating items of the same type, i.e., in the same part of the test one item may deal with vocabulary, the next with structure, the third with pronunciation, and the fourth with vocabulary again, without warning to the student that this item or that will test pronunciation, grammatical structure, or vocabulary.

To approach the integrated skills in terms of situations rather than language brings in extraneous factors such as the selection of the subject matter, sampling of problems, what constitutes handling a situation, etc. And even if some of these factors can somehow be controlled we would find that the sampling of language problems would remain inadequate. It is more economical and will result in more complete sampling to work from the language problems and then to seek situations in which particular problems can be tested.

14.2   AUDITORY COMPREHENSION

1. What is auditory comprehension? We do not mean by auditory or aural comprehension in a foreign language those matters that trouble the native speaker in his use of the language. Among the things thus excluded are for example technical vocabularies, technical matters of literary interpretation, subject matter which is not common knowledge in the culture where the language is spoken, intelligence beyond that needed for everyday non-technical activities of a literate people, and memory beyond that needed in common everyday living. We include, on the other hand, those language elements that native speakers understand by the mere fact of being native speakers of the language and not by any special training of particular native speakers. As a matter of fact, one of the means of validating a test of auditory comprehension is precisely to give the test to native speakers. If native speakers have difficulty in a test of aural comprehension, we assume that the test is not exclusively one of auditory comprehension in a foreign language; it is either a test for native speakers of the language or a test of factors other than language.

Dealing with auditory comprehension without regard to the fact that we are dealing with the complex but highly structured system of communication which is language leads to many blind alleys. At one extreme are tests that take into account only vocabulary and are therefore inadequate as measures of auditory comprehension. Other tests give only passing attention to syntax. These cannot be much better since the sampling of syntax and other elements is bound to be spotty and inadequate. As a matter of fact, pronunciation is seldom considered a factor that needs systematic treatment. The assumption seems to be that presenting passages orally will handle adequately the factor of pronunciation, whereas we have seen earlier that pronunciation may not be tested at all, even in a listening test, unless problems are built into the items.

At the other extreme are tests and discussions that show preoccupation with a great variety of supposed factors in auditory comprehension but fail to take into account systematically the major language elements. Our object is not to explore the effect of various speeds of delivery, various lengths of passages, or various voices on auditory comprehension. By this kind of view of the problem one might go on to include the acoustics of the room, the amount of background noise, the physical and emotional state of the students, etc. equally as primary factors to be explored. These are not, however, the crucial variables in testing. They are of concern only insofar as they must be held constant or within normal bounds in order not to distort the data that is of primary concern.

Auditory comprehension of a foreign language means recognition control of the signaling elements of the language in communication situations.

2. Auditory comprehension problems. According to the theory not all the signaling units and patterns of the foreign language are equally difficult to master. The student tends to transfer the signaling system of the native language, and as a result those units and patterns that are different in the two languages represent the learning problems. Testing the student on these problems is testing him in his mastery of the foreign language. These problems will occur in the pronunciation, stress, intonation, grammatical structure, and vocabulary of the language.

In the preparation of auditory comprehension tests a linguistic description of the goal language and a similar description of the native language of the students is needed in order to compare the two descriptions and thus locate and describe the problems. As in the case of tests of pronunciation, stress, intonation, grammatical structure, and vocabulary we need a list of the important problems to be tested. Then, depending on the length and purpose of the test, the most representative problems are selected on the basis of frequency of occurrence, range of usefulness, and level of mastery.

3. Separate tests for each native language background. The above definition and discussion imply that we should have separate tests for each native language background. In the case of the study of foreign languages in a country like the United States, the native language of the students is of course the same for practically all the students, but in the reverse case, that of the study of English in the United States by speakers of other languages, we should ideally have separate tests for the various native language backgrounds of the students. The difficulties of Spanish speakers learning English, for example, are different from those of the speakers of Japanese.

4. Tests for several language backgrounds or separate norms for each. Since the preparation of such separate tests will require considerable time and expensive research they may not be available for years to come. Meanwhile it is possible to use a test prepared for a different language background provided we do not assume that the norms are equally valid. It is also possible to prepare a test based on a variety of problems that have been found to be common to several language backgrounds and to keep separate norms for each language group that takes the test. The norms will be meaningful only within each language group, and we should also realize that some of the items will be useless for some language groups so that the testing power of the whole test will be less than the size of the test might lead us to believe.

14.3   TESTING AUDITORY COMPREHENSION

1. Initial steps in writing the test. We begin with a list of problems that has been obtained by comparing the language to be tested with the native language of the student. This list of problems will contain the problems of the student in learning each of the separate elements of the language. From this list are selected the problems to be included in the test in view of the time allotted, the level of the students, etc.

Words, minimal pairs, phrases, sentences and sequences of sentences that contain the problems to be tested are used in test items which are arranged so that the various elements are rotated. The items within any part of the test will be of the same format in order not to give the student any extraneous clues to the element being tested in each. Because the test is one of auditory comprehension the testing technique should at this stage be one that requires communication of meaning rather than one that may require comparison of form with form.

We can control the weight we assign to each of the language elements by the number of items devoted to each in the entire test. Thus if we wish to assign one-third of the weight to the combination of segmental phonemes, stress and intonation, we would devote one-third of the total number of items to these elements. If we wish to devote half of this third to sound segments and the other half equally to stress and intonation, we would include one-half segmental items, one-fourth stress items, and one-fourth intonation items. Grammatical structure might be given a second third of the total number of items, and vocabulary the last third. This particular arrangement would give equal weight to each of the three major elements, i.e., pronunciation, grammatical structure, and vocabulary.

2. The general technique to test auditory comprehension. The general technique to test auditory comprehension consists of presenting orally to the students an utterance in the goal language and checking to see if the students understand the complete utterance or certain crucial parts of it. The utterance presented to the students contains the problem being tested, and will be referred to as *the lead*.

3. True-false items. Let us assume that English is the language being tested and that Spanish is the native language of the students. The two languages have been compared and the list of problems to be tested is prepared. It is now time to decide on the type of item and to proceed with the writing of the lead material for the items.

There are various ways to check the student's comprehension of the lead utterances. We may ask the student to write what he has heard and, on the basis of what he writes, decide whether or not he has understood the specific problems being tested. Such a technique would normally be unsatisfactory, because the student may understand the key utterance but not write down the particular thing that we are after, or in trying to remember everything as he writes he may forget the crucial point. Scoring such answers takes a great deal of time and usually involves an excessive amount of subjective judgment on the part of the examiner.

A solution that has sometimes been used is that of including the problem in a statement and asking the student to say if the statement is true or false. An example testing the vowel contrast between *sheep* and *ship* follows:

A sheep is an animal.

True——. False——.

The student merely checks the blank following "True." If the examiner says "A ship is an animal," the student who hears the vowel difference and understands the simple utterance will check the blank after "False."

This technique is restricted by the need to present a number of wrong statements to the students and by the effect of guessing on all two-choice tests. The effect of saying to a group of students taking a test that "A ship is an animal," is a humorous one. The students who understand what is being said will chuckle and thus give a clue to those who do not understand.

The stronger objection to this type of item, however, comes from the heavy effect of guessing. Since only two answers are possible, the right one and the wrong one, fully half of the items can be answered right by out-and-out guessing. A formula for correction of the effect of guessing is of help in evaluating the performance of groups of students but is ineffective in the interpretation of individual scores.

The classic way to overcome this problem of guessing is to increase the number of items of the test. Increases in size, however, are no longer possible when the students have reached a point of fatigue that will influence their performance from this extraneous factor.

4. Multiple-choice items. Multiple-choice items seem to provide the most satisfactory technique for testing auditory comprehension. In multiple-choice items to test auditory comprehension, the lead contains the problem being tested and the choices or alternatives contain the distractors that the interference of the native language habits would normally suggest to the student according to our theory of language testing. One of the alternatives is more nearly right than the others and is chosen by the student as the "best" answer he finds among the choices.

5. Sample leads for auditory comprehension items. We will select one problem to represent each of the elements of language discussed in previous chapters: segmental phonemes, stress, intonation, grammatical structure, and vocabulary. English will be the foreign language and Spanish the native language of the students.

The segmental phoneme problem will be the contrast between the vowel in "ship" and that in "sheep." Spanish has one phoneme in the same phonetic area. The key words will be "ship" and "sheep."

The stress problem will be the contrast between the sentences

^2He $lòoked$ $ôver$ the $^3wáll^1$. (He examined it.)

^2He $lôoked$ $òver$ the $^3wáll^1$. (He looked above and beyond it.)

The intonation problem will be represented by the following pair.

^2The $^4bóy^2$, ^1who $stòod$ $^1úp^1$, ^2was $^3táll^1$.

^2The $bòy$ who $stòod$ $^3úp^2$, ^2was $^3táll^1$.

The structure problem will be the direction of modification in the combination "house dog" and "dog house." The Spanish speaker will tend to take the first element as the head of the modification structure because of the modification patterns of Spanish, and may understand "house dog" to mean a house and "dog house" to mean a dog.

The lexical problem will be "ash tray," representing a different pattern of lexical form, since Spanish uses a single word *cenicero* made up of a stem and a suffix.

We prepare leads for the items containing the problems just listed. We control the context so that the sound contrast, the stress contrast, the intonation contrast, the word order contrast of the modification structure, and the lexical unit "ash tray" will be decisive in choosing the right alternatives. The leads are the following:

1. ^{2}*It's a* ^{3}*shéep*^{1}.

2. ^{2}*Hè lóoked òver the* ^{3}*wáll*^{1}.

3. ^{2}*The* ^{3}*bóy*^{2}, ^{1}*who stòod* ^{1}*úp*^{1}, ^{2}*was* ^{3}*táll*^{1}.

4. ^{2}*Hàve you sêen our new* ^{2}*hóuse dôg*^{3}?

5. ^{2}*Do you wânt the* ^{2}*ásh trày*^{3}?

It should be noticed that in every case a contrasting pair is possible in the same context:

1. ^{2}*It's a* ^{3}*shíp*^{1}.

2. ^{2}*Hè lòoked óver the* ^{3}*wáll*^{1}.

3. ^{2}*The bôy who stòod* ^{3}*úp*^{2}, ^{2}*was* ^{3}*táll*^{1}.

4. ^{2}*Hàve you sêen our new* ^{2}*dóg hôuse*^{3}?

5. ^{2}*Do you wânt the* ^{2}*ásh càn*^{3}?

6. Types of alternatives. The alternatives in these items can be given in (1) pictures, (2) the goal language, or (3) the native language of the students. All three media have been used successfully in tests of auditory comprehension and will be illustrated separately for the same set of problems.

(1) *Picture items.* Items with pictures as choices have been used in tests for children and for literate adults at the lower range of mastery of the language. These picture choices should also prove successful if used systematically with illiterate adults. In this type of item the examiner reads the key material and the student selects from several pictures on his answer sheet the one that best represents or best answers the key material read by the examiner. The pictures represent the lead material and the distractors that the student would find because of native language interference in learning the goal language.

EXAMPLE 1. *It's a sheep.*

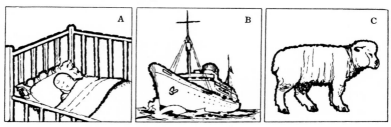

EXAMPLE 2. *²Hè lôoked òver the ³wáll¹.*

EXAMPLE 3. *²The ⁴bóy², ¹who stòod ¹úp¹, ²was ³táll¹.*

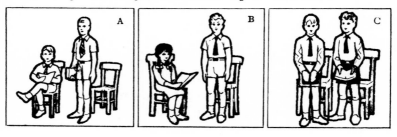

EXAMPLE 4. *Have you seen our new house dog?*

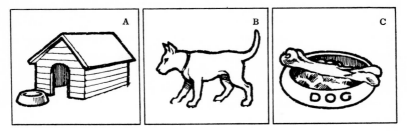

EXAMPLE 5. *Do you want the ash tray?*

In Example 1 the distractor represented by picture A, which would be right if the examiner had said, "It's asleep," is rather far-fetched. In experimental runs it may turn out that this distractor is not effective, in which case another more likely distractor would have to be substituted. It might possibly be the picture of a goat, which in one Spanish translation would be *chiva*, thus constituting a form-induced distractor.

Picture C of Example 2, "a player looking at or over the goal" is a form-meaning distractor through the similarity of English *wall* and Spanish *gol* (from English *goal*). Picture B is the crucial distractor and represents "a man examining a wall." The right choice is picture A representing "a man looking above and beyond the wall."

Example 3 has the chief distractor in picture A representing a short boy, who did not stand up, and a tall boy, who did. If the examiner had said, " [2]*The bôy who stòod* [3]*úp*[2], [2]*was* [3]*táll*[1]," this would have been the right alternative. With the lead as given, picture B is the right alternative, representing only one boy, who stands up and is tall, and a girl, who does not stand up. Picture C is a more remote distractor representing two tall boys.

In Example 4, "Have you seen our new house dog?" picture A represents a dog house and is thus the chief distractor. Picture B is the right alternative, and picture C represents a rather far-removed form distractor on the basis of possible similarity between English "house" and Spanish *hueso*. If the student chooses this alternative, we still know that he took the modifier of the construction as the head, which is the point we are trying to test.

And in Example 5, picture A represents the form distractor in the possible resemblance between Spanish *estruendo* 'thunderous noise' and English "ash tray." Picture B is a meaning distractor exploiting the pattern similarity between "ash tray" and "ash can." Picture C is the right alternative.

In the actual test, the key utterances would be available in writing to the examiner only, and the pictures would appear in a booklet for the student with appropriate instructions at the beginning of the test.

(2) *Items with choices in the goal language.* The same five problems can be tested by means of alternatives in the language being tested. This is a highly desirable type of technique because it permits the superior student to remain set in the goal language rather than having to switch back and forth between the native language and the foreign language. It also solves some problems encountered in representing alternatives in pictures.

Probably the greatest single problem in writing these items is to keep the language of the choices simpler than the key utterance itself. The alternatives for Example 1, "It's a sheep," might be "asleep," "a boat," and "an animal." All three are made up of very common English words. "Boat" and "animal" in addition resemble the Spanish words *bote* and *animal* which mean about the same and therefore constitute the easiest vocabulary level. We may be reasonably certain that most students who choose the wrong alternative may do so because of difficulty in hearing the sound contrast we are interested in.

The alternatives for Example 2, "[2]*Hè lôoked òver the* [3]*wáll*[1]," might be "looked above and beyond the wall," as the right choice, "examined the wall," as the crucial distractor, and "looked at the goal," as a form-meaning distractor.

For Example 3, "^{2}*The* ^{4}*bóy*^{2}, ^{1}*who stòod* ^{1}*úp*^{1}, ^{2}*was* ^{3}*táll*^{1}," the alternatives might be " One of several boys stood," as the crucial distractor, "The only boy stood," as the right choice, and "Two boys stood," as another distractor. Since the word "stood" appears in all three choices, we might attempt to put it into an introductory section so that the alternatives themselves will have a minimum of reading matter. We might select the question, "Who stood up?" and then give the alternatives without the word "stood" in them.

The alternatives for Example 4 "Have you seen our new house dog?" might be "a house," as a form distractor representing the crucial contrast of word order, "a dog" as the right choice, and "a bone" as a form-meaning distractor.

The alternatives for Example 5, "Do you want the ash tray?" might be "great noise," as a form distractor, "star for the tree," as another form distractor, and "dish for used cigarettes," as the right alternative.

Presenting now the key utterances with instructions as the "Examiner's Material," we have the following sample:

EXAMINER'S MATERIAL

Read the instructions aloud and then the test items in a *clear, natural style*. Do not attempt to render the items easier or more difficult by speeding or slowing your delivery. Pause twelve seconds after you finish reading each item to give the students time to read the alternatives and record their answers. Read aloud: INSTRUCTIONS. I WILL READ A SENTENCE ONCE. YOU WILL MARK THE ALTERNATIVE THAT BEST FITS THE SENTENCE. FOR EXAMPLE: [examples would follow]

ONE.   IT'S A SHEEP. (Pause 12 seconds).[1]

---

[1] It is important that the pauses after reading of each item be (1) uniform, (2) sufficient for the students to understand the choices, and (3) not so long that the students have time left to look around at other students and their papers. This 12-second pause is suggested from experience with very similar tests. A longer pause encouraged students to look around, and shorter pauses tended to produce unrest among the students.

TWO. ^{2}HÈ LÔOKED ÒVER THE ^{3}WÁLL.^{1}
(Pause 12 seconds).

THREE. ^{2}THE ^{4}BÓY^2, ^{1}WHO STÒOD ^{1}ÚP^1, ^{2}WAS

^{3}TÁLL^1.   (Pause 12 seconds)

FOUR.   HAVE YOU SEEN OUR NEW HOUSE DOG?
(Pause 12 seconds)

FIVE.   DO YOU WANT THE ASH TRAY?
(Pause 12 seconds).

The alternatives with appropriate instructions for the student would constitute the "Student's Material" as follows:

STUDENT'S MATERIAL

Read the instructions silently while the examiner reads them aloud. INSTRUCTIONS. THE EXAMINER WILL READ A SENTENCE ONCE. MARK THE ALTERNATIVE THAT BEST FITS THE SENTENCE. FOR EXAMPLE: [alternatives for the examples would follow here]

1. (A) "asleep"
   (B) "a boat"
   (C) "an animal"

2. He (A) "looked above and beyond the wall."
   (B) "examined the wall."
   (C) "looked at the goal."

3. Who stood up?
   (A) One of several boys.
   (B) The only boy.
   (C) Two boys.

4. He is asking about
   (A) "a house."
   (B) "a dog."
   (C) "a bone."

5. He is asking about a
   (A) "great noise."
   (B) "star for the tree."
   (C) "dish for used cigarettes."

(3) *Items with alternatives in the native language.* The preparation of auditory comprehension items with alternatives in the native language of the students is the easiest technique from the standpoint of the preparation of alternatives. Since the student by definition knows his native language, any possible difficulty in understanding the alternatives is practically eliminated, leaving the problem in the key utterance as the only one being tested. This assumes that the student is literate. If he is not, we must fall back on pictures as described above. Major reservations in connection with the use of the native language in the choices are (1) the influence that this practice will inevitably have on teaching in the classroom, and (2) the extra burden that switching back and forth between two languages puts on the good student, the one who no longer needs to translate.

The five sample items already presented might be tested through the native language, Spanish in this case, by the following alternatives:

1. (A) Está dormido.
   (B) Es un barco.
   (C) Es una oveja.

2. (A) Miró por encima de la pared.
   (B) Examinó la pared.
   (C) Miró al gol.

3. ¿Quién se levantó?
   (A) Un niño entre varios.
   (B) El único niño.
   (C) Dos niños.

4. Habla de
   (A) una caseta para el perro.
   (B) un perro casero.
   (C) un hueso para el perro.

5. Habla de un(a)
   (A) estruendoso ruido.
   (B) estrella decorativa.
   (C) cenicero.

7. Cautions for the preparation of good comprehension items. Preparing test items is a complex undertaking and cannot be reduced to a simple routine. Undoubtedly in preparing tests as in other complex activities, great individual differences exist, yet no rare talent is actually needed to prepare good tests once the problems to be tested have been clearly described and the test maker has the necessary language training to work with these problems. A number of cautions will, however, prove helpful to those who have little or no experience in the preparation of controlled language materials and tests. These notes of caution deal with the writing of the test leads and with the use of pictures, the goal language, and the native language in the choices.

Caution 1, context. Give only as much context as needed and no more. The problem in teaching differs from that in testing. In teaching we often seek to make a point clear by means of context. In testing, the context must be carefully restricted so as not to provide a by-pass to the answer. The context should be enough to resolve any ambiguity as to the crucial problem, and no more. For example, if we say "The house dog ate its food" we have given too much context to check comprehension of "house dog" versus "dog house." A dog house would obviously not eat food.

Caution 2, length of the lead material. There is no hidden virtue in the use of a long paragraph or even a complete article or essay as the optimum length of a comprehension passage. In fact, a full paragraph and certainly a complete selection are often unreasonably long and may constitute a test of memory rather than one of comprehension. Long paragraphs and essays may be used in tests in the native language to measure achievement in note taking or in specific subject-matter fields but they are not a good starting point in tests of a foreign language. In fact they are often wasteful of testing time since they require the repetition of material which does not reveal the language difficulties of the students. There is no optimum length for auditory comprehension leads. In general they should be free utterances, that is, they should be chunks of talk which appear independently in the language. They should be long enough to contain in a natural way the linguistic problem being tested. If the problem happens to involve a sentence sequence signal, the passage or lead will have to have at least two sentences. If the problem is one of pronunciation or of grammatical structure, a single sentence will usually suffice.

Caution 3, content. There is danger especially in auditory comprehension in using content that requires special information since some students may be familiar with such content and thus have an undesirable advantage that will distort the results obtained with the test. Using say the story of Peter and the Wolf even with different names, or using some anecdote in the life of a well-known figure such as Henry David Thoreau, or an incident in the history of the United States may result in distorted scores if some students are familiar with the story or incident and others are not. The content of the lead material should as much as possible be equally familiar or equally unfamiliar to all the students.

Caution 4, problem dominance. One can easily, in preparing a lead to test a certain problem, inadvertently include another problem that may be even more difficult than the one we wish to test. In multiple-choice items the alternatives should force a decision based on what we wish to test, but an extraneous problem in the passage may mean that the student does not have the chance to decide on the basis of the test problem. If for example, we use an unusual word in testing a pronunciation contrast through meaning, the student may fail the item because he does not know the word even though he may have fully mastered the pronunciation contrast.

Caution 5, limitations of pictures. Pictures are an excellent medium for the testing of auditory comprehension, yet they are definitely limited and they can be thoroughly ambiguous. Pictures have been used effectively for a long time to teach vocabulary and more recently to test it. They have also been used effectively in picture dictionaries. The writer tested the segmental phonemes of English as a foreign language through pictures, and pictures can be used to test grammatical structure as shown above. However, they probably cannot be used to test all the structural problems or all the lexical items we may need to test. And there is a point of diminishing returns in the use of pictures, a point which is reached when the pictures become so complicated or so remote from the idea they are supposed to suggest that they cannot be understood at a glance but have to be deciphered. We should also remember in using pictures that even as language can be ambiguous, pictures can be even more so. We must edit the pictures carefully and then test them with the kind of students for whom they are intended.

Caution 6, choices in the goal language. The use of the goal language in the alternatives to check auditory comprehension is particularly susceptible to the introduction of irrelevant problems. The choices should be as simple, as short, and as similar to the native language as possible. The preparation of separate tests for each native language background is especially important when the choices are in the goal language. For example, in a test of aural comprehension in English for Spanish speakers we may use the word "difficult" to test the word "hard." The Spanish speaker finds it easy to identify the word "difficult" because he knows *difícil* in a similar sense in Spanish. A speaker of Chinese, on the other hand, may have more trouble learning the word "difficult" than the shorter word "hard."

Caution 7, choices in the native language of the student. The use of the native language of the students to check auditory comprehension requires no particular caution if we proceed from our list of problems to the preparation of test items. The caution here is against the exclusive use of the native language, because of the deadening effect it will have on classroom teaching. Certainly advanced students should stay as much as possible within the goal language.

8. Special arrangement of the items to yield diagnostic information. Although the scores obtained with auditory comprehension tests should primarily represent proficiency in the integrated skill of auditory comprehension, it is possible to arrange the items of the test in such a way that the scores on the items dealing with each of the language elements can be computed separately. We can thus obtain in addition to the total auditory comprehension score five separate partial scores for segmental phonemes, stress, intonation, grammatical structure, and lexical units. These separate scores can show gross difference in performance in any of the elements and enable us to test that element more thoroughly with a special test or to advise the student as to the kind of work he will need to do.

The simplest type of arrangement is to have the items appear in cycles of five in the same order within each cycle. For example, if the first cycle has the order (1) segments, (2) stress, (3) intonation, (4) structure, (5) vocabulary, all cycles follow the same order. The result is that items 1, 6, 11, 16, etc., deal with segments; items 2, 7, 12, 17, etc., deal with stress; items 3, 8, 13, 18, etc., deal with intonation, and so forth. This arrangement requires that each of the five elements be given the same weight in the total auditory comprehension score.

When different elements are assigned different weights, there can be as many parts to the test as there are weights. If, for example, in a one-hundred item test we wish to assign weights, 20, 10, 10, 30, 30 to segments, stress, intonation, structure, and vocabulary respectively, three parts can be set up. The first part will have cycles of five items dealing with the five elements in the same order. This will use up ten items of each element and exhaust the stress and intonation items of which there were only ten to be included. We now have a second part in cycles of three items testing segments, structure, and vocabulary. This second part will have only ten cycles because there are only ten segmental items left. A third part will contain the remaining structure and vocabulary items in cycles of two.

This sort of arrangement makes it possible to remember easily the items testing each element. From the point of view of scoring, a random arrangement of the items can be equally satisfactory. Separate punched stencils for each of the five elements can be prepared and as each is superimposed on the answer sheet only the items dealing with that one element will be seen for scoring.

14.4 PROCESSING OF EXPERIMENTAL FORMS OF THE TEST

Once the auditory comprehension test has been written in an experimental form, with more items than will be included in the final form of the test, it should be tried with native speakers of the language or with non-native speakers who have fully mastered the language to detect defects that as a rule are in the material. The test is then given to a sample of the students for whom it is intended. This procedure has been adequately discussed in previous chapters and will not be repeated here.

If the choices are given in the native language of the students, it will not be possible to try the test on speakers of the goal language. Translating these choices into the goal language might solve this problem but the translation of the choices is full of problems of its own. Validation by other means such as interviewing the students for whom the test is intended to determine if the item does give the information sought is a valid but elaborate substitute. A sample of bilingual speakers fully proficient in both languages is the best solution if such a sample can be found.

Problems of the preparation of norms and of the construction of parallel forms of the tests will be discussed in the last part of this book.

Chapter 15

READING COMPREHENSION IN A FOREIGN LANGUAGE

15.1 WHAT IS READING IN A FOREIGN LANGUAGE?

1. Definition. Reading in a foreign language consists of grasping meaning in that language through its written representation. This definition is intended to emphasize two essential elements in such reading: the language itself and the graphic symbolization used to represent it.

2. Reading comprehension versus auditory comprehension. The similarities and differences between reading comprehension and auditory comprehension are of two kinds, language matters and matters of graphic representation.

Language problems. The language difficulties that a student has in reading a foreign language are substantially the same as he has in understanding it aurally, with three chief differences. In reading he is able to proceed at his own speed and go back to re-read what he may not have grasped at once, while in auditing he must adjust to the speed of the speaker. In ordinary conversation he may ask that something be repeated, but in a testing situation this is rendered impossible because different students would ask for different utterances to be repeated and the scores would lose their comparability. This difference in speed explains in part why students who do not have a major problem in learning the graphic representation of a language find it easier to read something than to understand it when spoken by natives.

Another difference between reading and auditing is the possibility of by-passing in reading some of the troublesome sound contrasts. Partly because we can read at our own speed it is easier to perceive graphic differences in symbolization than minimal differences in sound articulation that are not significant in the native language of the students. It is true that some sound contrasts may be by-passed in auditing as well, because of other clues in the discourse, but the fact is that in reading it is possible actually to distinguish the graphic differences without having to rely on the context.

The third difference between reading and auditing results from differences in style between the language used in speaking and the language used in writing. Questions, for example, are frequent in conversation, and conversation in turn is more frequent as speech than as writing. We can therefore expect to find fewer examples of questions in reading than in auditing. The sentences used in writing tend to be more complex and to contain more complex modification structures than those used in speaking. The vocabulary met in reading is of a far greater range than the vocabulary ordinarily used in speaking. And the length of the utterances that are found in reading is greater than the length of the utterances heard in conversation and in lectures and speeches, though the length of a reading paragraph may be somewhat similar to the length of a parallel unit in lectures and speeches.

These differences between reading and auditing in language matters—the less controlled speed, the by-passing of pronunciation problems, the greater complexity and length of the structures and utterances, and the wider range of vocabulary—are sufficient to require separate materials for reading tests. The tendency to prepare auditory comprehension tests by simply taking a reading test and presenting it orally to the students cannot be recommended. Wholesale transfer in either direction is not justified by the facts.

Problems of graphic representation.[1] In addition to language difficulties in reading, the student will have difficulties caused by the system of graphic representation of the language. These problems tend to be neglected when the native and the foreign languages use the same alphabet or other writing system. The problems of graphic representation are not overlooked when the two languages use writing systems so fundamentally different as

[1] For a fuller discussion of the analysis of graphic problems in learning to read and write a foreign language, see *Linguistics Across Cultures*, Chapter 5, by Robert Lado.

Chinese and English for example. Yet in testing reading in a foreign language we must take into account the problems caused by differences in graphic representation between the native language and the goal language whether they come from the same alphabet or from entirely different writing systems.

The reading problems due to graphic symbolization can be the result of the kind of units represented, the actual symbols used, and the direction in which the symbols are written. The units represented by writing systems are of three kinds: words or morphemes, syllables, and phonemes. Chinese traditional writing is logographic, that is, it represents words or morphemes. One of the systems of Japanese writing represents the roots in Chinese characters (*kanji* in Japanese) and the affixes in syllabic script (*hiragana* or *katakana*). The languages of Europe are written in alphabetic systems. When an English reader learns to read Chinese, part of the learning problem is due to the fact that he expects to read sounds out of the symbols. When the Chinese reader learns to read English, part of the learning problem is due to the fact that he will attempt to read similar ideas out of similar letters or sets of letters when actually a change of one letter in a word usually changes the entire word.

The graphic problem might be due to the use of different symbols for the same unit of language. Burmese, Korean, Thai, and the languages of Europe have alphabetic systems of writing, but the symbols are strikingly different. The symbols of Korean writing look more like Chinese writing than like the Latin alphabet used for many languages, yet Korean writing being an alphabetic system is much more like the writing systems of the European languages than like that of Chinese. And even within the same alphabet, graphic problems arise when an English reader learns to read another European language and finds that the same letter represents different sounds in English and in the other language.

The direction of eye movements in reading may also vary from one language to another and may therefore constitute a different learning burden particularly in rapid reading. Chinese is written in vertical columns running from top to bottom of the page and successively from right to left. These directions differ from those of English writing in two dimensions. Arabic, on the other hand, is written horizontally from right to left and the lines follow each other successively from top to bottom. Thus Arabic writing differs from English writing in only one dimension in this matter of the direction of writing and reading. These differences are simple enough to grasp intellectually, but the habits involved tend to reduce the speed of reading when a literate adult of one of the languages tries to learn to read the other.

A simple experiment shows how important the factor of reading from left to right can be when learning to read from right to left.[1] This experiment requires only a book, a mirror, and a watch with a second hand. The writer took an essay by Edward Sapir, "The Emergence of the Concept of Personality in a Study of Cultures," and timed himself on reading each of seven pages. Pages 2, 4, 6 and 8 were read in ordinary fashion from left to right. Pages 3, 5, and 7 were read backwards from right to left as they were reflected on a mirror in front of him. Page 1 was not counted because the title took up part of the page. The reading time for each of the four pages read in normal fashion was 1′ 30″, 1′ 40″, 1′ 35″, and 1′ 25″. The reading time of each of the three pages read from right to left was 6′ 35″, 6′ 00″, and 6′ 40″. The average reading time for normal reading was 1′ 33″. The average reading time per page when reading from right to left was 6′ 25″. In other words, this factor of direction of reading increased the reading time to approximately four times that of normal reading. A reading assignment which would take the writer two hours to complete would require eight hours and forty minutes to read from right to left. In addition, the writer felt physical discomfort and did not understand what he read with the completeness that he achieved when reading the same kind of material from left to right.

Additional evidence confirming the theory that differences in graphic representation of the native language and the foreign language constitute a learning problem is provided by the following objective data. The performance of Spanish readers was

[1] There are two ways to define reading in reverse. In the mirror image reversal used in this experiment the letters appear backwards along with reversed direction of the text. If we consider reversal only the order of appearance of the letters, keeping the individual letters in the usual direction, the speed of reading might be different.

compared with that of Persian readers on two parts of the same test of auditory comprehension in English.[1] The first part used picture alternatives. The second part used reading alternatives in English. Thirty-three Spanish readers were paired with thirty-three Persian readers on the basis of their scores on the picture part of the test. Then the average score of the Persian group on the reading part of the test was computed and compared with the average score of the Spanish group on the same reading part of the test. The average score of the Persian group was 65 per cent. The average score of the Spanish group was 71 per cent. The difference in favor of the Spanish group is 6 per cent, which is statistically significant at the 5 per cent level. Since the two groups are the same in auditory comprehension through pictures, we may conclude that the reading material of the alternatives was more of a problem for the Persian readers than for the Spanish ones. Persian writing uses Arabic symbols and is written from right to left. Spanish writing uses the Latin alphabet as does English and is written in the same direction as English, i.e., from left to right.

To find out if the reading factor was operative at both low and high levels, the thirty-three Spanish-Persian pairs of cases were divided into two groups, high and low, with sixteen pairs each, leaving out the middle pair. This tabulation showed 10 per cent higher scores for the Spanish readers in the low group and 3 per cent higher in the high group.

3. Problems of non-readers. In the above discussion and illustrations we have assumed that the students had already learned to read their native language. The case of those who have not learned to read at all is a different one. With illiterates there are no previous habits to be considered either as aiding the process of reading the foreign language or interfering with it. In testing reading comprehension in a foreign language among non-readers the language factor is substantially the same as for readers, but the factor of graphic representation is obviously not the same. Graphic representation in this case will constitute problems more in the nature of the problems of the native speaker who learns to read his own language.

[1] Robert Lado. Test of Aural Comprehension for Foreign Students, Form A. (Ann Arbor: English Language Institute, 1946.)

4. When has a student "learned" to read a foreign language? We can say in working terms that a student has learned to read a foreign language when he has mastered the specific difficulties of those of his language background and writing system. These difficulties are related to interference from the native language and writing system.

5. Reading the native language versus reading a foreign language. And since there are various purposes in reading—reading for literary appreciation, for specific items of information, for significant information in a given field, for examples of usage, etc.—we further define reading in a foreign language as the grasping of the full linguistic meaning of what is read in subjects within the common experience of the culture of which the language is a central part. Other types of reading are more properly the realm of reading in the native language, e.g. for literary appreciation.

Linguistic meanings are meant to include the denotations conveyed by the language to all the speakers of it as opposed to meanings that are perceived only by those who have specific background information not known by the other speakers in general. If one reads a quotation on a given industrial stock for the first time he will probably grasp only the linguistic meanings of what he reads. On the other hand a person who has been studying the fluctuation of the price of this stock will perceive in addition whether the price has gone up, down, or remained the same. And if this person has invested in the stock he may also perceive a meaning of "favorable" or "unfavorable" for his interests. These latter meanings are not within the realm of a reading comprehension test in a foreign language, since they are not linguistic but require special training or information in addition to control of the language. If, however, the necessary previous information is provided in the passage it then becomes linguistic meaning and may be included in the test, provided the subject is not one that requires special training or exceptional intelligence for its interpretation.

Properly included in linguistic meaning are the uses of lexical items in meanings that are normally brought out by the context even if such meanings would not be defined in the dictionaries of the language. This is the case of "glass" in describing a prize fighter as having a "glass jaw." This flexible use of words as bundles of features of meaning which come alive in each context is very much a part of the testing of reading in a foreign language.

6. Individual meaning and the educated person. We have made a distinction between linguistic-cultural meaning on one hand and individual meaning on the other. Linguistic-cultural meaning is "known" by "all" the members of a linguistic community and can be included in language tests. Individual meaning is the result of a person's total experience, which differs at least in detail from that of any other, and of his personality, which is unique. Individual meaning lies outside the field of foreign language testing.

This distinction between individual and linguistic-cultural meaning is too coarse as it stands and needs further elaboration to be more useful. Linguistic-cultural meaning is not as uniform and general throughout a linguistic community as might be supposed. There may be literate and illiterate members of a linguistic community, and their lexical inventory probably differs substantially. We would consider as part of linguistic-cultural meaning those matters that can be assumed to belong to the lexical stock of the general run of the literate members of the community. This criterion is a relative one, to be sure. The representativeness of the literate people of a community varies greatly from culture to culture around the earth today. And it has varied tremendously since the use and spread of movable-type printing by Gutenberg and since the idea of educating the masses became widely established in some cultures. Nevertheless the criterion helps to decide what lexical units to exclude from language tests.

The criterion of educated versus folk members of a linguistic community has also proved useful in selecting "standard" forms versus folk forms of the language. The term "educated" has to be defined specifically in order to be useful. Here again, the formal criteria to identify the educated members of a linguistic community would vary greatly from culture to culture today and would vary equally as greatly over the past few hundred years in any one culture.

The individual meanings which we cast out of foreign language testing are not as amorphous as might be assumed from the fact that we did not consider them part of the patterned system of established meaning distinctions of the linguistic community. There is the individual meaning that each person builds from his total life experience as it interacts with his personality. There is the "individual" meaning that becomes part of the family group, or a group of friends, or of two persons. Much of this meaning is trivial. To one person, dogs are lovable while to another they are to be feared; and so with cats, horses, and even snakes. To man and wife a certain date may call for a celebration and another for sad remembrance. Much of it can refer to a person or a family with fine traditions or a bad reputation. The particular meanings of a particular individual or family that are not part of the common knowledge of the linguistic community may not be tested as a sign of knowledge of the language. But the process by which a language unit acquires this individual meaning is part of knowing the language and may be tested through specific examples in which the development of the individual meaning is observable.

There is the professional or technical meaning that the individual needs for the discharge of his trade, profession, art, spiritual work, etc. The druggist reads a doctor's prescription that is unintelligible to the patient but clear to him. The physician reads the description of the chemical composition of a medicine and knows what it means and what it may be used for. The pilot reads his flight instructions and understands what they mean. These professional or technical meanings have to be learned by native speakers of a language as well as by the foreign speaker; they may not be used in tests to measure reading comprehension in a foreign language except in the special case in which the members of a profession are learning the foreign language and include professional meanings in their learning material.

And then there is the vast universe of meaning encompassing scientific information, aesthetics, cultural information, morality, religion and theology and history, which an individual may learn not for the discharge of his profession nor through his cultural and personal experience but through study, observation and insights of his own. These insights and information make him grasp more richly the history, present significance, and future expectation of each event or exhibit. These meanings make him understand better his own body, spirit, and personality, and those of his fellow men. He understands more fully within the limitations of his humanity and of his time the living world around him, the physical universe in which he lives, and God and His Will. These are attributes of true education, of the educated man. This means that in any circumstance in which he finds himself he sees more, hears more, and can predict more than his companion who knows only what his culture taught him and what he had to learn for the discharge of his profession. This means also that the educated man can understand more meanings in what he reads and can derive a richer, fuller meaning from it. The learning of a foreign language contributes significantly to true education and insofar as we test ability to read a foreign language we are testing a mark of the educated man. But beyond this, we would be testing a man's total education, and this lies beyond the testing of reading comprehension in a foreign language.

15.2 LISTING THE READING COMPREHENSION PROBLEMS

As in other tests of language we begin by listing the problems to be tested, in this case problems that are characteristic of reading.

At the beginning stage are the problems resulting from differences between the native and the foreign languages in the graphic symbols and in their relation to the language units they represent. The minimally constrasting shapes of the letters in an alphabetic system may be problems. The fact that a circle " o " and a vertical stem "1" constitute six different letters depending on whether they are combined or not and how they are combined can be a learning problem for one who has not used the Latin alphabet previously: the circle at the left of the stem produces " d ", at the right of the stem, " b "; the stem going down at the right of the circle gives " q ", at the left of the circle, " p ". The stem alone is "1" and the circle alone is " o ". A broken circle gives "c", etc. The fact that not all the elements of a letter are contrastive may constitute a problem. The fact that letters combine in certain larger groups of letters that fit syllables in certain ways and not in others may be a problem. In "dishearten" the "s" is part of "dis-" and "h" part of "heart." But in "dishevel" the "s" is part of "-shev-", and how does one who is learning to read English know?

The direction of the written line, the symbols used to identify word boundaries, sentence boundaries, types of sentences, stress, parts of sentences, paragraphs, sequences of sentences and of paragraphs, may constitute problems to be tested at an early stage.

At an intermediate level of achievement are the meanings of words and phrases within a limited vocabulary and the meanings of the basic patterns of structure that constitute recognition problems to the particular students for whom the test is intended. The more frequent sequence signals in paragraph organization, and the more frequent organizational types within paragraphs are also part of this intermediate level of reading.

At the advanced level are the contextual abstraction of partial meanings and extended meanings of lexical items in their full vigor, the stylistic variations that are readily understood by native readers, the full range of sequence signals and organization, and the handling of longer paragraphs and series of paragraphs into lexically unified selections.

15.3 TESTING READING COMPREHENSION

1. General technique. The general technique to test reading comprehension consists of presenting to the student passages containing reading problems and testing his comprehension of the passages precisely at those points at which the problems are crucial.

2. Pre-reading technique. With students for whom the graphic representation will be a heavy learning problem one may need to test their ability to identify the graphic symbols themselves without going through the full process of reading. The problem symbols, or words and phrases containing the problem symbols, are presented as the lead; and minimally contrasting symbols or series appear as distractors along with the right alternative which is essentially the same as the lead.

EXAMPLES: Circle the alternative that matches the model best.

Model	Alternatives
b	p d q h b
bale	pale dale bale hale kale
hand	bank land dank hank hand

Different types can be introduced to see if the student identifies the letters in them.

bale   pale **dale** *bale* **hale** kale

dale   pale **dale** *bale* **hale** kale

3. Reading techniques for beginners. Beyond identifying the graphic symbols on this pre-reading level the student's problem at the elementary level becomes one of identifying and understanding words and sentences through their graphic representation. Following is an example testing the lexical unit "boiling" through picture alternatives.

He is boiling water.

A   B   C

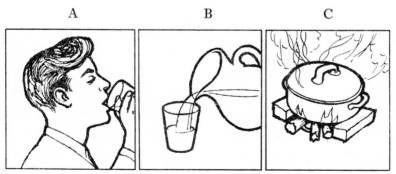

The same item with the alternatives in the goal language might be as follows:

He is *boiling* water.

(A) "making hot"

(B) "putting in"

(C) "drinking"

It is difficult to write good alternatives for beginning students in the goal language. The alternatives can be more difficult to understand than the key item being tested. This problem becomes less acute as the level of the test advances, and it practically disappears at the advanced level.

The same item with alternatives in Spanish as the native language of the student might become

He is *boiling* water.
(A) "hirviendo"
(B) "poniendo"
(C) "tomando"

Since at this level the items would deal with vocabulary and grammatical patterns in similar fashion to the items described in the chapters on the testing of vocabulary and grammatical structure, no further discussion of these techniques is necessary here. The additional problem of graphic representation is handled by the pre-reading technique and by an extension of the comprehension techniques already described. The following is an example of an item testing the spelling contrast between "sun" and "son."

It's a bright son you have here.

A   B   C

4. Reading techniques for intermediate and advanced students. Since we are testing complete linguistic comprehension, the type of item that presents several multiple-choice items

for each passage read is well-adapted to our purpose. The following is an example testing lexical meaning of a word, figurative meaning of words, and identification of the head in a subject structure:

> The sky highway over the top of the world has become a milestone in the history of intercontinental travel, ushering in a new age of commercial aviation. (Scandinavian Airlines System Map.)

1. "Highway" in this sentence means
   - (A) 'road for automobiles'
   - (B) 'route for airplanes'
   - (C) 'group of stars'
   - (D) 'animal with wings'

2. The place this sentence talks of is
   - (A) 'high mountains'
   - (B) 'high clouds'
   - (C) 'the Moon'
   - (D) 'the North Pole'

3. The thing that has become a milestone is
   - (A) the highway
   - (B) the sky
   - (C) the top
   - (D) commercial aviation

4. "Age" in this sentence means
   - (A) 'the years of something'
   - (B) 'the years of a person'
   - (C) 'epoch in history'
   - (D) 'a spice'

These items and alternatives are designed for Spanish readers learning English. Hence the use of "epoch in history" in a choice to test "age." "Epoch in history" is easily understood by Spanish speakers because of the similarity of *época* and *historia*. "A spice" is a form distractor for "age" because with spelling mispronunciation it would become something like /áxe/, which is similar to Spanish *ajo* /áxo/ 'garlic.' "Garlic" is not learned readily by Spanish speakers but "spice" is similar to Spanish *especie*, which would be applicable to "garlic" as 'seasoning.'

The fact that Spanish is assumed to be the native language also explains the choice of "highway" and "age" as items to be tested rather than "intercontinental" or "aviation." The word "intercontinental" does not even appear in Thorndike's 30,000 word list, yet it is known by Spanish readers because it is the same as Spanish *intercontinental*. "Aviation" is almost the same as Spanish *aviación* and, therefore, does not represent a learning problem.

Another example of a reading technique will illustrate a variation in style and will concentrate on testing sequence signals.

There are two considerations, often intermingled in practice, which arouse the thought of an international language. The *first* (1) is the purely practical problem of facilitating the growing need for international communication in *its* (2) most elementary sense.

The opposed *consideration* (3) is not as easy to state and can be so stated as to seem to be identical with the first. *It* (4) should be put in something like the following form: An international auxiliary language should serve as a broad base for every type of international understanding, *which* (5) means, of course, in the last analysis, for every type of expression of the human spirit *which* (6) is of more than local interest, which in turn can be restated so as to include any and all human interests.[1]

1. The word before "(1)" refers to
   (A) "considerations"
   (B) "practice"
   (C) "thought"
   (D) "language"

2. The word before "(2)" refers to
   (A) "international language"
   (B) "growing need"
   (C) "elementary sense"
   (D) "international communication"

[1] Excerpts from "The Function of an International Auxiliary Language," by Edward Sapir. In *Culture, Language and Personality; Selected Essays*. (University of California Press, 1956) pp. 47–8.

3. The word before "(3)" means
   (A) "the practical problem"
   (B) "elementary international communication"
   (C) "the second consideration"
   (D) "identical with the first"

4. The word before "(4)" means
   (A) "the first consideration"
   (B) "the opposed consideration"
   (C) "the following form"
   (D) "an international language"

5. The word before "(5)" refers to
   (A) "a broad base"
   (B) "every type of international understanding"
   (C) "in the last analysis"
   (D) "every type of expression"

6. The word before "(6)" refers to
   (A) "in the last analysis"
   (B) "every type of expression"
   (C) "the human spirit"
   (D) "more than local interest"

The above example is rather difficult. The following is easier and has fewer items for the length of the passage. It represents a more informal style of writing from a letter.

We boys in my neighborhood had no place to play except the *streets* (1). If we wanted excitement the easiest way was to smash something or steal something. I found something better at the Boys' Club. I learned how to swim. I played basketball on one of the *teams* (2). I made furniture—one of the tables is still in my living-room. I became a Volunteer for the Boys' Club and worked around the Club helping the younger kids. I was President of the *Volunteers* (3) for two years. The Boys' Club gave me the start I needed to lead a full and decent life. (From literature soliciting aid for Boys' Clubs of America.)

1. "(1)" represents
   (A) the only place to play
   (B) the place where boys did not play
   (C) a good place to play

2. "(2)" refers to something of
   (A) the neighborhood
   (B) the street
   (C) the Boys' Club

3. "(3)" means
   (A) boys who offer to do something
   (B) the name of a group of boys
   (C) the Boys' Club

The third item of the above example tests the comprehension of a common noun, "volunteer," transformed into a proper name. This special use of "volunteers" is brought out by the context and by the initial capital of the text.

Other styles and formats of reading comprehension items are used in printed tests. Some present the passage on the left half of a page and the multiple-choice items on the right half at about the same height as the reference on the passage. Others present the choices horizontally rather than vertically as above. Matters of format should be decided on the basis of clarity and ease of reference to the student within the space limitations imposed by cost of paper, printing, handling, etc.

The items testing comprehension of a reading passage may deal with the total passage, with a particular sentence or part of a sentence in the context of the passage, or with individual words or even parts of words. In writing these items it is easy to go astray unless a deliberate effort is made to sample the range of problems of the list we wish to test.

The discussion and examples have dealt with testing reading comprehension as an integrated skill on the part of a student of a foreign language. The same techniques can be used to test comprehension of a specific book or article. This problem is actually a simpler one since we do not have to choose items that are representative of general problems. The preparation of reading comprehension tests to go with specific reading material can be of considerable help to students and teachers.

Chapter 16

SPEAKING A FOREIGN LANGUAGE

16.1 WHO KNOWS HOW TO SPEAK A FOREIGN LANGUAGE?

1. Need to clarify the issues. The ability to speak a foreign language is without doubt the most highly prized language skill, and rightly so, because he who can speak a language well can also understand it and can learn to read it with relative ease unless it happens to be a language like Chinese or Japanese, whose writing systems constitute major learning problems of their own. Also, the ability to speak a language will greatly expedite and facilitate learning to write it. Yet testing the ability to speak a foreign language is perhaps the least developed and the least practiced in the language testing field.

This situation is probably due in part at least to a lack of clear understanding of what constitutes speaking ability or oral production. A quotation from the report of the Investigation of Second-Language Teaching mentions the problem:

> In the field of speaking ability, we were faced with even fewer established standards of achievement than existed for aural comprehension. There was no consensus among teachers regarding the range of vocabulary or the degree of grammatical complexity which the language student could be expected to use actively at the end of the first and the second year. As for actual tests of oral production, we knew of none in published form for general use.[1]

One can safely say that as a rule, even when speaking ability is one of the teaching aims, it is not tested directly in anything like an objective, systematic way.

---

[1] F. B. Agard and H. B. Dunkel. *An Investigation of Second-Language Teaching* (Boston: Ginn and Company, 1948), pp. 55–6.

Teachers who have to assign grades and interviewers who must judge the ability of a student to speak a language depend largely on their over-all impression of the student's speech or on informal interviews. Yet these impressions from memory or haphazard interviews can separate accurately only students who speak like natives and students who are beginners. The vast majority of cases, which normally fall somewhere between these two extremes, are not reliably separated into levels of speaking ability by this approach, because of the complexity of the language and non-language factors involved.

16.2   WHAT IS SPEAKING A FOREIGN LANGUAGE?

1. Approach through situations outside of language. We may attack the problem of clarifying this business of speaking a language from outside of language or from language itself. Most of the attempts to produce systematic tests of oral production have attacked the problem externally. Speaking ability is described as the ability to express oneself in life situations, or the ability to report acts or situations in precise words, or the ability to converse, or to express a sequence of ideas fluently.

This approach produces tests that must range over a variety of situations to achieve validity, and then there is no assurance that the language elements of speaking have been adequately sampled. Scoring is done by means of a rating scale describing the type of responses to be expected and the score to assign to each. The following is an example of a rating scale for short responses elicited by pictures:

2—Conveys a simple description completely and correctly. Conveys the simple description completely and correctly, but elaborates and in so doing makes some error or errors of vocabulary, grammar, or pronunciation— errors which interfere little with the understandability of the utterance.

1—Conveys the simple description with one or more errors of vocabulary, grammar or pronunciation, these errors being such as *not* to interfere with the understandability of the simple description.

o—Conveys very little meaning.
   Conveys the wrong meaning.
   Makes errors which obscure the meaning.
   Says nothing.[1]

Sometimes sample responses representing each rating are provided to help the examiner compare his judgments with those of the test makers.

In these rating scales one finds references to fluency, vocabulary, pronunciation and enunciation, and grammatical correctness which show that as soon as an examiner begins to listen carefully for speaking ability he notices differences in the various elements of speech which he can grade more accurately than the over-all impression of speaking or the desirable but elusive criterion of intelligibility.

2. Approach through the elements of language. By admitting that the ability to speak a foreign language is a complex matter and deliberately attempting to attack it through its linguistic elements we can hope to achieve better coverage of the language itself and more objective scoring of the student's responses.

We define oral production or speaking ability as the ability to use in essentially normal communication situations the signaling systems of pronunciation, stress, intonation, grammatical structure, and vocabulary of the foreign language at a normal rate of delivery for native speakers of the language.

Through this approach the situations become of secondary importance, since they must not be a decisive factor in the test. The language difficulties become the central testing problem. And such variables as talkativeness, introversion-extroversion, the ability to tell interesting stories, etc., which might influence an examiner if he is listening for the total impression of a student's speech, are properly eliminated. And the factor of oral fluency becomes simply the ability to produce at a normal rate of speed the words and structures of the language in the stress and intonation patterns of that language.

[1] *Ibid.*, p. 57.

16.3   LISTING THE ORAL PRODUCTION PROBLEMS

The first step in preparing an oral production test is then not the preparation of ingenious items, important as this is at the proper time, but the preparation of the list of the linguistic problems that the speakers of one language will find in learning the other. If speakers of a variety of languages must be tested on the same test the list must be a composite one of representative problems from these various native languages. Such a list will include the sound segments, stress patterns, intonations, grammatical structures, and a range of lexical units, that constitute learning problems because they are not paralleled in the native language or languages of the students.

The need to begin from a list of problems has been stressed in the chapters dealing with the separate elements of language. In speaking tests, we need to alternate the various problems and add the idea of fluency in the form of normal rate of delivery.

16.4   HOW TO TEST SPEAKING ABILITY

1. General technique. There is no difficulty in formulating a general technique to test oral production. The general technique is simply to give the student sufficient clues to produce certain utterances that contain the problems we wish to test. Complicating factors lie in the need to elicit a quick response; to elicit it without giving the student the very information we wish to check, and to make sure that the student will attempt to produce that problem and not some other utterance that may be correct but is of no interest to us at the time. Also complicating the testing problem is the difference between producing an utterance with the attention chiefly on its form and producing the same utterance in the normal flow of speech where the concentration is on content. Because of the practical impossibility of observing the student in the varied situations in which he uses the language we try to devise test items that will as nearly as possible duplicate the essential stimuli and conditions of actual speech.

2. Specific stimuli to elicit the key utterances. Pictures, the native language of the student, and the foreign language being tested are the practical stimuli that can be used in production tests. Pictures are probably the most valid medium if properly devised and edited, and as we have seen in previous chapters they can be used to test the entire system of segmental phonemes, a sample of a given vocabulary, and at least some of the structures of the language. The various ways to use pictures with pronunciation, grammatical structure and vocabulary need not be repeated here; it is only necessary to add that since total production is being tested, the items checking vocabulary, pronunciation and grammatical structure should be alternated, preferably in such a way that the student is not aware of what is being tested in each particular item.

The native language as a production stimulus has the virtue of permitting precise information to be given without providing at the same time give-away clues to the response we wish to observe. When picture stimuli fail to elicit all the problems we need to test, the native language may be used to supplement them.

The foreign language can be used as a stimulus also, but special care needs to be exercised to avoid giving too much information in the stimulus, or making it so difficult that the student fails the item because he does not understand the stimulus itself.

When we are preparing a test that will range over the entire list of problems of the speakers of a particular language learning to speak another we will usually have to use more than one type of stimulus. Pictures alone, desirable and valid as they may be, will not elicit all the problems; they certainly will not elicit them in the most economical manner. We will need to combine the stimuli to achieve completeness.

3. **Oral production test designs.** The design of a production test and the scheme of its items are separate from its content. We have advocated here on the basis of our theory and experience a test content based on linguistic problems. This content can be built into a variety of test designs.

The following design is that of the oral production tests of the Investigation of Second-Language Teaching.[1]

---

[1] *Ibid.*, pp. 56–60.

Part I, Picture Series. Twenty pictures representing simple actions to elicit single sentences. Two sample pictures with expected response printed below them.

Part II, Sustained Speech. The student talks for two to three minutes on an assigned topic presented to him at the time of the test. Separate topics assigned to lower level and upper level. Sample topics:

Lower Level:

You are talking with a Spanish-speaking person who has never been to the United States. Describe to him the town or city in which you live. (If further stimulus is necessary before time is up:) This person is also interested in what a North American home looks like. Describe to him the home in which you (or your parents) live.

Upper Level:

You have met a young German in Europe who seems to you to have the makings of an outstanding American citizen. You resolve to try to convince him that he should emigrate to the United States. Talk to him about the United States so that you may help him decide whether he would like to come. (If further stimulus is necessary:) Your young German friend is interested in American schools. Describe to him life at the school you attend.[1]

Part III. Conversation. Fifteen exchanged utterances between the student and a native speaker whose voice is recorded on a phonograph disc. The student is asked to imagine that he is speaking with a friend who is a native speaker of the language he is learning. The friend speaks to him, and immediately afterward another voice on the record tells the student in his native language what to reply. For example, the friend may say: "¿Cómo está usted?" and the English voice says: "Tell him you're fine and ask him how he is." Pauses are provided in the record while the student makes his response. At the end of each pause, a buzzer warns him to stop speaking and prepare for the next interchange.

[1] *Ibid.*, pp. 57–8.

The above design took from fifteen to twenty minutes to administer.

A shorter design lasting from six to seven minutes to administer was used by the writer in an experimental test presented to the student on $5'' \times 8''$ cards. It consisted of three parts:

Part I, Picture Series for Grammatical Structure and Vocabulary. Line drawings depicting situations and actions that elicited problem grammatical patterns and a few vocabulary problems. Each picture contained only one problem. The pictures were tried with native speakers of the language. More than 50 per cent of the original ones were eliminated because of variations in the responses of natives, or because of failure to elicit the key utterance consistently.

Part II, Reading. Eight short sentences presented in ordinary writing to the student with instructions to read them aloud. Each sentence contained one or two pronunciation problems.

Part III, Story Picture. A single picture depicting the scene of an automobile accident with people arguing vigorously over whose fault it had been. The student was instructed to tell the story. His rate of speech was sampled in one or two timed 30-second spans.

A validity coefficient between the scores obtained with this test and the composite judgment of eight teachers was ·72. This is high for the length of the test but too low for predictions or interpretations based on individual scores. A more comprehensive design would be preferable. The following is a design that might prove more rewarding than the two above:

Part I, Picture and Context Grammatical Structure Series. Twenty-five pictures connected with questions or incomplete sentences designed to elicit problem patterns.

Part II, Picture Stories for Fluency. Two composite pictures with instructions to tell the story. The examiner takes a representative count of the rate of words produced in $30''$ for each picture.

Part III, Completion Series for Pronunciation and Vocabulary. Twenty-five incomplete sentences designed to elicit problem vocabulary items and problem sound segments, stresses, and intonations. The pronunciation problems might be built into the vocabulary items elicited by the lead material of the incomplete sentence.

Probable time of administration: fifteen to twenty minutes. Prompting in the native language to be provided when the stimuli fail to elicit the desired response.

4. Improving the objectivity of scoring. Unless we list specifically what the examiner is to listen for in the responses, we cannot expect dependable scoring: one examiner will notice vocabulary matters, another, pronunciation, others will be impressed by fluency or by grammatical inaccuracies; and some may be led astray by halo effect, or personality characteristics of the students.

Rating scales such as the one quoted above, and rating scales of sample responses at each rating level are of course an improvement, but unless the rating scale tells the examiner exactly what elements to consider right and what to consider wrong, he is still left to his own opinions and listening habits at the moment of scoring.

The best solution to this problem is to list for the examiner the specific point in the problem which decides whether the response is right or wrong and to instruct the examiner to disregard everything else. If the item tests a grammatical problem depending on word order, the examiner is instructed to disregard pronunciation, vocabulary, and fluency. If the item tests a vocabulary problem, the examiner disregards everything else. This solution is dictated by the limitations of the powers of observation of human beings. If the responses are recorded, it is possible to score several problems in each item. This would reduce the number of items necessary for a reliable test, but it would not reduce the scoring time, since the examiner would want to listen to the responses perhaps as many times as there are problems in each item. It might be possible to score accurately combinations of problems such as pronunciation and vocabulary at once. This might profitably be explored and if found satisfactory would theoretically cut the scoring time in half.

The items should be tried with native speakers of the language to eliminate those items that do not elicit the key responses. The examiner's scoring sheet should contain the standard response expected and obtained from native speakers and non-crucial variations, that is, variations that do not eliminate the problem being tested. By trying the test experimentally on a representative sample of the students for whom it is intended we can arrange the items in order of difficulty, eliminate those that do not separate the superior students from the lower ones, and secure samples of the responses that are typically wrong. Two or three of these samples of wrong responses might appear in the examiner's scoring sheet.

Responses are counted either right or wrong. Any intermediate classifications such as half credit for an almost right response tend to complicate the scoring and render it unreliable.

5. Group testing of oral production. If a number of recording machines are available as in many language laboratories now in use, the test of oral production described can be administered as a group test. Group administration has a number of advantages that make it more desirable than individual testing, e.g., avoiding the exchange of information among students, reducing the time consumed in administration, simplifying the schedule of administration, etc.

6. Objective, partial production techniques. Even with highly efficient speaking tests, the time it takes to score them and to administer them militates against their use on a wide scale as a routine part of the testing program of educational institutions. Objective, partial production techniques such as we have discussed in connection with the testing of separate language elements might eventually provide a practical solution for wide, routine testing of production. Meanwhile, the ability to speak a foreign language, though it is the most highly prized of the integrated skills, will go largely untested.

Chapter 17

WRITING A FOREIGN LANGUAGE

17.1   **WHAT IS WRITING A FOREIGN LANGUAGE?**

1. Writing a foreign language versus creative writing. Perhaps because we have usually associated writing with more carefully thought-out content and style than everyday conversation we find it difficult to think of writing in a foreign language apart from some worthwhile content. Yet we find that the ability to write a worthwhile composition is not possessed by all the speakers of a language; the ability to write creatively requires special talent and special training. A person can write his native language without being able to create anything beautiful or of intrinsic value for its content. We cannot then use this creative power as a sign that a student knows how to write a foreign language. In fact, since we do not agree too often on what constitutes good content or beautiful presentation we will not agree on the scoring of compositions in a foreign language as long as we mix content and style with language in our scoring.

We should not however go to the opposite extreme and claim that content and style are to be abandoned in writing a foreign language. They are vital, but they constitute a different testing problem, and we will make more progress by measuring language as language and content and style as content and style. Also, it does not seem promising to test students on creative writing in a foreign language until they have mastered the language itself, and then the problem becomes more and more like that of testing native speakers.

2. A working definition. We will then define writing a foreign language as the ability to use the language and its graphic representation productively in ordinary writing situations. More specifically we mean by writing a foreign language the ability to use the structures, the lexical items, and their conventional representation, in ordinary matter-of-fact writing. This definition parallels those given for the other language skills and like them it provides definite criteria for the preparation and scoring of tests. We recognize then two major elements in writing a foreign language: the language elements and the graphic representation of the language.

With this kind of analysis it is obvious that the problem of writing will be different for each native language group, because the language burden differs according to the native language and because the graphic representation burden is different according to the experience of each group with the writing system of the native language. The problem is also a special one for those whose native language has never been written or who never learned to write it. For those who have never written a language the entire process of writing is new—from handling the writing instrument to producing the graphic symbols and making sense in the language. For those who already write their native language the problem of representation implies the establishing of new habits where the foreign language writing habits conflict with the native ones. And the effect of these conflicting habits will persist through fairly advanced stages of control of the new language.

To be thorough and efficient we need to prepare a list of the language matters, and their graphic representation, that will constitute problems for the particular linguistic background we wish to test. We can say that when a student has mastered these problems he knows how to write the foreign language. With such a list we will be able to prepare better tests of writing and achieve more objective scoring.

17.2   HOW TO TEST WRITING A FOREIGN LANGUAGE

1. **General technique.** Techniques used to test writing in the native language can often be used in the foreign language as well; the difference lies in the problems to be tested. These techniques vary according to whether they deal with the integrated

process of writing or with separate factors such as punctuation, spelling, structure, or vocabulary. In every case, however, we set up a stimulus to obtain a controlled response containing the problems we wish to test.

2. The written composition as a testing instrument. A single picture, or a single composition topic given in the goal language or in the native language of the students is widely used as a writing test especially when the student's ability to produce a connected piece of writing is the chief skill being tested. The virtues claimed for this kind of approach are the realistic nature of the response and the fact that it can show how well a student can think in the language. The shortcomings are the difficulty of scoring the responses objectively and the inadequacy of the sample contained in most compositions. Any single composition touches a limited range of the problems that a student might have, and the student is often able to avoid some of these problems deliberately in writing a test composition. Telling him that he will be scored on the range of structures and vocabulary that he uses encourages artificiality of style and makes the scoring even more complicated. A single composition is probably not the best means to test writing a foreign language.

A series of pictures or topics in the native language of the students or in the goal language to stimulate a variety of responses instead of a single composition maintains much of the naturalness of integrated writing and provides a broader sampling of the problems which the student may have. Scoring, however, still remains a complex process that requires time and can be done with precision only by highly trained personnel.

3. Approach through the elements of writing. When we abandon the attempt to elicit complete written samples to test writing, we are better able to cover the entire range of difficulties in the language and in its writing or any representative sample of these problems. In any case, we are able to secure a wider sample by this approach, and the scoring can be made either more objective or completely objective depending on the technique.

The validity of the kind of test that thus samples the synthetic elements of writing is not readily conceded. After a student does well on one of these tests the question remains whether or not he will do well in an actual composition. Such a question can be answered by correlating the scores obtained on the test with performance scores on a number of actual compositions which for the sake of validation are scored by a jury of competent judges with identical instructions on what constitutes superior and inferior work.

An eclectic design using both the synthetic approach for wider sampling and easier scoring and the composition approach with its more readily acceptable validity, does not of itself guarantee a good test since the total test will be only as good as the sum of its parts, and any part that is unsatisfactory will weaken the total test accordingly.

4. Completion technique. A technique that can be used to test punctuation, spelling, vocabulary, and grammatical structure objectively consists of providing an incomplete piece of writing and asking the student to complete it. To test punctuation we leave out some of the punctuation, to test spelling we leave out a letter or letters, to test vocabulary we leave out a word or words, and to test grammatical structure we omit some structure signal. The context must define unambiguously the element that is missing.

The adaptation of the technique to the various elements of writing can be seen with the aid of a few examples. No variations are shown but with some ingenuity any number of them can be developed by the teacher.

Punctuation. To test punctuation we can use parentheses or brackets at the point where the student has difficulty:

"( ) Do you plan to come tomorrow ( )" "Yes, I do."

The student is asked to supply the punctuation needed if any. Spanish literate speakers might place an upside down question mark at the beginning as well as the right one at the end, for that is their practice in Spanish.

Spelling. To test spelling we omit the problem letters and define the word by context.

"Pro—e—or Smith teaches history in college."

The student is asked to supply the missing letters. Spanish speakers and others learning to write English find it difficult to remember whether the spelling is with single or double "f" and with single or double "s."

This technique is superior to dictation as a test of spelling because it does not require any more writing than the crucial letters and as a result a large number of problems can be tested in a relatively short time. In addition it does not mix spelling problems with pronunciation ones as may be the case in dictation.

There are various ways to define the incomplete word, and ordinarily it may be safer to leave only one spelling blank per item.

"Did you re—ve a letter from home today?"
"A group of words is a —rase."
"He is not in favor of it; he is actually o—osed to it."
"There were three men and two w—en present."

Grammatical structure. The following item would test an irregular plural in English:

"How many child—— do you have?"

It is not always easy to write items such as this to test structure. Pictures, more detailed linguistic context, or the native language of the students are helpful in such cases. The following item tests the use of an irregular preterite in English:

"We needed more food so we —— it and went on our way."
(buy)

Vocabulary. Best-known among these completion-type techniques are those that omit vocabulary items in a self-defining context.

"My nephew's sister is my ———."

5. Limitations of the completion techniques. Completion items are more difficult to answer than ordinary multiple-choice items for the same problems and are sometimes preferred because they force the student to produce the answer. Since writing is a production activity, production items requiring completion are assumed to be more valid in testing writing than multiple-choice recognition items. One weakness of the completion item, however, is the difficulty in preparing a context that will allow only one possible answer. "A vehicle of transportation," for example, may be a ship, a plane, a car. Providing additional context to limit the number of possible answers is not always easy. "A vehicle of transportation used on roads" may still be a truck, a car, a bicycle. "A passenger vehicle of transportation used on roads and having four wheels" may be a car or a bus. "A private passenger vehicle of transportation used on roads and having four wheels" may still be a car or a bus. And in this process of adding context to remove ambiguity, we may easily make the context more difficult to understand than the very problem of recalling the word we set out to test.

Another weakness of the completion item is the time required for scoring. For informal classroom use one can and does devote a few minutes to each student paper, and certainly the time required to score a completion test is much less than that required to score an essay type test. For classroom review and assignment testing the completion item is a useful and handy tool. But for large-scale testing, even five minutes' scoring time per test can become a major consideration. In terms of masses of papers, three-thousand tests at five minutes each would require the work of a person for a month and a half at forty hours per week.

6. Objective, partial production techniques. Partial production techniques approximate the process involved in answering the completion items and at the same time are easier to score. The problem of supplying unambiguous context is considerably lightened by the incomplete, multiple-choice clues supplied in such items. Following are examples of multiple-choice items that may be used in testing the elements of writing. The validity of such items cannot be taken for granted of course and must be established in each case.

Often the process involved in answering a completion item requires a choice of easily-recallable items. The recall feature of the completion item is in such cases of secondary importance. We may in fact safely substitute a multiple-choice item without serious loss of efficiency. Spelling and punctuation often involve problems of choice rather than of recall. Certainly when a Spanish speaker hesitates in the spelling of the word "professor" he is not troubled by the recall of the letters "f" or "s"; he has to choose among various spellings that appear possible to him. We therefore do not impair the validity of the item by providing those possible spellings as choices and asking the student simply to check the number of the correct answer in a separate answer sheet. Similarly, the problem in punctuation is not so much to recall how to write a question mark or a period but to choose between them or between them and a comma. We do not lose validity by supplying the punctuation marks as choices and having the student record his answer by simply checking a number representing the symbol he would use.

Some of the problems tested above in completion items can be turned into multiple-choice items of similar effectiveness as follows:

Instructions: Think of the item that would complete the sentence, then check the alternative that matches your choice.

"Do you plan to come tomorrow ( )" "Yes, I do."
  1 (¿) 2 (.) 3 (?) 4 (:)

"Profe—or Smith teaches history in college."
  1 s 2 th 3 z 4 ss

"Did you rec—ve a letter from home today?"
  1 ei 2 ee 3 ie 4 i

"A group of words is a —rase."
  1 f 2 gh 3 p 4 ph

"He is not in favor of it: he is actually o—osed to it."
  1 p 2 ph 3 pp 4 cp

"There were three men and two w—men present."
  1 i 2 e 3 u 4 o

"How many child— do you have?"
  1 s 2 ren 3 es 4 ss

"We needed more food so we —— it and went on our way."
       (buy)
 1 b - y 2 b - - - - t 3 b - - - d 4 h - - e b - - - - t

"My nephew's sister is my ——."
 1 a - - t 2 n - - - e 3 c - - - - n 4 s - - - - r in l - w

Sequence signals and other elements of connected writing can be tested by the above techniques applied to longer passages especially if the native language of the student or pictures are used to supplement the context.

Instructions: Complete the blanks from the context or the translations, then check the alternative that fits your answer. A hyphen (-) represents one letter. A long dash (—) represents the end or beginning of a word, or a full word. The parentheses ( ) indicate places for punctuation. A line ——— represents a phrase.

Dear John:

I — three things during my short stopover in Paris that would	1 s-e	2 s-w	3 s--n
— interested you very much.	1 h--e	2 h-d	3 h-s
One was Napoleon's tomb ( ) cold, massive, somber. —other	1 (.)	2 (?)	3(,)
was the River Seine, light and	1 A-	2 T-e	3 T--s
cheerful, moving swift— along in the brisk autumn air. And	1 l-	2 -r	3 --t
the — was Notre Dame, tall, elegant, elaborately beautiful, with its Gothic spires pointing skyward	1 a-----r	2 o---r	3 f---l
to — heavens. (los)	1 t--s	2 t---e	3 t-e

————————visit Paris?
(¿ Cuándo vas a)

1 W— a— y— g— t—
2 W— y— g—t—
3 W— g— t—

17.3 TEST DESIGN

A test of writing should consist of several parts with different types of items and problems to sample the elements of writing. Below is one of many possible designs:

Part I. Objective, partial production, multiple-choice items. Fifty to eighty items dealing with specific problems of spelling, punctuation, grammatical structure, and vocabulary.

Part II. Objective items based on one long passage. Twenty to thirty items of the objective, partial production type on a single connected passage testing chiefly matters of sequence and transition signals.

Part III. Three pictures with instructions to write a paragraph about each. Written context should force the student to use other than simple preterite constructions. Grade mechanics only. Number of errors per 100 words.

Part IV. Two short compositions on assigned topics. Thirty minutes each. Style and content are graded as well as mechanics.

17.4 IMPROVING THE OBJECTIVITY OF SCORING COMPOSITION TESTS

In scoring short or long compositions without dealing separately with the language and graphic problems, it is possible to improve the consistency of the grades by providing the examiner with sample compositions at each level or grade. The examiner is thus able to compare his own judgment with the grades suggested by the test maker.

17.5 EVALUATING CONTENT AND STYLE

1. Content. Content much beyond the general knowledge and experience expected of any literate speaker of a language lies outside the range of foreign language tests as such. Composition tests are therefore usually confined to matters of common experience or topics for which the students are given the content. Composition topics such as the following are frequently used:

" Describe your home town to a friend from France."
"Tell about your recent trip to . . ."
"Describe your home."
"What would you do if you had a million dollars?"

If a picture is used as the stimulus for a composition, the subject of the picture is usually one of common experience. A technical picture showing the operation of an atom smasher would not ordinarily constitute a valid subject for a composition test because most students would not be able to understand it. A picture of a family seated at table with a child feeding something to the cat, the mother holding a spoon with food to the baby's mouth, etc., might be valid under certain circumstances.

Given a valid topic for a composition, there are at least three things that can be measured in connection with content: (1) the points of information to be brought out; (2) the organization and sequence in which these points are presented; and (3) the formal signals given the reader to guide him in understanding the topic fully.

Regarding (1), the points of information to be brought out, there is no limit to what can be said about almost any topic, yet the examiner can judge what points are relevant and he can list them. Another way to determine the information points that should be brought out in connection with a particular topic is to administer the composition test to a representative sample of students and to list the points of information mentioned by the superior students. The test maker edits the list on the basis of what he or a group of competent judges deem relevant. Points of information mentioned by the weaker students can be compared with the list from the superior students to show critical differences for scoring purposes.

A refinement of this approach is to pair the students on the basis of a test of general intelligence in the native language: each student in the advanced foreign language group is paired with one of about the same intelligence score from the low language group. We would thus have students of the same intelligence in the advanced group and in the beginning group, and the differences in content between the compositions of the two groups could not be said to reflect intelligence. This refinement is recommended for the preparation of a standardized test and not for an ordinary classroom test.

As to (2), organization and sequence, the points of information that are relevant for a particular topic can be organized in a limited number of ways. Depending on the nature of the information the points or constituents may be organized on some logical basis, on a time sequence, on a special arrangement of some kind, on the basis of some movement or itinerary, on some arbitrary conventional system such as according to the letters of the alphabet or the decimal system of numbering, on the basis of what the writer considers favorable and unfavorable, or on some combination of these and other criteria.

If the topic is the daily schedule of a person, a time arrangement is indicated. History is usually written on a time arrangement intermingled with space considerations in the form of different countries, etc. Other arrangements are possible, but it seems to fit the data better to present them chronologically. A legal argument often follows a logical sequence of some kind with historical and other pertinent information intermingled on a time basis. Geography is written on a space arrangement. Logical sub-systems are sometimes used in addition. The countries of South America might be described at one sweep by moving clockwise from Venezuela to the Guianas, Brazil, Uruguay, Argentina, Chile, Perú, Ecuador, Colombia and inland to Bolivia and Paraguay. A logical arrangement or classification might be used also in the form of inland countries and coastal countries. The vocabulary of a foreign language textbook is usually arranged alphabetically at the end, that is, by an arbitrary conventional system.

It is then possible to exercise some judgment with regard to the arrangement chosen by the students for a particular set of information points and with regard to how effectively the arrangement chosen has been carried out. As in the case of the information points themselves, the test maker may himself indicate the arrangement and sequence that is to be considered superior, and the arrangements that are to be considered less satisfactory. Or he may study the compositions of superior students or compositions judged to be superior by competent judges and abstract the features of arrangement and sequence that are to be graded as high and those that are to be considered low.

Since each language has its own system of signals to indicate the structure of the arrangement of the information points or components in written communication, we can check the student's composition with regard to (3), the formal signals he has used or failed to use to guide the reader in understanding the information points and their arrangement. Fully integrated descriptions of these systems of signals are not available. Studies report word signals, or punctuation, but not the typical sets of signals used in compositions. Perhaps it is assumed that these sets are known by everybody, but they are not.

It is interesting that in writing we tend to use a larger stock of words to indicate the constituent points of a composition. This may be due to the fact that intonation and contextual stress are not marked in ordinary writing, although they play an important part in speaking, and have to be replaced by sequence words in writing to avoid ambiguity. Their more extensive use in writing, especially formal writing, accounts for the fact that they appear to be overly formal when used in ordinary conversation.

Paragraph indentations are a formal mark that usually signals a new constituent or point. Then there are special words or words whose special function is to indicate the logical classification of each next item. Sequence signals such as *also, besides, moreover, furthermore, likewise, similarly*, etc., introduce additional equivalent points; if the point is presented as a consequence of previous matters, *therefore, so, consequently, thus, as a result*, etc., may be used. *However, yet, nevertheless, still*, etc., are used to introduce points that are an exception to previous statements.

There are sets of sequence signals indicating series of points of information. These sets usually have an opening signal, intermediate signals, and a closing one. There is considerable variety in these sets. Here are some examples: *First, next, then, finally. Begin, then, later, next, afterwards, at last. North, east, south* and *west. At six, at seven, at ten. One, another, the other*, etc. These series can be related to time, order, direction, etc.

When a student uses an exception signal for a consequence or an addition, we can usually mark his usage as wrong. The same is true when he uses an opening signal in the middle of a series, etc. Some of these signals can be tested effectively with the more objective techniques described earlier. Others might be approached by asking the student to write in connected style the outline of the subject of a composition. Their testing in actual compositions can be aided by having the structure of the composition with alternative permitted signals at various points outlined clearly for the scorer.

2. Style. The marks of literary style that set apart great works of art are not the responsibility of foreign language tests to discover. Literary criticism, the favor of discriminating readers, and survival over the years are part of the test of great works of art. But such matters of style as appropriateness or inappropriateness of the use of certain contractions in a friendly letter, the use of the first person pronoun, the use of colloquial language, etc., can be part of a test of writing at the advanced level. Some of these matters of style—i.e., selection of one form in preference to another that would also fit the situation linguistically—are interestingly different in each particular language or culture. The use of the first person singular in some styles of English, as when F. D. Roosevelt addressed his audience as " My friends," are a mark of friendly informality. In other languages this usage would be interpreted as excessive pride, and the first person plural would be used as a sign of being modest.

Differences in writing direct conversation, quoted conversation, or indirect speech are in part matters of style that can be tested. Differences between the style of a factual report, a friendly letter, a defense of something, etc., might be legitimately included in an advanced test of writing a foreign language. Differences between the style of poetry, as distinguished from prose, may be more properly considered in the teaching of creative writing than in the teaching and testing of the ability to write a foreign language.

Chapter 18

THE TESTING OF TRANSLATION

18.1   **TRANSLATION AS A TEST OF TRANSLATION**

Translation has been misused in foreign language testing as a test of everything connected with proficiency in a foreign language. Because of the excessive use of translation for purposes other than measuring translation itself, the attitude of this writer has been to discourage translation when other means exist to test language without translation.

The ability to translate well is an art. It requires special talent and special training. Translation is a highly complex skill of its own and will usually introduce problems as well as solve them in testing other linguistic skills.

In testing the ability to translate from and into a foreign language, however, translation tests have self-evident validity: they are performance tests. Yet, ironically, translation tests that are so common in testing other skills are not available as tests of the ability to translate. In this chapter we will discuss some of the features and considerations that might result in good tests of translation through the performance of sample translations.

18.2   **WHAT IS A GOOD TRANSLATION?**

1. Types of translation as an activity. There is considerable difference between the activity involved in (*a*) written translation and (*b*) live translation performed by interpreters.

Written translation in turn may be of two kinds: (1) factual, intended primarily to convey information with precision, and (2) literary, intended to reproduce a work of art. Factual translation is used in letters, books, magazines, newspapers, the radio, and for commercial purposes in sales booklets, instructions on the use of a product, etc. Literary translation is used in prose, poetry, the drama, and opera, which are intended not as factual reports on the originals but as literary works in their own right.

Live translation, the translation that an interpreter does directly from the speech of the original speaker, is somewhat different when performed as consecutive interpretation while the speaker is silent and when it must be done at the same time that the speaker continues to talk. This latter is known as simultaneous interpretation and is practiced in the United Nations and in other international meetings where several languages may be used by the speakers. The interpreter listens to the address and while it is in progress he renders it in another language which may be piped through earphones to members of the international gathering or to radio listeners many miles away.

2. Dimensions of goodness of fit of a translation. Regardless of the type of translation involved we could define goodness in a translation as the degree to which it reproduces the original material. This essential simplicity, however, develops into at least five dimensions which complicate the job of producing good translations and assigning scores or grades to translations. These dimensions are goodness of fit to (1) the letter and patterns of the original, (2) the meaning of the original at the sentence level, (3) the connotations of the original for its readers applied now to the readers of the translation, (4) the original as the readers understood it plus the flavor of the original language and culture for the readers of the translation, who know they are reading a translation, (5) the original in artistic effect rather than in detail, but keeping at the same time the form to adjust to music as in the translation of operas or to meter and rhyme as in the case of poetry.

For literary or scientific purposes, the first dimension, goodness of fit to the letter and patterns of the original, is the least important one. Yet in teaching the grammar of a foreign language it is sometimes very revealing to give the students literally a word-for-word translation of a pattern sentence into their mother tongue and then render it in the pattern that functionally would reproduce it.

For scientific and news reports, that is, for factual information, the second dimension of goodness of fit, the meaning of the original at the sentence level, is the relevant one. If we are translating Columbus' reports on the discovery of America we neither render them word-for-word in the Spanish patterns in which they were written nor do we substitute "ocean-going steamer" for "caravel" in a supposed attempt to equal the impression that "caravel" must have had on readers in Columbus' time. We use English sentences that convey the meaning of the Spanish sentences and we use the closest translation we can make of the words. If the translator is afraid that the closest translation of a word will have such a different connotation for the new readers that they will be misled as a result, he may choose to write a footnote telling the reader that at that time a caravel was an ocean-going ship.

In literary translation goodness of fit may preferably be (3) or (4), reproduction of the artistic effect that the original has on its readers, or this plus the awareness that this is the effect upon readers from another culture in their language. Both of these criteria can be carried too far, of course, but the border between achieving an artistic effect and producing a bad translation by going too far from the original is not easy to define. Dating of the material and cultural placement should probably not be violated, i.e., anachronisms should not be introduced in a translation in order to give the modern reader of the translation the same artistic effect the original had upon the readers of its day; and misplacement of the setting should not be introduced either. As a rule, it will produce a better translation to change some words for their functional counterpart in translation rather than to keep slavishly to the original. To achieve the impression on the readers of the translation that the artistic effect they are perceiving is that of the readers of the original, a few words may be kept in the original language or some of the patterns of the original may be retained, both of which would normally be considered bad translation.

Translation of operas and poetry, except for free verse, require adherence to the form of the music in one case and to certain forms of meter and rhyme in the other. The translator may freely change words and sentences as long as he maintains the artistic impact of the lines and the measured syllables, rhymes, and rhythm of the work of art in translation.

3. Dimensions of goodness as to quantity. Speed in the translation of a work of art as in the production of a work of art is irrelevant. How many hours it took Cervantes to write *Don Quijote de la Mancha* or how many hours it took John Ormbsy to translate it artistically into English is of no general interest. On the other hand, if a man wishes to translate letters and commercial reports as a means of livelihood, the speed with which he translates material is important. Speed in non-literary translation is then a criterion that may be tested and graded on a scale.

In both literary and non-literary translation, there is no objection to having the translator consult any and all works of reference. In the case of non-literary translation, since speed is a factor, the student who needs to make heavy use of reference material is retarded in his speed of translation and is therefore scored lower.

Live consecutive interpretation requires the ability to speak and render correctly the ideas and the style of the speakers, sometimes in a condensed form. The speed factor is greatly accentuated in simultaneous interpretation, in which fast rendition of the material is essential.

4. Problems of linguistic and cultural change. Because languages and cultures change over the centuries a translation that is superior in its time becomes less and less effective to new generations of readers. Hence the fact that great literary works have to be translated again and again. The Bible being what it is has had by far the greatest number of translations. When one must translate a book written in another age in another language, one has to study the language and the culture of the time in order to produce a good translation. Competence to do this kind of translation can be tested at least in part with objective and completion types of test items. These problems will not be discussed further. Instead, we will now consider practical means to test translation of a non-literary nature.

18.3 TESTING TRANSLATION

1. General technique. Probably the most valid and practical technique to test ability to translate is a performance test of translation. The general technique consists merely in giving the student selected sentences and paragraphs or spoken utterances to translate, and then scoring his translation.

2. Testing translation in different directions. Since translation from the native language to a foreign language is usually more difficult than the reverse type of translation, and since oral interpretation is different from written translation, a translation test may include various parts depending on the skills that are to be tested.

The most comprehensive translation test, one that would be given to a student wishing to establish his competence as a full interpreter-translator in both directions and in writing and speaking should include the following parts:

Written translation:
　Native to foreign language. Various styles.
　Foreign language to native language. Various styles.
Consecutive interpretation:
　Foreign language to native language. Various fields.
　Native language to foreign language. Various fields.
Simultaneous interpretation:
　Foreign language to native language. Various fields.
　Native language to foreign language. Various fields.

The number of people who are fully qualified in all these skills is probably not very large. And the demand for people with all of these skills is not great. In most cases there will be need for translators who are fully qualified in one or several of these skills. The interpreters that accompany heads of government in the great international meetings of this century must be outstandingly qualified in consecutive and simultaneous interpretation with a mastery of both the native and the foreign language.

The interpreters who do the simultaneous interpretation at the United Nations need to be exceptionally well qualified in simultaneous interpretation from the foreign to the native language.

Commercial translators working on translation of advertising and instructions, and translators working on the translation of magazines need to be qualified in written translation from the foreign language to the native language. Foreign language and native language are rather ambiguous terms at this stage of language testing. It is not rare to find translators who are fully qualified and work full time in translation from what to them is one foreign language to another foreign language.

3. Translation test design. Following are suggestions for a battery of translation tests covering the six operations or skills of translation between two languages. Each test of the battery is complete in itself and is intended to be of sufficient length to be reliable enough for practical use of individual scores. The design alone does not produce reliability, of course, and any test prepared to these specifications will have to be checked for reliability as would any other test.

TEST I. Written Translation from the Foreign Language to the Native Language.

Part I. One hundred items requiring the student to complete a translation already begun. Each item consists of a sentence in the foreign language and the translation of the non-crucial parts of it. The student fills the blank to complete the translation. The items test translation problems of grammatical structure, pattern selection, vocabulary, punctuation, and spelling. Each item contains preferably only one problem and is scored either right or wrong without intermediate categories.

EXAMPLE: *Es difícil saber de antemano lo que costará este puente.*
It is difficult to know beforehand what ————.

The student is expected to write "this bridge will cost" in the space provided. The response should be scored only for the subject-verb word order. Any response that has "will" or "cost" before "bridge" is wrong. Any response that has "bridge" before "will cost" or any recognizable rendition of it will be counted right. Other problems such as spelling, the proper tense, the vocabulary involved, etc., will be tested in separate items.

Part II. A two- to three-hundred word passage with approximately thirty blanks in the translation at points where sequence signals might be necessary. The original and the partial translation are given to the student.

EXAMPLE: En esto, pues, y en el desarrollo de la nueva técnica maderera, estaba el germen de un conflicto entre los dos grupos. El choque inevitable revistió todas las características de un conflicto social. De una parte, los nuevos industriales se encontraron libres para crear riqueza en cantidades hasta entonces desconocidas. Por otra parte, los que se preciaban de defensores de la cultura y la tradición rehusaron la cooperación económica de los industriales y sin embargo no hicieron nada por mantener el vigor de la cultura y la tradición. . . .

Here, ——, —— in the development of the new wood technology, was the germ of a conflict —— the two groups. —— inevitable clash took on all the characteristics of a social conflict. ————, the new industrialists found themselves free to produce wealth in hitherto unknown magnitude. ————, —— who prided themselves on being the defenders of culture and tradition refused —— economic cooperation of —— industrialists and ———— did nothing to maintain the vigor of the culture and tradition. . . .

To facilitate the scoring, duplicate blanks can be placed close to the right margin of the page, and a scoring key provided, giving the expected responses, acceptable variations, and the typical wrong responses.

Part III. Two shorter passages of about one hundred words each representing two different styles for full translation. For example, one of the passages might have samples of quoted conversation and the other might be straight exposition or description. The student is instructed to render each passage in two translations, one representing the original accurately as in a scientific report, the other a freer version capturing the flavor of the original but using where necessary different constructions and even different words. The "accurate" version is scored on the basis of mistranslations on the one hand and of foreign constructions on the other. The freer version is graded on the basis of the over-all quality of the result.

TEST II. Written Translation from the Native Language to the Foreign Language. It parallels TEST I except for the fact that the translation is in the opposite direction.

TEST III. Consecutive Interpretation from the Foreign Language to the Native Language.

Part I. One hundred short sentences for complete translation. Each sentence contains a single problem and is scored on the basis of this problem alone. The sentences are recorded on a disc or tape. After each sentence there is a pause to allow the student to produce his translation orally. A buzzer warns the student to get set for the next item. The response need not be recorded since the examiner will be able to score it at the first hearing. The test sentences will contain translation problems involving stress, intonation, vocabulary, grammatical structure and sequences. The examiner has a scoring sheet giving the expected response, permitted variations, and the typical incorrect responses. Translations are either right or wrong without intermediate categories.

Part II. Three longer utterances of perhaps 50, 75, and 100 words respectively for consecutive interpretation. Each utterance is given without interruption, preferably from a recording. A sufficiently long pause is allowed after each passage to permit the student to translate the entire passage. A buzzer warns him to get set for the next utterance even if he has not finished the previous one. The responses have to be recorded in order to make possible the rather complex scoring necessary. The translation is scored on the basis of three criteria: number of information points of the original omitted by the translator, number of points translated to mean something significantly different from the original, and foreignisms introduced in the grammar and the vocabulary of the translation. Each one of these criteria is applied by means of a scoring sheet that clearly marks in the running text or in a separate outline the specific information points considered relevant for the utterance, the typical distortions that are significantly different from the original, and the typical foreignisms. These latter two are given in addition to the correct translation and acceptable variations.

TEST IV. This test would parallel TEST III only involving translation in the opposite direction, that is, from the Native Language to the Foreign Language.

TEST V. Simultaneous Interpretation from the Foreign Language to the Native Language. This test should be an extension of TEST III, Consecutive Interpretation from the Foreign Language to the Native Language, because a student who is not able to do consecutive interpretation as tested in Part III will not be able to do simultaneous interpretation, which involves interpretation under more difficult conditions. Part I and Part II of the test may be those of TEST III, then.

Part III. This part will consist of three longer utterances in the foreign language of approximately 300 words each. The three utterances will vary in difficulty and in speed of delivery, so that one is produced at a slow but normal rate and increases in difficulty from very easy to intermediate. The second utterance is given at an average normal speed and increases in difficulty from intermediate to difficult. The third utterance is delivered at a fast but normal rate and varies in difficulty from hard to very hard.

The student records his interpretation as he listens to the original through earphones. The interpretation is scored on the basis of information points omitted, information points reported significantly wrong, and foreignisms introduced in the translation. These matters are listed for the examiner in his scoring material. The test is intended to find a level where the student can no longer go on with the translation. If this occurs as expected, the remaining scoring points are all marked as missed. This design is somewhat on the pattern of the Stanford-Binet Intelligence Test.

TEST VI. Simultaneous Interpretation from the Native to the Foreign Language. The same as TEST V only in reverse.

Since these are purely theoretical designs never put to practical use, it is expected that the design would be varied and improved if a translation battery were to be produced.

Chapter 19

TESTING OVER-ALL CONTROL OF THE LANGUAGE

19.1   HOW WELL DOES HE KNOW THE LANGUAGE?

In Part II we dealt with tests of the various elements of language. Each chapter attempted to answer questions such as "How well does he pronounce and hear the sounds?" "Does he recognize the grammatical signals and does he use them properly?" "Does he understand an adequate vocabulary and can he use it?" Part III deals with similar questions regarding listening, reading, speaking, writing, and translating as separate skills. In all of these, we came upon the central factor, language. It is also possible and relevant to ask the general question, "How well does the student know the language?"

This question in the present context would imply absence of specific interest in any one of the separate elements of language or any one of the separate skills as discussed. It also implies that language being the central factor in the elements and skills, a test of language would also give us at least a rough estimate of mastery of the elements and some of the skills.

19.2   OBJECTIVE, PAPER-AND-PENCIL TECHNIQUES TO TEST CONTROL OF THE LANGUAGE

1. "New type" tests. The early "new type" foreign language tests were attempts to measure achievement in the foreign language as a whole. The Cooperative tests in French, German, Latin, and Spanish are representative.[1] Their design was based on reading comprehension, vocabulary recognition, and grammatical usage. Revised versions included a section on the culture

---

[1] Cooperative Test Division, Educational Testing Service, Princeton, N.J.

of the people that spoke the language. This section was in the native language of the students and dealt with the geography and historical accomplishments of the culture. The *Cooperative Spanish Test* (1948, 1950) for example, has three parts. Part I contains 50 Spanish words, each with five numbered English meanings; 10 Spanish idioms, each in a Spanish sentence and with five Spanish paraphrases as alternatives; and 9 to 10 paragraphs with multiple-choice items to check comprehension. Part II consists of 50 English sentences followed by multiple Spanish translations one of which is the best. Part III consists of 50 multiple-choice items in English about Spanish culture.

With the growing interest in aural-oral skills in foreign language teaching, separate tests of aural comprehension have been developed in the Cooperative Test series. These will be mentioned in a section on achievement tests using auditory techniques.

2. The Cooperative Inter-American Tests[1] which are in part achievement tests in English and in Spanish as foreign languages test also reading comprehension, vocabulary, and grammatical usage. These tests added a novel feature in vocabulary by providing incomplete choices that require active recall of the item in context rather than passive recognition of the word in isolation. The design of the pertinent tests of this series is the following: READING: Part I, Vocabulary consisting of 65 sentences with an omitted key word which the student selects from four alternatives. Part II, Comprehension, made up of 57 multiple-choice items testing comprehension of sixteen paragraphs. LANGUAGE USAGE: Part I, Active Vocabulary. Sixty-five sentences with the key word omitted. The student thinks of the key word and checks his selection against incomplete choices in multiple-choice design. Part II, Expression. Forty-nine items of three sentences from which the student selects the one that constitutes best usage.

3. An early design that introduced pronunciation as a full-fledged part of a paper-and-pencil test is that of the **English Language Test for Foreign Students.**[2] It consisted of separate sections on grammatical structure, pronunciation of consonants and

---

[1] *Ibid.*, 1950.
[2] R. Lado (Ann Arbor: George Wahr Publishing Co.), 1951.

vowels, word stress, and recognition vocabulary, including two-word verbs. The distribution is as follows: Part I, Grammatical Structure, through meaning rather than correctness. Forty multiple-choice items. Part II, Section 1, Consonants and Vowels, through comparison with other consonants and vowels in the context. Forty items. Section 2, Word Stress. Fourteen items. Part III, Vocabulary Recognition, in sentence context. Forty items.

4. The most complete paper-and-pencil test now in use is the **Examination for the Certificate of Proficiency in English.**[1] A new form of this test is produced each year for use in a program of English certification abroad. These forms vary slightly in design from year to year but they have sections and parts as follows:

Part I.   Consonants and vowels.

Part II.   Word stress.

Part III.   Sentence stress and intonation.

Part IV.   Sentence comprehension (Grammatical structure).

Part V.   Continuing a Conversation (Grammatical structure).

Part VI.   Active vocabulary in sentence context.

Part VII.   Recognition vocabulary in sentence context.

Part VIII. Reading comprehension.

The total number of items ranges from 196 to 235. Testing time is approximately two hours.

5. **A full design possible at present.** By bringing together the best paper-and-pencil techniques described in the various chapters above we now have the tools and the knowledge to develop highly effective tests of over-all control of a foreign language. One of several promising designs might be as follows:

Part I.   Consonants and vowels. Twenty items.

Part II.   Word stress. Twenty items.

Part III.   Context stress. Ten items.

Part IV.   Intonation. Ten items.

Part V.   Spelling. Ten items.

[1] R. Lado *et al.* (Ann Arbor: English Language Institute, 1954–). Not available for use outside the certification program.

Part VI.   Punctuation. Ten items.

Part VII.   Grammatical structure. Sentence comprehension. Twenty items.

Part VIII.   Grammatical structure. Partial production. Twenty items.

Part IX.   Vocabulary recognition in sentence context. Twenty items.

Part X.   Active vocabulary in sentence context. Twenty items.

Part XI.   Reading comprehension. Seven paragraphs. Twenty items.

Part XII.   Translation from the foreign language. Twenty items. Partial production type.

This represents a 200-item test that can be administered in approximately two hours. By careful statistical study of the performance of each part and each item, it might be possible to eliminate a number of items, leaving the remaining ones spaced more widely apart in difficulty. If any part turns out to be very highly correlated with some other part, it may be possible to eliminate it without serious loss of reliability or validity. With these refinements it might be possible to shorten the test to a one-hour paper-and-pencil instrument.

The separate scores on each part of the test would in all likelihood not be reliable enough for interpretation of individual scores beyond very rough estimates at the ends of the scale for each.

19.3   AUDITORY TESTS TO SUPPLEMENT LANGUAGE BATTERIES

If adequate equipment and rooms are available it is considered more valid to add to a set of paper tests one of aural or auditory comprehension. The Cooperative foreign language tests have added one of aural comprehension to their battery. The *English Examination for Foreign Students*[1] has a full aural comprehension part. The English Language Institute administers an aural comprehension test as part of its battery of English language

---

[1] Educational Testing Service, 1947.

tests.[1] The rationale for the construction of tests of auditory comprehension has been fully discussed in the appropriate chapter.

19.4 ORAL PRODUCTION AS PART OF A FOREIGN LANGUAGE TEST BATTERY

The inclusion of oral production as part of an examination to determine a student's general proficiency in a foreign language is generally considered of importance. The usual practice is to have a more or less formal interview with the student and to rate on a scale of some kind his ability to speak. This is the practice followed in the Examination for the Certificate of Proficiency in English.[1] A more reliable practice would be to include a short test of oral production of the type discussed in the appropriate chapter.

[1] Test of Aural Comprehension, 1946, 1957. R. Lado. (Ann Arbor, English Language Institute.)
[2] R. Lado *et al., op. cit.*

PART IV

BEYOND LANGUAGE

Chapter 20

HOW TO TEST CROSS-CULTURAL
UNDERSTANDING

20.1 CULTURE AND THE STUDY OF LANGUAGE

One cannot learn a foreign language well unless he learns something of the experience and beliefs of the people who use that language natively. This is readily understood and admitted when we put it in time perspective and say that we cannot read Cervantes with full understanding unless we know something of Cervantes' time. We understand this fact also when two cultures are very different from each other. A western man will not understand Japanese well unless he knows something of Japan and the Japanese people. Without this knowledge we will not understand or will actually misunderstand constant references, overt and implied, to their historical accomplishments, heroes, works of art, folk tales, customs, etc.

The relevance and educational value of studying the culture of a people in the sense of their outstanding contributions to art, literature, and the history of civilization has long been highly regarded in teaching foreign languages. Knowledge of a culture in this sense has been tested in various ways and offers no particular difficulty. It has also been tested in objective type items in the Cooperative foreign language tests which have a full section on the culture of the particular language being tested.

There is another sense in which culture is relevant to full understanding of a language. This other view of culture is not to be considered in conflict with or in any sense a substitute for the study of the culture of a people as their outstanding achievements. It is rather a necessary adjunct to full understanding of these achievements and the language of that people. This aspect of culture has not been sufficiently well understood in teaching and has not even been touched in testing. The present chapter deals with the clarification of this view of culture and means of testing it.

20.2   WHAT IS CROSS-CULTURAL UNDERSTANDING?

A. Assumptions and definitions.

1. *Unity of the human race.* In the discussions of this chapter there is a basic assumption of and belief in the unity of all mankind. All races have the same origin and are capable of the same emotions and the same needs encompassing the whole range of human experience from hunger and the craving for food to theological inquiry and the seeking of God.

2. *Cultural diversity of man.* Within this genetic unity of mankind, different groups or communities of people have evolved different ways of life which facilitate their own in-group interrelations but at the same time set them apart from other groups. When these ways of life are sufficiently different from others they constitute separate cultures.

3. *Defining a culture.* A culture, as used here, is synonymous with "the ways of a people," and not with refinement or broad learning. As the ways of a people a culture is not a haphazard conglomeration of actions but specific ways of doing things, showing organization or structure for any group of people. The way Spanish people live, for example, shows organization of behavior, a system of actions, which is different in many ways from the system of behavior of the people of Japan or the United States. We can say that a culture is a structured system of actions or behavior.

Although each action is a unique event, and therefore different from all other actions, for any given culture these actions fall

276

into frames or patterns which have characteristic identifying features. A culture might be defined as *a structured system of patterned behavior.* This definition attempts to describe human cultures as they exist; it does not attempt to invent culture. If a culture, identifiable as such, does not fit into this definition or summary statement, it is assumed that the definition is wrong, not the culture; the definition merely summarizes our understanding of what a culture is.

Cultural anthropologists, or ethnologists, are engaged in the study of cultures. A definition of culture by them should be of interest to us. The following is such a definition which in addition offers the advantage of having been selected and elaborated by one of the leading anthropologists of the United States:

> Cultural anthropologists, during the last twenty-five years, have gradually moved from an atomistic definition of culture, describing it as a more or less haphazard collection of traits, to one which emphasizes pattern and configuration. Kluckhohn and Kelly perhaps best express this modern concept of culture when they define it as "all those historically created designs for living explicit and implicit, rational, irrational, and non-rational, which exist at any given time as potential guides for the behavior of men." Traits, elements, or, better, patterns of culture in this definition are organized or structured into a system or set of systems, which, because it is historically created, is therefore open and subject to constant change.[1]

4. *Inability of natives to describe their own culture.* As an example that could be duplicated in other settings, let us take a visitor that goes to the United States to study the "American" way of life or United States culture. But what do the hosts show him? The average adult in the United States is aware of the industrial might of his country so the hosts show the visitor an automobile assembly line if possible, and they show the tourist attractions in the city. They will find a way to tell him the favorable generalities that they have been taught about themselves, which may happen to be the same favorable generalities he too

[1] Harry Hoijer, "The Relation of Language to Culture," in *Anthropology Today* (ed. A. L. Kroeber, Chicago: University of Chicago Press, 1953), p. 554.

may have learned about himself and his culture. Occasionally someone may criticize a thing or two, or everything. But the fact remains that we are rather helpless to interpret ourselves accurately and to describe what we do. Much of what we do is governed by our habits, acquired almost unnoticed from our elders and our cultural environment.

Our inability to describe our cultural ways parallels our inability to describe our language unless we have made a special study of it. The paradox is that we are able to use the complex structure that is our language with astonishing ease and flexibility, yet when someone asks us when to use *between* and *among*, for example, we are apt to tell him the most surprising fiction, believing we are telling the truth. Similarly we may be able to tie a bow tie with speed and ease, but the moment someone asks us to explain what we do, we become thoroughly confused and may give him false information. For example, in the United States we pride ourselves in being "free" and often tell our foreign visitors that we can do as we please, but at the same time we may demand that our student visitors attend classes regularly, a restriction that is considered an invasion of personal freedom in some countries. Although verbalizations about patterns of behavior are often inaccurate, they are nevertheless part of a culture, and our definition of culture must be understood to include, therefore, both what people say and believe about their culture and what they actually do.

B. Functioning units of culture.

For the purpose of testing cross-cultural understanding it is not sufficient to describe a few over-all characteristic traits of a culture. Such information would be of value in combating false cliches, but even if all false cliches were exploded we would not necessarily achieve cross-cultural understanding. We need much more specific information on how people do specific things and what those things mean. We need to refer to specific patterns of culture.

And these patterns are made up of subordinate patterns or sub-units. Having orange juice, coffee, fried eggs, and white toast one morning and grape-fruit juice, coffee, scrambled eggs, and whole wheat toast the next morning would usually be considered in the United States two occurrences of the same unit of behavior: eating breakfast. Yet they are different. The mold or design by which the act of eating becomes breakfast is the unit. This unit can be part of a larger unit, such as having a meeting to discuss something at breakfast, where breakfast is only the setting. Or it can itself be the large unit made up of smaller substitutable elements such as performer, act, objects, setting, time, manner, purpose, etc. These elements, though always unique and always different, are identified as "sames" and "differents" through cultural molds which are themselves patterns.

C. Form, meaning, and distribution.

These functioning units of culture, these patterns which constitute the designs that together are a culture, have form, meaning, and distribution.

1. *Form.* The forms of these patterns of culture are identified functionally on inspection by the members of that culture, although the same individuals may not be able to define accurately the very forms they identify. We can describe breakfast by observing a representative number of occurrences of breakfast and by noting the contrasts with those occurrences which resemble breakfast but are identified as lunch, dinner, a snack, or supper by natives.

2. *Meanings.* Like form, meanings are culturally determined at least in part. They represent an analysis of the universe as grasped in culture. Patterned forms have a complex of meanings, some representing features of a unit or process or quality, some grasped as primary, others as secondary, tertiary, etc. Eating breakfast, lunch, and dinner are engaged in usually as providing food and drink for the body. We say then that breakfast, lunch, and dinner usually have that primary meaning. In addition a particular form of breakfast at a particular time or day may have a meaning of good or bad on a moral or religious scale, on a health scale, on an economic scale, etc. A particular form of breakfast may carry as secondary meaning a social class identification, a national origin identification, a religious identification.

In short, any of the distinctions and groupings of a culture may be part of the meaning of a particular form unit.

3. *Distribution.* All of these meaningful units of form are distributed in patterned ways. Their distribution patterns are complexes involving various time cycles, space locations, and positions in relation to other units. Breakfast, for example, shows time distribution on a daily cycle, a weekly cycle, and a yearly cycle as well. Breakfast shows a space or location distribution. It is also distributed after some units of behavior and preceding others.

Form, meaning, and distribution probably do not exist independent of each other in a culture, but they are spoken of operationally here as separate. Forms are relevant when they have meaning; meaning presupposes a form in order to be of relevance to us here; and meaningful forms always occur in patterned distribution.

Within a culture we can assume that when an individual observes a significant patterned form in a patterned distribution spot, it will have a complex of culturally patterned meanings for him. Breakfast in the kitchen at 7 a.m., served by the same person who eats it, and including coffee, fruit juice, and cereal, will have a different complex of meanings than breakfast in bed at 11 a.m. served by a formally dressed waiter, and including caviar and other trimmings. The observation of this form may occur directly, indirectly through still photography or drawings, the motion picture, television, etc., or indirectly again by means of a language report.

D. Cross-cultural understanding and biculturalism.

If, within the above view of culture, an individual can identify the forms, meanings and distribution of behavior in another culture, we say that he understands that culture. With understanding he will be able to interpret accurately what people do in that culture; he will be able to interpret their behavior when he observes it directly or when he observes it through language, motion pictures, newspapers, and other means of reporting human activity. If, with or without understanding, a person learns to function in the other culture, to act so that his actions have the meanings intended, we can say that he has become bicultural. Presumably a person can become bicultural without full understanding, just as natives can function in their culture without understanding it.

20.3 PROBLEMS OF CROSS-CULTURAL UNDERSTANDING

1. **Habit as a major factor.** The patterns that permit unique occurrences to operate as sames within a culture do not develop for operation across cultures. Within a culture they operate with great ease as a result of their repeated use. When they are fully acquired by the growing child, they become deep-seated habits largely below the threshold of conscious thought.

2. **Not a tabula rasa.** When an individual of one culture comes in contact with another culture he does not learn its patterns as he did his native ones. In learning his native culture we could assume a *tabula rasa* in which the native patterns gradually impress themselves. In learning a foreign culture his native patterns are already impressed in his system and will interfere with or facilitate learning the new ones.

3. **Transfer.** From observation of behavior in contact across two cultures, and by analogy to language transfer, we assume that the individual transfers his native culture system to the foreign culture when in contact with it. We assume that when an individual of culture A observes a form in culture B in a particular distribution spot, he grasps the same complex of meaning as he does in his own culture. When the form in culture B is not present in his own culture he will nevertheless tend to interpret it as one of the forms of his native culture. We further assume that when he engages actively in a unit of behavior in culture B he chooses the form which he would choose in his own culture to achieve that complex of meaning. In other words, he will use his native patterns both productively and receptively.

4. **Problems of production or active participation.** We have drawn a difference between understanding—identifying or interpreting the patterns of a culture—and active participation—being able to function in that culture. The distinction is a necessary one even though the two are closely integrated into one system.

In production we assumed that the individual goes from a "complex of meaning," including purpose, to a form—an action or abstention from action. When the form, meaning, and distribution of a pattern are functionally the same in the native and the foreign cultures, we have facilitation, and the individual seems to "learn" that pattern in the foreign culture with great ease. He actually does not learn it but merely transfers it from his native culture. When the form, meaning, distribution, or a combination of these are functionally different in the two cultures there will be a learning problem.

These learning problems vary greatly in difficulty depending on the nature of the difference. We can classify the problems in four main types:

(1) The meaning is "same" but the form is different in the two cultures. The individual will use his native culture form and will therefore be misunderstood. Within this type, we further note that

    (*a*) if there is a form in his native stock that is similar to the foreign culture form, the learning problem is to establish a new association between the meaning and the form. Or

    (*b*) if the new form is not available in the native culture, the learning problem is both to learn the new form *and* to associate it with the meaning.

(2) The meaning and the form are the same but the pattern shows different distribution.

(3) The meaning is the same but the form and distribution are different.

(4) The meanings are not equatable in the two cultures because the meaning in one culture does not exist in the other or it is so differently limited that it can be said not to exist in the other culture.

(5) Different meanings attached to what can be said to be the same form in the two cultures.

5. Problems of recognition or interpretation. Recognition is identification and interpretation of the meaning of cultural behavior. The individual observes a form in another culture and draws a complex of meaning from it which is culturally the same meaning as another individual of the same culture would draw.

As in production, when the patterns have the same form, meaning, and distribution, there is facilitation. Problems arise in the following cases:

(1) Same form but different meaning. Under different meaning we recognize either a meaning in the experience of the observer but not associated with that form in the native pattern, or a meaning not in his experience.

(2) Same form, same meaning, different distribution. The pattern may be non-operative in a situation in which it is in force in the native culture. Or there may be different quantities in various environments as compared with the native culture.

(3) Strange form—A form not in the experience of the individual.

6. Structural comparison of cultures to predict learning problems. From the above considerations it should be clear that the problems of cross-cultural understanding arise from structural differences in the two cultural systems. Therefore, we need to compare the two cultures systematically. We need a structural comparison, taking up at least the major patterns of behavior in regard to their form, meaning, and distribution in order to predict and describe the learning and testing problems.

20.4   HOW TO TEST CROSS-CULTURAL UNDERSTANDING

1. Describing cross-cultural understanding as opposed to testing it. Before we can test cross-cultural understanding we must know with precision what the problems of understanding are, since it is these problems that we seek to test. Furthermore, before we can list the problems of cross-cultural understanding, we must know what the cultural patterns of the two cultures are. In studying cultures, anthropologists use two main tools: observation and interview. The additional use of questionnaires and psychological tests is marginal at present. The anthropologist deals with objects and events or behavior. He observes at length, and he interviews at length, to discover the patterns of the culture which he assumes are there.

Our problem in attempting to test cross-cultural understanding is different in several ways. (1) In testing, we do not have to discover the patterns, we assume they are known from previous research. We attempt to find out if an individual of another culture knows them, i.e., if he has learned them. (2) Since we are in a pedagogical situation, we do not have unrestricted time to test each individual but must strive for group testing, preferably within a period of one or two hours. (3) Because of the time limitation, we cannot observe the individual as he acts in the foreign culture but must resort to verbal techniques in highly concentrated form to permit quick coverage of a large sample of the problems of cross-cultural understanding. (4) Again because of the time factor and the pedagogical purpose, the questionnaire technique seems impractical, since evaluation of questionnaires is a delicate and time consuming matter. We will restrict ourselves to objective testing techniques.

2. Validity of objective techniques. Can we rely on "objective" techniques to test cross-cultural understanding? Will the subjects not answer what they think will please us rather than what they actually think? Will they give the "real" answers since they are on guard because we are testing them?

Our definition of cross-cultural understanding is needed at this point. Cross-cultural understanding is the knowledge of what people of a culture do and what it means, i.e., what function it has in the culture. Cross-cultural understanding does not mean a guarantee that the individual of another culture will like or dislike that way of doing things or that he will or will not do things that way himself if permitted. Cross-cultural understanding in itself does not show moral valence. It can be used to promote sympathetically the welfare of the foreign culture or it can be used to attempt its destruction more effectively. To attempt to control the use made of cross-cultural understanding by an individual is a different problem from testing his cross-cultural understanding.

In the above sense, then, we are testing knowledge, and knowledge can be tested objectively. And as a matter of fact, lack of understanding of a culture cannot be covered up in taking a properly devised objective test. The individual may choose what he thinks we want him to choose, but unless he knows the culture he may choose the wrong thing.

A further consideration adds validity to our testing point of view regarding cross-cultural understanding. When we give a test of cross-cultural understanding, as with other educational tests, the student is usually interested in obtaining a high score. Thus we are assured of his desire to give the right answers. If then he fails to give the right answers, we are justified in concluding that he does not know them. When test items have been properly screened for extraneous factors, we can infer that missing a number of items means lack of understanding of the other culture.

In anthropological interviews, on the other hand, the investigator has to guard against wilful deceit on the part of the informant for any number of possible reasons. He must also guard against false statements made naively by the informant. The anthropologist does not know the answers himself; he is seeking to discover them. He protects his findings by using multiple informants and by checking for internal consistency in the data he obtains, but he cannot completely overcome a margin of error introduced by the fact that he does not know the answers when he begins. In testing, we assume that the patterns have been discovered, and we try to find out if an individual who wants to know them actually knows them.

3. Techniques. If understanding is knowledge that can be applied in interpreting another culture, we can use a variety of objective techniques to test understanding. The following are some samples which may be productive:

Same versus different. At the heart of all human knowledge lies the ability to identify things which are same and things which are different. Cultural sames and differents are not physical sames and differents. If in the native culture two forms of behavior have the same function but in the foreign culture they have different functions, there will be a problem of understanding. A same versus different technique might test this as follows: Three actions are described, two of which are different in the foreign culture but the same in the native one. The subject is asked which of the three actions are the same. For example:

> You are in a small village of southern Spain. Which of these situations are equally normal everyday occurrences without a special meaning?
> You attempt to visit three persons and all three are in bed resting so you cannot see them just then.
>> (A) The first person is resting in bed at six in the morning.
>> (B) The second person is resting in bed at two in the afternoon.
>> (C) The third person is resting in bed at six in the evening.

The expected answer would be A and B, since they would fit the normal rest pattern there. "C" is different. It would mean something special: an illness, or a person who works at night for example.

Multiple choice. If the problem is caused by the same form with a different function we can use a multiple-choice technique in which one of the choices represents the meaning of that form in the native culture but not in the foreign one, where it becomes a wrong choice. Another choice must be the meaning of that form in the foreign culture, that is, the right choice. A third alternative should be a distractor that seems plausible from the context but is not right. A fourth and a fifth might also be incorrect meanings induced from the context. A simple example will illustrate the technique.

Situation A: A soccer match is in progress in Spain. There is a moment of fast action in front of one of the goals. Most of the spectators stand up and WHISTLE LOUDLY. They are:

> (1) showing enthusiastic approval of the play.
> (2) showing displeasure.
> (3) showing relief after a moment of danger.
> (4) asking for a repetition; more of the same.
> (5) signaling the end of the game.

The expected answer is "(2) showing displeasure." Since in the United States the same action might mean a form of enthusiastic approval, an American not familiar with that action in Spain would be tempted to choose "(1) showing enthusiastic approval of the play" thus revealing lack of understanding of that item of behavior.

In the sample item the testing is achieved by alternatives that refer to the primary meaning of the action. The same multiple-choice technique could be used with alternatives that labeled the action as normal, or special in its meaning. The particular situation of the sample item does not lend itself to this check because whistling at a sports event would not be considered unusual in either culture. Eating breakfast under the conditions described earlier could be tested by choices labeling it normal, special, not practiced, etc. in the alternatives. Following is an example involving the mid-day meal in Spain:

> It was spring again in Madrid, March 21, and a cheerful sun filtered through the window. The large clock in the dining-room struck the half hour. "Two thirty," said father, "and the food looks good."

The time of this meal is:
    (1) normal everyday time.
    (2) special occasion time.
    (3) not Spanish.

The expected response is "(1) normal everyday time."

In some cultures there is a social and economic distinction between wooden houses on the one hand and stone, concrete, or brick houses on the other. Wooden houses tend to be the shacks that belong to the lower socio-economic groups. In the United States wooden frame houses can be as luxurious and expensive as any other. Below is an item that attempts to test misunderstanding due to this difference. The distance of a house from the center of a city is also viewed differently in the United States and in other cultures. It is an additional distractor in the item.

> The Smith family live in a wooden frame house very far from the center of Detroit, Michigan, where the father works. It takes him an hour to get to work every morning and an hour to get home in the evening.

These circumstances indicate that this family

(1) is rather poor.

(2) is rather rich.

(3) could be rich or poor.

The best alternative is "(3)" since in effect a well-to-do family as well as a poor one might very naturally live in a wooden frame home away from the center of the city.

Since full-time maids are as a rule no longer to be found among middle-class families in the United States, the following item might test functional understanding of this fact.

Mrs. Jones telephoned an employment agency and said that she wanted to interview some maids to replace hers who was getting married. "How many days a week did you want her?" the agency asked. "Full time, and she will live in. The maid's quarters are very adequate," Mrs. Jones replied.

These circumstances indicate that the Jones family probably

(1) are poor, lower-class people.

(2) are average, middle-class people.

(3) are rich people.

(4) could be average middle-class or rich.

The best alternative is "(3)."

These have been rather trivial problems chosen for their ease in illustrating the possibility of testing cross-cultural understanding objectively. More subtle problems that interfere with full understanding of a culture and its language are quite pervasive and far-reaching.

20.5   BIBLIOGRAPHICAL NOTES

In matters concerned with anthropology and cultural anthropology the writer found helpful the volume *Anthropology Today, An Encyclopedic Inventory*, edited by A. L. Kroeber (The University of Chicago Press, 1953.)

The main source of method and grasp of the problem comes from the attempt to understand culture on the model of the structure of language. The volume *Language in Culture, Conference on the Interrelations of Language and Other Aspects of Culture*, edited by Harry Hoijer (The University of Chicago

Press, 1954) critically evaluates the extreme position of Benjamin Lee Whorf regarding the relation of language and culture.

The role of cultural understanding in the teaching of language is discussed by Charles C. Fries in a chapter on "Contextual Orientation," in *Teaching and Learning English as a Foreign Language* (Ann Arbor: The University of Michigan Press, 1945).

Anthropological studies of a variety of cultures are numerous. For the non-anthropologist *Cultural Patterns and Technical Change*, edited by Margaret Mead, and *Patterns of Culture* by Ruth Benedict are readable and revealing.

Chapter 21

TESTING THE HIGHER VALUES

21.1   **ARE THERE HIGHER VALUES?**

We have thus far dealt with languages as signaling systems and with testing languages as testing the practical control of those systems. But no thoughtful teacher of foreign languages would want to say that the only value in learning a language is the practical control of it as a signaling system, valuable as this accomplishment is. Other and higher values are assumed to result from the proper study of another language.

These higher values usually remain in vague undefined terms not only in our defense of the teaching of foreign languages but in our very thinking. Yet if they are important values they should be clarified and if possible they should be tested to see if our teaching has produced them along with the control of the language as a signaling system.

Do these values exist and if they do what are they? The evidence is not of the same kind as that of linguistics itself. We do not have minimal test frames readily available for the higher values. Yet the fact that the study of languages has in so many cultures, and particularly in Western Civilization, formed a central part of the education of scholars and those who would be educated may be evidence that thoughtful men have seen important values in learning foreign languages. Perhaps we cannot be certain that any value beyond language will be attained, but we can be reasonably sure that those values exist and that they have been sought in the study of foreign languages through the ages. We can also be certain that they have been attained often enough to keep alive the faith in the study of foreign languages of those who seek education for themselves and for those who are entrusted to their care.

Since we cannot be certain that every language class produces these additional values, it is important that they should be tested. And since mysterious intangible values cannot be tested, they must somehow be made real and tangible. We cannot hope at this stage of our knowledge of human behavior to lay bare these higher values with anything like the clarity now possible in the analysis of language, but we should strive to clarify them as much as possible.

21.2   WHAT ARE THE HIGHER VALUES AND CAN THEY BE TESTED?

We will mention four values related to foreign language study that seem to lie beyond mere mastery of a signaling system.

1. Education itself. Perhaps the highest value that learning a foreign language can produce is education itself. There are the outward signs of education and the inner qualities and wisdom of the educated person. For centuries men have sought the outward signs of education and the inner content. Knowing Latin and Greek, and later knowing French and in some cultures knowing Spanish, German, Arabic, and later English and now other languages have been considered essential marks of education. But the contributions of the study of foreign languages to the inner content of education are of greater interest to us.

What is education? To educate is to develop the complex potentialities of a human personality. One of the most precious of these potentialities is the ability to think, freely, constructively, and accurately. Adult human thinking is inextricably bound up in language, and language allows freedom in some dimensions and enslaves in others. A person who knows only his native language and that without insightful analysis knows less what parts of his thinking are determined and bound by the system of his language and which are his own choices than a person of equal capacity who has mastered a foreign language. Other things being equal, the unsophisticated monolingual is more apt to falsely assume that everything he thinks is entirely his own and is universal, final, and correct than the person who has studied and learned a foreign language.

Testing such a statement is not easy of course. Language

learning is not the only way to achieve freedom to think. And such freedom is not easily measured regardless of how it is achieved. We do notice that this freedom to think without error outside our own language frame is not found equally distributed among individuals. We can attempt to test these differences in their relation to the native language. We can set out to test whether or not the person who studies and masters a foreign language does in fact acquire a certain amount of freedom to grasp reality not only in the set grooves of his language but in other ways as well.

We may make statements in which inferences based on the native language are incorrectly projected to other cultures or historical periods. The student can be asked to point out possible inaccuracies and give his evidence for suspecting that they are inaccuracies. The same students can be tested at the beginning of their study of a foreign language and after a given period of such study. Their increase in freedom to think beyond their native language patterns could then be compared with the increase for others who do not study a foreign language and for those who study foreign languages under different conditions.

Richness of individual meanings beyond the basic information taught every member of a community is part of the inner content of education. What cultures teach their members about foreign languages is usually very limited and often more in the nature of a caricature than information. A person that studies a foreign language well will have a richer experience and individual meaning of that foreign language and of all other foreign languages. This statement can probably be tested not only for the foreign language studied by students but for other foreign languages as well. The test might consist simply of various statements regarding the nature of foreign languages and of particular foreign languages.

2. Insight into own language. To achieve a fuller understanding of one's own language it is almost essential to learn a foreign language. This does not mean that the study of Latin grammar will help an English-speaking student to write without split infinitives or dangling participles or without spelling errors. This is a narrow gauge interpretation of the value of the study of a foreign language for the understanding of one's own language. Understanding means fuller appreciation, perspective, and feeling for its creativeness.

In this sense the value of the study of a foreign language in depth is almost self-evident. As we learn that in Chinese, for example, "difference" is expressed as 'black-white,' the "universe" as 'heaven-earth,' "speed" as 'fast-slow,' "switch" as 'open-shut' we more readily recognize the effect of metaphors in the continuing evolution of our own language. As we discover that the Spanish word *que* can mean 'who,' 'whom,' 'which,' 'that,' 'what,' 'as,' 'one who,' 'those who,' 'one whom,' 'those whom,' 'that which,' 'when,' 'how,' 'to,' 'than,' 'because,' 'since,' 'for,' 'and,' we will be better able to realize that in our own language we also use words in a great variety of meanings.

Having studied and learned to use the inflectional devices that signal 'actor,' 'action,' and 'undergoer' in Latin or in Old English we will have the perspective to grasp more fully the significance of word order signals in present-day English.

It may be argued that language perspective and maturity do not necessarily result from the study of a foreign language. It remains, however, that when properly taught, the foreign languages are probably the most effective means of achieving that perspective and maturity in the grasp of one's own language that constitutes richness of understanding.

The study of language as a general subject rather than a foreign language may also contribute to the achievement of language perspective, the study of a course in language would be hollow and meaningless if it did not use an abundance of specific phenomena from a variety of languages. And here again, the teaching of such a subject would not in itself insure the desired result without the proper orientation. As a matter of fact, the study of language without the actual study of a foreign language can easily remain a dry uninspiring experience without sufficient educative impact to justify it; and at the same time the study of a foreign language without observing the significance of its linguistic phenomena may become more training than education.

Can this language sophistication or perspective be measured?

It seems possible, at least in part. The various erroneous views of language and of the native language of the students that are so widely held can be presented in the form of specific statements of fact which the student is asked to mark as either "true" or "false." One such statement might be "To pronounce English correctly we must pronounce every letter as written." Another, "English is a grammarless tongue."

3. Insight into a foreign culture. Another educational value derivable from the proper study of a foreign language is a greater understanding of and insight into another culture. The lack of this insight can result in cultural provincialism. If the language is taught with relation to its cultural setting the student will acquire a broader cultural horizon even as he learns the language itself. To understand another people means to grasp their patterns of behavior and their values in their own terms rather than in ours. This is what broadens our cultural horizons, not merely to add a few curious facts about another people in the system of values of our own culture—and we do not mean here that we must adopt their values or consider them superior or inferior to our own.

The usual argument that information about another culture can be obtained just as well by the study of translations from its literary works is weak on two counts. To understand a foreign people through one's own native language is indeed a difficult task. First, one will tend to interpret the foreign culture in terms of the values that its patterns would have in one's own, because of the intimate associations between our language and our culture. And second, the assumption that the works of another culture will be found in our language is naively optimistic. What is translated is often determined by economic considerations. Will there be a wide enough audience to make it economical to translate and publish? And in modern times, what is translated is often what governments or groups wish to disseminate as propaganda. If one is interested in things that do not appeal to the masses he may have to seek his own translator, which represents an expense that most readers cannot afford. And if one wishes to make his own selection of the works he will read in another language, he cannot wait for translations supplied by the propaganda agencies of this century. In other words, to depend on translations is to have no freedom in this respect. On the other hand, the person who masters the foreign language is set free to choose and to interpret what is of importance to him.

Can we measure the insight into another culture that we claim will result from the proper study of foreign languages? In each culture there are folk misrepresentations of other cultures and of foreign cultures in general. If we present these in multiple-choice items containing also true statements about the foreign cultures we should be able to determine whether or not those who have studied foreign languages show greater understanding or less misunderstanding.

4. Insight into own culture. A fourth and perhaps less tangible value of learning a foreign language in its proper cultural setting is a corollary of the third, that of gaining insight into the foreign culture. If such insight is achieved, and in the degree that it is achieved, we will gain perspective of our own native culture. One who has never glimpsed any other way of doing things except his own will tend to think of his own patterns as the only way to live. He will be less aware of those patterns in his behavior which are bound by cultural habit and those in which he has varying degrees of freedom of choice than if through the study of a foreign language he has succeeded in understanding at least in part the patterns of behavior of another people. In short, he will know himself less by not knowing those who are culturally different from him.

Testing cultural perspective and maturity is not simple. Cultures have not been analyzed with the precision achieved in language analysis, and we will not as readily agree therefore that a certain specimen of behavior is or is not culturally determined. We can, however, select items which are in all probability cultur-ally determined, write some of them with explanations that are not cultural, and ask the students if such statements are true or false. For example, we can write, "We drive on the right side of the street because, being right-handed, we control the car better from the right side of the road." Another example might be, "We write from left to right on the page because it is easier for us due to the shape of our hand and fingers."

Another approach might be to make statements that do not restrict the content to what is actually true, and we can ask the students to label the statements as true or false. For example, "We are free to do what we please in the United States."

5. Attitude toward minority groups. Also related to the understanding of foreign cultures is the problem of attitudes toward minority groups in places where two cultures exist side by side. Groups such as the Spanish speakers of the Southwest of the United States, French speakers of Louisiana, Pennsylvania Dutch, the Welsh people of Great Britain, the American Indians of the Americas, and hundreds upon hundreds of other groups who find themselves as cultural minorities enclosed in larger linguistic areas, have traditionally suffered from lack of appreciation and understanding on the part of the politically dominant community and corresponding hostility on the part of the submerged group. In such cases, there usually develops a folklore of misrepresentations that builds a wall of separation which breeds further misunderstanding and warps the personalities of both the dominant and the submerged groups. In such communities, the study of the language of the submerged group as well as that of the dominant one would in all probability greatly improve the attitudes of communities and their mutual relations.

Any increased understanding and true tolerance might be reflected in the rejection of such familiar cliches as usually develop in these cases. These can be presented to the students directly or indirectly. By directly is meant that the student would be asked to accept or reject statements about the other group. The usual false statements might then be interspersed with true statements. For example, the statement might say, "X is a cheat because he is of such and such a group." Or, "The people of such and such a group are lazy," etc. These statements will be so obvious in their purpose that students whose attitudes have not changed may decide to reject them for purposes of the test only. Better results might be obtained by setting up situations in which the people of the minority groups are the actors. Multiple-choice items can then be devised with alternatives that give the right answer, the prejudiced answer, and an answer that goes to the opposite extreme and assumes that nobody in the submerged group can do wrong.

6. Interest in other peoples. The attitudes of students toward peoples of a different speech and culture, that is, toward "foreigners," should be affected by the study of a foreign language and culture. An attitude of fear, distrust, and disapproval of all that is foreign should tend to disappear with the study of a foreign language. A willingness to accept a foreign person into our circles, and even to welcome him because of the stimulation and educational values which such a person will bring should be a likely outcome of foreign language learning. Impressionistically it seems that students learning a foreign language show greater interest in foreign students than those who do not study a foreign language. Such comparisons are not always valid, because of initial interest shown by the student in choosing the study of a foreign language and because of the desire of students to practice the foreign language with a native speaker as an aid to their class performance.

Such attitudes can nevertheless be tested by various means. For example, we can present the case of a person in trouble in a foreign country and ask the student to suggest solutions. The student's suggestions might reveal his attitudes toward things foreign.

7. Non-utilitarian practical values. In addition to these higher values of the study of foreign languages and of the utilitarian practical benefits to be derived from their study in business, employment, scholarship, etc., there are benefits to be derived from the study of foreign languages that are practical but not utilitarian. Among these are the possibility of a richer experience in pleasure travel, the possibility of establishing friendships across languages and cultures, of hearing broadcasts and seeing plays or listening to operas in the foreign language, etc.

These benefits are self-evident. One cannot see why good foreign language teaching can be considered unnecessary either for the highest aims of education or for the practical purposes of earning a living and enjoying whatever leisure one may find.

21.3 BIBLIOGRAPHICAL NOTES

William Parker's *The National Interest and Foreign Languages* is very good reading. On the purely utilitarian side, there are various booklets and articles available to students; for example, *Vocational Opportunities for Foreign Language Students*, Third Revised Edition, by Schwarz, Wilkins, and Bovée, published by the *Modern Language Journal*.

PART V

REFINING AND USING FOREIGN
LANGUAGE TESTS

Chapter 22

NORMS

22.1   WHAT DOES A SCORE MEAN?

1. A score alone means nothing. To say that a student made
a score of 60 on a test of auditory comprehension has no significance whatsoever. It may be the highest score ever made on the
test, or it may be the lowest. If the test is a very easy one, it may
represent practically no knowledge of the foreign language; and
if the test is an extremely difficult one, it may represent near
native control. If the average score on the test is 200 it is an
extremely low score, but if the average score is 30 it is probably a very high score. A score taken by itself has no value.

2. To measure is to compare. To measure is to compare a
quantity that we cannot fully estimate with another quantity
that is known and familiar. We can then say that the quantity
we are measuring is more than, less than, twice, three, four, five
or whatever times larger than the known quantity with which
we are comparing—measuring—it. The known quantity with
which we compare those we wish to measure is the *unit*. In
measuring a length of cloth we may use the *meter* as the unit, or
we may use a *yard*, depending on where we are. When we say
that the piece of cloth is three meters long, we mean that it is
three times as long as a length we know, the meter. If the unit is
the yard, which is smaller than the meter, we would say that the
piece of cloth is three and three-tenths yards, or we may express

the fraction of a yard in a smaller unit that is also familiar to us and say the piece of cloth is three yards and eleven *inches*.

3. The quantity being measured and the unit with which we measure it must be comparable. To attempt to measure the weight of a person with a unit of length such as the meter or the yard is nonsense. There are no length meters or yards in the weight of a person. This comparability of the quantity being measured with the unit we use to measure it, which is so obvious in the case of the weight of a person, can be difficult to see when we measure less tangible things such as a person's control of a foreign language or his ability to understand native speakers of it. When the comparability of the unit to the quantity we wish to measure is not obvious and requires elaboration, the problem of determining how comparable they are is called validity, but it is essentially the same as deciding whether or not a unit of length, the meter or the yard, can be used to measure the weight of a person.

4. Six ways to measure, i.e., to compare quantities with units. In measuring a piece of cloth, we will usually want to know more than merely the length of it. We may want to know the width, the weight, the cost, etc. All these quantities will help us decide whether or not to buy the piece of cloth. In foreign language learning and in other learning we may be interested in measuring quantity in six ways: (1) content, (2) rank, (3) level, (4) growth rate or progress, (5) profile or perspective, and (6) probability of success. The units used in each case will vary.

5. Norms. In addition to knowing the number of units that the quantity contains we usually want to know whether this is enough for what we need or too much or not enough. In the case of the piece of cloth we may want to know the number of yards or meters usually needed for a suit of clothes, or the usual width or weight of this type of cloth, etc. In foreign language testing we may need to know, in addition to the number of units, how many units natives know, how many units other students with the same amount of study have mastered, etc. The amounts known by groups of students that may help us to compare the measurements we make are *norms*. There are as many types of norms as there are ways to measure quantities with units.

22.2   CONTENT NORMS

Probably the most tangible norms are those that can be expressed in units of content of what it is to know a foreign language. If knowing how to pronounce Japanese, for example, means among other things knowing how to pronounce the five vowels of Japanese in their various environments, the unit might be a vowel, and norms might be expressed as the number of vowels mastered by students. Since knowing a foreign language involves mastering problems in sound segments, stress, intonation, grammatical patterns, and vocabulary, content norms might be expressed in terms of the specific problems of each element that students have mastered. In other words, instead of saying that these students have made such and such a score, we would say that they have mastered these particular problems or units of the various elements of the foreign language.

In practice, however, mastery does not occur in all or nothing fashion for each unit. Each vowel or other unit is mastered in some environments while it remains a problem in others, and in certain situations such as reciting in class while not in others such as addressing an audience. If the test has more than one item for each problem, the norms can indicate the proportion of times that the problem was handled correctly in the test. Thus if a test has four items for each problem we may be able to say that the student has no difficulty with (has "mastered") these problems; and he has 25 per cent difficulty with these others, 50 per cent difficulty with these others, 75 per cent difficulty with these others, and has not mastered any of the rest. The use of per cents may imply a refinement that four items per problem do not justify. The actual number of items passed out of the number of items devoted to the problem may be more meaningful. Norms and scores might then be expressed as passing all items for these problems, passing one out of four for these other problems, etc. When different numbers of items are assigned to different problems, giving the numbers passed out of the number tried is still quite clear.

Content norms are particularly meaningful in measuring and interpreting performance on the elements of language as discussed in Part II of this book. Tests of aural perception of English for Japanese speakers and Spanish speakers[1] that test 25 problems four times each in a 100-item test lend themselves perfectly to the computation and use of content scores and norms. The problems are arranged in the same order the four times they appear in the test, without awareness of this fact on the part of the students. In scoring the test it is a simple matter to count the number of times that each problem has been missed, and consequently, the scores can indicate the problems not missed, and the problems missed one, two, three, or four times. From the accumulation of such scores, norms can be computed and reported. Teachers can then look at a particular test paper or at the papers of a particular class and decide whether the students have learned enough or must study further and if so, what they must study.

Content scores and norms should ultimately rest on the units that constitute knowing the foreign language, but they may be expressed in partial terms also, that is, a particular test may be devised to test only the consonants of the foreign language, or only some of the consonants, instead of the entire stock of sounds of the language. The scores and norms are meaningful as long as they are stated in terms of the units tested and not as representing mastery of the entire language.

Content scores and content norms can be expressed simply as raw scores, i.e., the number of items missed or passed for each problem or for the entire set of problems. When raw scores are made sufficiently meaningful in expressing content mastery, no transformation is necessary, and no transformation of such raw scores should be adopted for a test unless there are other specific purposes involved.

22.3   RANK NORMS

1. What are rank scores? Probably the most widely used norms are based on ranking the student as high or low; top, middle, or bottom; first, second, third from the top, etc., in comparison with other students. Rank measurement is used in everyday affairs and conversation when dealing with such matters as the

---

[1] *Test of Aural Perception in English for Japanese Students*, by R. Lado and R. A. Andrade. (Ann Arbor: English Language Institute, 1950.)

weather, children, etc. We say that such a day was the coldest of the month, that Lucia is the oldest of the children and Robert the second oldest, that Carmen is the best student in the class, etc.

2. Types of rank scores. The simplest rank score is the number of the position of the score when all the students are ranked from high to low. John is the fifth from the top out of forty students in the class. This simple ranking is useful for many things, but it is rather crude for tests that are to be used more than once.

Percentile scores are a much more refined and useful type of rank scores. Essentially a percentile score indicates the per cent of students that scored below it. A percentile score of 60 means that 60 per cent of the students who took the test during the preparation of the norms made scores below this one. A percentile score of 50 means that 50 per cent or one-half of the students made scores below it, etc. This percentile score is not directly dependent on the number of items passed by the student but on the number of students who passed fewer items than this one. Obviously in a very difficult test, most of the students will miss many items and what appears to be a low raw score, low in the number of items passed, may turn out to be a high percentile score, because many of the students made lower scores.

A simple way to think of percentile scores is to think of two scales side by side; one is a scale of raw scores in terms of the number of items passed by students; the other is a scale of percentiles giving the number of students that passed at each raw score, divided in one hundred equal groups. (Figure 22.1.)

If a student passes seven items, his raw score is 7 on the raw score scale. At that same level we find on the percentile scale a 2, meaning that 2 per cent of the students made scores lower than 7. Similarly, if a student passes 10 items, his raw score is 10. Locating 10 on the raw score scale we read 15 across on the percentile scale, meaning that 15 per cent of the students on whom the norms are based made raw scores lower than 10.

Because literate people are so accustomed to using per cents, the percentile scores are readily understood by the layman and the teacher, who immediately sense the significance of a score better than that of 90 per cent of the students tested for the norms.

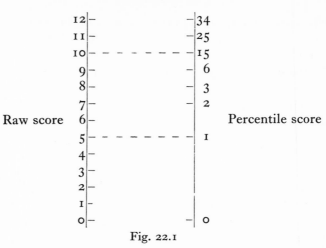

Fig. 22.1

Percentile scores, like all other scores have some shortcomings. One of them is that scores do not scatter evenly throughout the scale but tend to cluster or bunch up near a center and to thin out near the wings of the scale. Consequently near the center of the scale a change of one raw score point may mean a change of five or even ten percentile points, while at the ends of the scale a change of several raw score points may not represent a change of more than one percentile.

This shortcoming is more fundamental than may appear on the surface, as is understood when we realize that it is relatively easy for a student in the middle range of scores to improve his raw score a bit, while at the upper end of the scale it is extremely difficult for a student to advance a single point. With percentile scores, the easily achieved advance in raw score at the middle range will represent a large jump in percentile score, while the difficult advance made at the upper end of the scale will represent a small percentile score gain.

Standard scores. To overcome the imbalance introduced by percentile scores between changes in the middle of a distribution and at the extremes, especially at the upper extreme, scores based on the mean and standard deviation of the distribution of scores have been worked out. The unit in such scores is usually the length of a standard deviation. We must understand what a standard deviation is in order to understand standard scores.

A standard deviation is a measure of distance away from the mean of a distribution. The mean is a middle amount to which all scores would be reduced if they were made equal. The mean (short for arithmetic mean) is expressed by the formula

$$M = \frac{\Sigma x}{N}$$

where M is the mean, Σx is the sum of all the scores, and N is the number of scores. By adding all the scores and dividing by the number of scores we obtain the mean score.

Each score will be larger or smaller than the mean, except for a few that may be the same as the mean. The distance of each score from the mean is known as the deviation and is obtained by subtracting the mean from the score. Thus a score that is equal to the mean has a deviation of zero. A score that is larger than the mean has a deviation with a plus sign. And a score that is smaller than the mean has a deviation with a minus sign. This minus sign does not mean, then, that the deviation is less than zero, for this would be impossible. The minus sign merely means that the deviation is below the mean. A deviation is expressed by the formula

$$D = X - M$$

where D represents the deviation of a particular score, X the raw score, and M the mean of all the scores.

If we square each of these deviations from the mean, add them up, divide them by the number of test papers, and obtain the square root of this, we obtain the standard deviation, a convenient unit that helps compare or measure how far from the mean a particular score may be. The formula that expresses the standard deviation is

$$SD = \sqrt{\frac{\Sigma (X - M)^2}{N}}$$

where SD means the standard deviation, $\Sigma (X - M)^2$ is the sum of the squares of the deviation of each score from the mean, and N is the number of test papers.

If the mean of the scores on a test is 50, and the standard deviation is 10, a raw score of 60 is one standard deviation higher than the mean and is expressed as $+1$ SD or $+1$ σ (sigma). Similarly a score of 40 is one standard deviation below the mean and is expressed as -1 SD or -1 σ. A raw score of 70 is two standard deviations higher than the mean and is written $+2$ SD or $+2$ σ. A score of 65 is one and a half times the standard deviation above the mean, or $+1·5$ SD, etc.

Since it is not convenient to handle plus and minus quantities and decimals in large numbers of scores, one can transform the mean to a convenient figure like 100 and the standard deviation to 20 and thus further transform a score of -1 σ into 80 ($100-20$), a score of $+1$ σ into 120 ($100+20$), etc.

In these standard scores, all we have done is to obtain a convenient linear unit for the scores, one that may be roughly comparable from test to test. But if the raw scores from which the transformed scores are obtained are clustered in any special way, not normally about the mean as in a normal curve we will have a considerable error in comparisons. For example, if the raw scores are bunched up above the mean but scattered widely below the mean, a standard score of $+1$ σ may represent a score better than 80 per cent of all the scores, while in a test in which the raw scores were skewed in the opposite direction from the mean the same standard score of $+1$ σ might represent a score better than only 60 per cent of the scores.

Normalized standard scores. To overcome the problem of skewed distributions of scores used in preparing norms, normalized standard scores have been developed and are widely used in tests. These normalized standard scores are based on the properties of the normal distribution curve, more specifically on the relation of the proportion of space enclosed by the curve at a distance from the mean. A brief illustration of this relation will help clarify the basis for these normalized scores.

3. The normal curve. Two features of a normal curve interest us at this time. One is the fact that measurements of many physical and psychological characteristics of human beings when taken for large numbers of people turn out to be distributed like a normal curve, hence its name: normal distribution curve. The curve shows a bulge at the center coinciding with central or average cases, and it shows symmetrical wings or ends that thin out as they separate from the center bulge. This thinning out of the curve coincides with the decrease in cases as the scores spread higher and lower than the average. This coincidence of the shape of the curve with the number of cases at various distances from the average can be observed by simple inspection of a normal curve as in Figure 22.2.

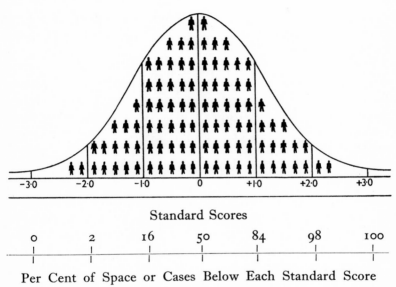

Standard Scores

0	2	16	50	84	98	100

Per Cent of Space or Cases Below Each Standard Score

Fig. 22.2

Second, the per cent, or proportion, of space enclosed by the normal curve at any particular distance from the center is known and is available in convenient tables. Roughly about one-third of the space (34·13%) is enclosed between the center and a distance of one standard deviation above, or below the center. About one-sixth (15·73%) is enclosed above, or below, one standard deviation. By adding these percentages of space from three standard deviations below the center to three standard deviations above the center as on a scale from low to high we have the following percentages of enclosed space rounded off to the nearest whole number.

TABLE 22.1

SD = % space	
3	100
2	98
1	84
0	50
−1	16
−2	2
−3	0

4. Transforming raw scores to normalized standard scores. If we let the per cent of persons (cases) below each score be represented by the per cent of space enclosed by the normal curve at each point we can use the normal curve to convert per cents of cases into normal distance from the mean in standard deviations and vice versa regardless of minor irregularities of the actual curve of scores used to establish the norms of a test. The irregularities are assumed to be due to errors of sampling and imperfections of the test.

Thus a raw score on the test which is better than 84 per cent (84·13%) of the scores will be one standard deviation above the mean on the normal curve and will be read as +1·0. A raw score that is better than 98 per cent (97·72%) of the cases will become +2·0. A score that is better than 16 per cent (15·87%) of the cases will be −1·0. And so on for all the possible raw scores on the test.

If we now slide these normalized standard scores up the scale to a convenient point that eliminates the use of minus signs and decimals we may have a scale with 100 as the mean and 20 as the standard deviation, for example. In this case a score of +1·0 would become 120 (i.e., 100+20). −1·0 would become 80 (i.e., 100−20), etc.

A graphic method of converting percentile scores to normalized standard scores facilitates the operations involved by using arithmetic probability paper.[1]

5. The use of rank scores in foreign language tests. Percentile scores and standard scores of various types are used with foreign language tests. They are particularly helpful in tests of

[1] J. C. Flanagan, "Units, Scores, and Norms," in E. F. Lindquist (Ed.), *Educational Measurement* (Washington: American Council on Education, 1951).

the integrated skills and of mastery of the language as a whole without differentiation into the elements of language or the different skills. They permit the comparison of a student's performance with that of large representative groups of students so that we may judge a particular performance as superior, extraordinary, average, poor, inferior, etc.

The Cooperative Inter-American Tests use percentile norms for school grade levels. The tentative norms are based on up to 26,000 Spanish-speaking and bilingual children in Puerto Rico and Mexico, and 10,000 English-speaking and bilingual children in the United States. The norms are listed separately for each of the twelve school grades tested.

Norms for selected groups requiring only one scale need not be based on such large samples, although the larger the sample the more dependable the norms provided that no extraneous factors are introduced.

The "Scaled Scores" used in the Cooperative foreign language tests are normalized standard scores with 50 as the average that students achieved in a given course of study.

Percentile scores and normalized standard scores may also be used with tests of the elements of language which permit specific scoring. In addition to knowing that the student has mastered such and such problems, it is important to know, for example, that only 10 per cent of the students in similar circumstances master those problems.

The desirability of using large samples to establish norms for a test should not result in mixing together scores made by different populations under varying conditions. The performance of each significant subgroup of students used in the normalizing sample should be reported separately in addition to the total performance. This specificity will permit more intelligent interpretation of scores by comparing them not only with the total norms but particularly with the performance of those students who most closely parallel the ones at hand.[1]

6. Tables of norms. The rather abstract considerations and operations involved in the development of satisfactory norms are

---

[1] See A. Anastasi on "The specificity of norms," in *Psychological Testing* (New York: The Macmillan Company, 1954.)

necessary for the test maker and should be generally understood by the test user, but the test should provide tables so that the test user may read the transformed scores simply by supplying the raw score of the test. These tables may be of many types and styles but they essentially pair off each possible raw score with its appropriate transformed score. If more than one set of transformed scores are provided they may be shown on the same table.

TABLE 22.2

Raw Score	Normalized Standard Score	Percentile Score
M = 70 (0–100)	M = 100 σ = 20	(0–100)
100	160	100
99	158	100
97	156	100
...	...	...
71	103	55
70	100	50
69	97	45
...	...	...
32	46	2
31	44	2
30	42	2
29	40	1

From scoring the test we obtain a raw score, say, of 70. We locate the raw score on the raw score column and then read the standard score horizontally across, 100, and the percentile score, 50.

22.4   LEVEL OF DEVELOPMENT

In addition to information regarding the content of the material mastered by a student and in addition to knowing that his score is better than, say, 90 per cent of the scores made on a test, it is meaningful to know if a student speaks as well as the average interpreter, or if he understands the foreign language as well as the average student who has studied, say, two years of the language in college.

The Cooperative Inter-American Tests give average scores for each grade level from 1 through 12. We can then interpret the individual Spanish reading score of a student as being at the level of twelfth-grade students in Puerto Rico, for example.

The Cooperative foreign language tests, higher level, give norms in terms of more than two years of high school work or more than one year of college work in the foreign language.

For students studying in a foreign country, norms indicating the average score of successful students in various fields such as engineering, graduate medicine, law, political science, etc., might be meaningful, since a greater control of the foreign language is necessary to study law in a foreign language than to study engineering or postgraduate medicine.

Average scores alone made by normalizing groups might wrongly give the impression that a student must achieve a level which is at least as high as the average in order to place. This is the old error of taking an average as the standard and expecting all students to be equal or better than the average. It might be more meaningful to give the range of scores of a particular level of development from one standard deviation below the mean to one standard deviation above the mean, so that instead of a point we have a range of possible scores for each level of development.

22.5   GROWTH RATE OR PROGRESS SCORES AND NORMS

1. Measuring amount of learning. We often want to assess how much a student has learned rather than how much he may know at a particular moment. This question regarding progress is particularly relevant in foreign language testing because of great differences in the contact that students may have had with the language before attending a particular course. Some students may have heard their parents use the language natively at home, others may have traveled to the countries where the language is spoken and may have acquired some knowledge of the language there, and still others may have unusual initial grasp of things in the foreign language through transfer insights. Whatever the reasons, a score on a foreign language test taken at the end of a course of instruction in the foreign language may mean many things besides learning gained during the course.

Comparisons of different teaching techniques on the basis of final test scores alone are open to question because we do not know if the groups being compared were equal at the beginning of instruction. If three or four students in one of the groups had lived in the country where the language is spoken natively, their final scores would in all likelihood invalidate the results of the comparison.

Some tests, such as the Stanford Spanish Tests,[1] wisely give different norms for students who have studied other languages, especially languages that are closely related (Latin and French in this case). This provision does not solve the problem of initial level, which may be due to various causes, and which even in the case of differentiated norms would not account for differences in amount of the other languages mastered and amount of transfer before instruction began.

In order to measure progress or amount of learning in a foreign language we need two scores at least, a score at the beginning of a certain time or experience and a score following that period of time or experience. Additional scores may be desired to estimate amount remembered after a certain period following instruction. Such is the case in the study of rate of forgetting.

Another condition required in measuring progress is that the two scores must be comparable. Still another is the condition that the tests must be reliable, that is, their scores must not fluctuate by chance factors more than a small amount so that any differences may be attributable to the learning that has taken place rather than to chance variation in the scores of the tests.

Some tests are subject to a considerable amount of "practice effect"—amount of improvement that taking the test once produces upon taking it again without intervening instruction. This practice effect may result from memory of the specific items of the test or from familiarity with the type of problem contained in the items. With tests that show a very high rate of practice effect it is difficult to know what part of the improvement in scores is due to learning from instruction and what part is due to familiarity with the test or the type of test. If we give the same test twice without intervening instruction to the same group of

[1] A. M. Espinosa and T. L. Kelley (Stanford University Press, 1927).

students we can estimate the practice effect of a test. This amount if not unduly large can be subtracted from the improvement in scores in order to keep the difference in scores more purely as the effect of learning.

The progress of a student is the difference between the second score and the first, corrected for practice effect. Letting X_2 and X_1 represent the second and the first test respectively we have the formula, Improvement $= X_2 - X_1$.

2. The factor of entrance level. It has been observed and reported[1] that the amount of learning in auditory comprehension and in other language proficiency is progressively less as the beginning level of the students increases. The amount of learning is the difference between raw scores made before and after a course of instruction in the foreign language. This observation shows that the rate of learning follows a negatively accelerated curve with a steep slope at the early stages and a leveling of the slope as the learning progresses. A parallel phenomenon has been observed in other fields of learning.

In language learning in particular this lower rate of learning at the advanced stages of mastery is not surprising. Learning of the large patterns takes no more effort than learning the minor ones, yet when a student learns one of the larger more frequent patterns at an early stage he has learned a significant amount of the language; while in learning the minor patterns at the more advanced stages the effort is approximately the same but the portion of the language learned is smaller. A factor of selection of easy problems at the beginning and more difficult problems later is also fairly obvious.

Whatever the explanation, however, the fact is that raw score increases at the lower end of the scale are not directly comparable with raw score increases at higher points on the scale. For example, an increase of 34 raw score points by a student whose entrance score was 20 is more than twice the raw increase of 13 points gained by another student whose entrance score was 70; yet in a sample table shown below both improvements equal the average improvement at their respective levels.

[1] R. Lado, "The Relation of Entrance Level to Rate of Progress in Aural Comprehension," *Language Learning*, 4, Nos. 1–2 (1951–2): 17–35.

Similarly, if two groups of students are compared as to amount of learning by giving a test before and after teaching for the purpose of determining which of two techniques is the more efficient, the results will not be valid unless the two groups are equated as to entrance level.

3. Progress norms at varying entrance levels. Information on the amount of learning shown by particular groups of students on a test under given conditions are of interest in interpreting the amount of learning shown by a particular student or a particular group. Such information can be reported in the form of norms which take into account the entrance level differential. A simple way to report such norms is to list the mean improvement of the normalizing sample of students at various entrance score levels, whatever different levels are necessary to show significant differences in rate.

An example, showing only the mean improvement rates at ten-point intervals, is shown in Table 22.3.

TABLE 22.3

PROGRESS NORMS

Entrance Score	Average Increase	Entrance Score	Average Increase
90–100	1	40–49	26
80– 89	8	30–39	30
70– 79	13	20–29	34
60– 69	17	10–19	35
50– 59	23	0 – 9	35

Table showing progress norms at ten-point intervals based on 1,000 cases studying English for eight weeks. Test used is "Test of Aural Comprehension," by R. Lado

The intervals in Table 22.3 are too coarse for any practical use with individual scores. Assuming a smooth distribution (not a normal one), justified by the shape of a line joining the average improvements for each interval after plotting them on graph paper, and further justified by inspection of the data, a more useful table would give the average improvement for each raw score.

TABLE 22.4

AVERAGE PROGRESS AT EACH ENTRANCE SCORE

Entrance Score	Mean Increase	Entrance Score	Mean Increase
96	1	79	12
95	1	78	12
94	2	77	12
93	2	76	13
92	3	75	13
91	4	74	13
90	5	73	14
89	6	72	14
88	6	71	14
87	7	70	15
86	7	69	15
85	8	68	15
84	8	67	16
83	9	66	16
82	10	65	17
81	11	...	...
80	11		

4. Mean improvement units and norms. By computing the mean improvement at each entrance level we can then know by inspection whether the improvement of student A is better than the average improvement at his entrance level, or if it is average or less than average. But we cannot tell if his improvement is better or worse than the improvement of student B who is also better than average at his entrance level. We need a unit that would render all improvements comparable. Such a unit would make it possible to compare at least partially a class of forty students with another class of similar size even when they cannot be paired as to entrance level, which would require large numbers of students to select from.

Zero improvement. Improvement data are different from test scores in one fundamental feature. Improvement has a zero point—no improvement ($X_2 = X_1$). Other test variables do not begin at zero on the test, hence the need to start from the center of the distribution—the mean.

Distance from zero to the mean as an improvement unit. In order to compute percentile or standard norms at each entrance level

315

we might need as many as a hundred thousand cases, a thousand at each entrance score on a one-hundred point scale; and even then, there would be insufficient cases at the end of the scale and more than needed at the center. The arithmetic mean of a distribution, on the other hand is one of the most stable statistics we have, and it becomes stable enough to be used as a measure with a relatively small number of cases.[1] "Mean improvement unit" is a rather long name to use for a unit of measure so we may use *meanim* for convenience.

If a student improves as much as the average for his entrance score his improvement score is 1 meanim. If he improves twice as much as the average his improvement score is 2 meanims. If he improves half as much as the average, his score is ·5 meanims. The improvement scores of all the students in a course can be averaged and compared with the average improvement of another course also measured in meanims.

To compute the improvement of a student in meanims from a table giving the average improvement at each entrance point we subtract the student's second score from the first and divide the difference by the mean improvement at that entrance score as given in the table. The formula is

$$X_{mnms} = \frac{X_2 - X_1}{M}$$

where X_{mnms} is the improvement score in meanims, X_2 is the second score, X_1 is the first score, and M is the mean improvement of the students at that entrance score.

For a particular test it is simple to prepare a double entry table of meanims giving on one axis the entrance scores and on the other the raw improvements from zero to three or four meanims. An example from the data of the Test of Aural Comprehension used above is shown in Table 22.5.

To avoid having to use decimals which add nothing to our data we can multiply all improvement scores by 10. The table would then be simpler.

---

[1] If the standard error of a population is 10, the standard error of the mean of a sample containing 25 cases could be 2. The standard error of the mean of a sample of 100 cases is 1.

TABLE 22.5
TABLE OF MEANIMS

Raw Score Improvement—

Raw Entrance Scores	1	2	3	4	5	6	7	8	9	10	11	12	13	14	15	16	17
96	1	2	3	4													
95	1	2	3	4													
94	·5	1	1·5	2	2·5	3	3·5	4	4·5	5	5·5	6	6·5	7	7·5	8	
93	·5	1	1·5	2	2·5	3	3·5	4	4·5	5	5·5	6	6·5	7	7·5	8	
92	·3	·7	1	1·3	1·7	2	2·3	2·7	3	3·3	3·7	4	4·3	4·7	5	5·3	5·7
91	·3	·5	·8	1	1·3	1·5	1·8	2	2·3	2·5	2·8	3	3·3	3·5	3·8	4	4·3
90	·2	·4	·6	.8	1	1·2	1·4	1·6	1·8	2	2·2	2·2	2·6	2·8	3	3·2	3·4
...	...	...	...	...	...	...	...										

TABLE 22.6
TABLE OF MEANIMS

Raw Score Improvement—

Raw Entrance Scores	1	2	3	4	5	6	7	8	9	10	11	12	13
96	10	20	30	40									
95	10	20	30	40									
94	5	10	15	20	25	30	35	40	45	50	55	60	
93	5	10	15	20	25	30	35	40	45	50	55	60	
92	3	7	10	13	17	20	23	27	30	33	37	40	43
91	3	5	8	10	13	15	18	20	23	25	28	30	33
90	2	4	6	8	10	12	14	16	18	20	22	24	26
...	...	...	...	...	...	...	...	...	...	...	...	...	...

To read a mean improvement score from a table of meanims like Table 22.6 we locate the raw entrance score on the raw score scale at the left and we move horizontally to the right until we come to the column under the raw improvement of the student. The figure in the box where the raw entrance score line and the raw improvement column coincide is the student's improvement in meanims. For example, a student's entrance score is 91; his raw improvement is 6. The place where the line and the column coincide gives the score in meanims as 15.

A special problem arises when the second score of a student is lower than the first one. This can be interpreted two ways. If we assume that a student cannot know less as a result of instruction than he did before instruction, we would count such cases as zero. Or we may assume that the instruction may have actually confused the student and as a result he can solve fewer problems after it. We would then compute the amount of loss in meanims and write them with a minus sign. Or we may assume that the minus scores are the result of variability in the test. If we are computing averages, these minus scores would then be offset by positive scores that may be higher than actual improvement. In interpreting the score for the individual student we can explain to him that the variation in the test is probably responsible for the negative "learning."

22.6   PROFILES

In reporting several parts of a test dealing with different elements such as vocabulary, grammatical structure, sound segments; or separate skills such as reading, auditory comprehension, etc.; or in reporting scores on separate tests of grammar, pronunciation, etc., by the same student it is meaningful to have all the scores on a comparable scale so that the student's comparative performance on each score may be viewed. A student may be very good in the range of recognition vocabulary which he understands, but weak in the construction of sentences; or he may be excellent in reading comprehension, but poor in auditory comprehension. Having these scores on the separate tests reported on different scales is meaningless for purposes of comparing his relative performance.

It is obvious that in order to have comparable scores it is necessary not only to use the same type of score but to have norms based on the same population or comparable populations. If the students used for one of the tests were selected from schools that take their students from a highly educated group, the percentile norms are not comparable with those prepared on the basis of unselected students.

22.7   PREDICTING SUCCESS

Two types of questions are asked in this area. Does this student know enough French or Spanish to study in France or a Spanish-speaking country? Or, does this student have enough language aptitude to learn French, Latin, English, or Spanish? Since the answer to both questions involves more factors than merely language proficiency or merely language aptitude, we must present it in the form of a probability. To establish success norms we usually compute the per cent of students at each test score that may be said to have succeeded in the criterion activity. We thus say that 50 per cent of the students who scored better than 69 on this test were able to carry a full load of studies in an English-speaking university of the United States, while 90 per cent of those who scored better than 79 carried a full load of studies successfully. If 90 per cent of the native speakers with comparable training carry a full load of studies successfully we can say that at this level (79) the foreign speaker will be successful as far as language is concerned. In the case of test norms correlated to success in a university it is difficult to use a correlation technique unless we assign arbitrary weights to a number of criteria of success.

In tests of language aptitude, the usual procedure is to correlate the scores made on the aptitude test with scores made later by the same students in courses in which they studied a foreign language. In addition to the correlation coefficient indicating the amount of predictive power that the test has, the norms will indicate what per cent or proportion of success was achieved by students in the various score levels of the aptitude test.

In conclusion it may be said that norms and scores being means of evaluating the performance of students in the complex operation of a foreign language, they should be provided in units that are meaningful to the users, and they should be provided in a variety of units because there are multiple ways of evaluating human performance as complex as that of language.

22.8 BIBLIOGRAPHICAL NOTES

Anastasi, Anne. *Psychological Testing* (New York: Macmillan, 1954). Chapter 4. Norms: Their Nature and Interpretation.

Flanagan, J. C., Units, Scores and Norms. In *Educational Measurement*, E. F. Lindquist, Ed. (Washington, D.C.: American Council on Education, 1951).

Guilford, J. P. *Fundamental Statistics in Psychology and Education*. Third edition. (New York: McGraw-Hill Book Company, 1956.)

Chapter 23

VALIDITY

23.1   WHAT IS VALIDITY?

1. Validity as relevance. Does the test measure what it claims to measure? If it does, it is valid. If it is a test of vocabulary, does it test vocabulary?

In this sense, validity is essentially a matter of relevance. Is the test relevant to what it claims to measure? You would not measure ability in French by the loudness of a student's voice because this is irrelevant. Nor would you measure a person's knowledge of French by his intelligence. Intelligence within the limits of normalcy is an irrelevant factor. Knowledge of a foreign language and intelligence are two distinct things.

Furthermore, one would not measure the ability to speak a foreign language by asking a student to explain the theory of relativity in that language if he does not understand the theory of relativity. The problem of the content is greater than the problem of the language. Many students who speak the foreign language would not be able to explain the theory of relativity in it or in any language.

In other words, for a test to be valid we expect the content and conditions to be relevant, and that there will be no irrelevant problems which are more difficult than the problems being tested.

23.2   HOW TO ESTABLISH RELEVANCE

1. Face validity. One way to establish relevance, a widely used way but a weak one, is to decide whether or not a test is valid by simple inspection. This accounts for the suspicion of objective tests; they do not always look relevant. Yet face validity can be very misleading. What looks like a very valid measure of auditory comprehension in a foreign language may not be valid. In an earlier chapter we saw how a test item in which the examiner reads the sentence, "He's watching the car," and the student chooses from among three pictures the one that best fits the sentence, may be valid or irrelevant depending on the pictures. If one of the pictures shows a man washing a car, and another watching it, the item is relevant for English as a foreign language for some language backgrounds. If, however, one of the pictures shows a man watching a car and another picture shows the man watching a ship, only a minor and probably irrelevant matter of "car" versus "ship" would be tested, a matter that could just as easily be tested without going through the complex machinery of an auditory test.

Similarly, the number of years a student has devoted to the study of a foreign language is not a very valid indicator of his ability to speak it. There are other factors involved in learning to speak a foreign language than the number of years devoted to it. Individual differences among students are astonishingly great. Different courses of study give different emphasis to the various skills. Different teachers achieve different results. Some students have had experience in the foreign language outside of class; for example, in a bilingual home, through travel abroad, etc.

2. Validity by content. Since language is a highly structured and highly complex activity we will need more than face validity to be convinced that a test measures the language element or skill it purports to measure. We will need to check the validity of the content of the items. If we use an interview as a language test, we will have to prove that the content of the interview either ranges over the entire system of the language or adequately samples it.

Modern linguistic analysis of the learning problems in a foreign language permits a highly refined study of the content of a language test. On the other hand, those tests that have used only face validity in selecting reading paragraphs or comprehension utterances have often failed to take into account the very specific nature of the significant elements of the language and have not adequately sampled these elements.

With the use of linguistic analysis and comparison of languages we are able to locate and describe the significant elements that will be most troublesome to a particular group of students. We are thus able to discuss content validity on more solid ground than previously. Having located for example the pronunciation difficulties that our students will have, we can examine a pronunciation test to see if these difficulties are tested. If they are not, the test is probably not valid as to content. And the same may be said with regard to grammatical structure problems and vocabulary content.

3. Control of extraneous factors. In foreign language testing we have a special way to check for extraneous factors that is not available in other types of testing. We assume that native speakers of the language of the same educational level as those for whom the test is intended "know" the language. Thus if the test is administered to native speakers of the language they should make very high scores on it or we will suspect that factors other than the basic ones of language have been introduced into the items. We expect the native speakers to miss a few items because of clerical mistakes or momentary lapses, but the distribution of scores by native speakers should be highly concentrated at the very top of the scale.

There are at least two situations in which failure of native speakers to pass test items does not represent the presence of extraneous non-language factors. One is the use of the native language of the students in the alternatives. Since the language of the students is foreign to the native speakers of the goal language, they will not be able to understand the alternatives. In this same situation would be the use of alternatives dealing with experience not familiar to the native speakers but well known to the foreign speakers for whom the test is intended.

The other situation is more subtle. It seems to involve cultural misinformation about the native speakers' own language through spelling traditions, and artificial rules of correctness. English-speaking people have no difficulty distinguishing the words "either" and "ether" in speech. Yet when asked in a silent test whether or not the sound represented by the th in "either" is the same as that of "ether" a considerable proportion of them say that they are the same. Another example is that of Spanish speakers who normally have only one phoneme /b/ in speech but who have been told in school that they should pronounce "b" as a bilabial stop and "v" as a labio-dental fricative. When asked in a silent test whether or not the initial consonant of *base* is the same as that of *vase* a large proportion of them will respond that they are different, and in effect in demonstrating their pronunciation to themselves they may pronounce them differently.

In both of these situations the performance of native speakers as a way to eliminate extraneous factors in a test cannot be used. We will have to rely on the direct observation of the behavior of the students for whom the test is intended.

4. Validation of the conditions required to answer the test items. Even when we are reasonably certain that a test includes the language problems we need to test and does not contain decisive extraneous problems, we cannot be sure that it is valid. Let's take a pronunciation item as an example. The student is asked to indicate which of the three sounds represented by the hyphens are the same. "We had to b--ld a fence. It k--ps the children out. Last year they k-cked and broke many little trees."

We know that the item tests the difference between the English phonemes /iy/ and /i/ as in *eat* and *it*, a valid problem for speakers of Spanish, Portuguese, Japanese and many others when they learn English. We know that native speakers have passed the item without difficulty. But the manner in which the student must apply his control of the problem in answering the item is not the same as when he is using the language for communication. Therefore, we do not know if a correct response by a foreign student actually indicates that he does make the pronunciation distinction when speaking. The item then is valid as to content but we do not know if it is valid as to the conditions under which the content is tested.

5. Empirical validation. At this point we need to compare the performance of the students on the test item and their actual use of the language—in this case their pronunciation of the two sounds /iy/ and /i/. In more general terms, we need to compare the scores on the test with some other criterion whose validity is self-evident, e.g., actual use of the language, or scores on a test whose validity has already been established. Since we are at a period of rapid advances in the description of language and language problems, the criterion will often be use of the language under normal or near normal conditions.

Scoring the criterion. Scoring the student's mastery of the language in actual use is a major problem. To solve it we need to have an expert judge observe the use of the language by the student and decide whether or not he has mastered the problem. When the criterion involves many complex variables that cannot easily be isolated, we may use several qualified judges who will render separate ratings of the student's performance. These ratings are then combined into a composite rating, which is assumed to be more stable and accurate than any of the separate individual judgments.

In validating the test item that asked the students which of the sounds represented by the hyphens were the same, the following procedure was followed: A representative group of students were asked to take the test silently as the instructions indicate. The test papers were collected and put away unscored. The examiner then asked each student individually and privately to read the items aloud to him. The examiner was thus able to score each student's pronunciation of the same problems the student had answered silently. The test papers were then scored, and the two sets of scores were correlated. The correlation was sufficiently high to warrant use of the test when direct testing of pronunciation is not feasible.

If the question is raised whether the student's pronunciation when reading aloud is the same, or sufficiently the same, as his speaking pronunciation, a further validation becomes necessary. The criterion could then be the student's performance on a production test which does not use reading as a stimulus but which tests the same pronunciation problems as the test we are validating. In either case we are comparing performance on the test with a criterion which is deemed to be more valid than the test.

Since scoring the live responses of a student is often not an easy matter, it may sometimes be desirable to have more than one judge score the criterion responses of the student and to combine the scores of the different judges.

23.3 REPORTING THE VALIDITY OF A TEST

The evidence regarding the validity of a language test can be presented in two ways: in "expectancy tables," and as a correlation coefficient.

1. Expectancy tables. Expectancy tables are used in aptitude tests and in predicting success from scores on a foreign language test. They are double entry tables with raw scores appearing on one scale and proportion or per cent of success or failure on the other. Table 23.1 shows a typical case giving raw scores on an English language test and grades made by the same foreign students during their first semester in universities of the United States. Table 23.2 gives the percentage of failure at each raw score interval. Figure 23.1 presents the same data graphically.

TABLE 23.1. Expectancy Table showing the relation between scores on an English language test and grades made by foreign students who elected twelve or more hours of Credit Courses during first semester in a United States university. Courses dropped without substitution of another are counted as failures. Students electing less than twelve hours are not included.

| Test Scores | Semester Hours Credit During First Semester | | | | |
	F	D	C	B	A
90–99	3		12	72	90
80–89	6		84	123	66
70–79	21	24	102	18	12
60–69	51	51	66	15	3
50–59	27	12	6		3
40–49	9	3			

TABLE 23.2. Expectancy Table showing percentage of credit hours failed during first semester in a United States university by foreign students electing twelve or more hours in relation to scores on an English language test.

Test Scores	Percentage of Failures	Number of Credit Hours
90–99	2	177
80–89	2	279
70–79	12	177
60–69	27	186
50–59	56	48
40–49	75	12

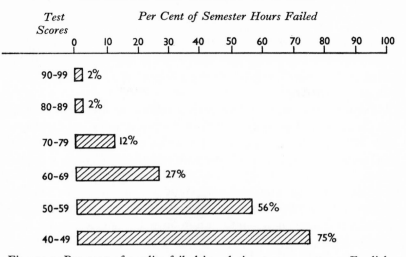

Fig. 23.1. Per cent of credits failed in relation to scores on an English language test

2. Validity coefficients. The usual method of reporting the validity of a test is to give the correlation between its scores and those of the criterion. In the case of the pronunciation test mentioned above, we would compute the Pearson Product-Moment correlation coefficient between the scores obtained by the students when taking the test silently and the scores assigned to the same students by the examiner when the test was read aloud individually by them. In the case of the relation between scores on an English language test and per cent of hours credit failed during a subsequent semester in a university, the biserial coefficient of correlation would be used because there are only two scores possible in the criterion: pass or fail. To compute the coefficient of correlation between scores on the English language test and the grades obtained by students during their first semester in a university of the United States we would assign numerical values to the letter grades and would then use the Pearson Product-Moment coefficient.[1]

In the case of the pronunciation test a correlation coefficient

---

[1] For the computation of the correlation coefficient see section 24.6 below or any standard text on statistics applied to psychology or education, e.g., Guilford, *op. cit.*

of ·80 or higher would be considered good in view of the difficulties involved in testing pronunciation and the variability of the criterion. A correlation coefficient of ·90 or higher would be unusually good. In the case of the success or failure of students in a university as related to their English language scores we would not expect such high coefficients because English language is only one of the many factors necessary for success in university studies.

When the problem is to establish the existence or non-existence of any relation at all, we compare the size of the correlation coefficient with its standard deviation and decide according to statistically accepted probabilities whether the coefficient indicates a significant relation or merely a chance variation. Since the standard deviation of a correlation coefficient indicates the variability of the obtained figure, it is customary to indicate the standard deviation after the coefficient with a plus and minus sign thus:

$$r = ·82 \pm ·2.$$

23.4 SUMMARY OF STEPS RECOMMENDED TO ACHIEVE MAXIMUM VALIDITY OF FOREIGN LANGUAGE TESTS

Below is a summary of the steps recommended in the preparation of foreign language tests to achieve maximum validity. These same procedures would apply in the thorough evaluation of the validity of a test already published.

1. Begin from a linguistically accurate list of the learning problems of the students. This insures better content validity.

2. Select or create a type of item that is practical and has validity with relation to content and conditions of the problems.

3. Edit the items for possible extraneous factors that may be more difficult than the linguistic problems the test is to measure.

4. Administer the test experimentally to native speakers of the language of comparable education and language experience as the students for whom the test is intended, or to non-native speakers who are known to have mastered the language. Eliminate or edit the items missed by significant proportions of these

speakers of the language. This increases validity making the test more purely a matter of language proficiency.

5. Administer the test experimentally to a representative sample of students for whom the test is intended and correlate their scores with scores by the same students on a valid criterion. The criterion is to be scored by an expert or by a panel of competent judges. If the criterion is another test or the grades made by students in college, reduce the data to a numerical scale and apply the appropriate correlation method. The coefficient of correlation between the scores on the test and the scores on the criterion is the validity coefficient of the test.

6. Present the data in the form of a correlation coefficient followed by its standard deviation, or expectancy tables and graphs or both.

23.5 SELECTED REFERENCES

Anastasi, Anne. *Psychological Testing* (New York: The Macmillan Company, 1954). Chapter 6. Test Validity. Discusses factor analysis validity and other problems of validation. Good bibliography.

Guilford, J. P. *Fundamental Statistics in Psychology and Education.* Third edition (New York: McGraw-Hill Book Company, 1956).

Thorndike, R. L., and Hagen, E. *Measurement and Evaluation in Psychology and Education* (New York: John Wiley and Sons. 1955, 1957), pp. 108–123.

Chapter 24

RELIABILITY

24.1   WHAT IS RELIABILITY?

1. Stability versus fluctuation or instability. Reliability has to do with the stability of scores for the same individuals. If the scores of students are stable the test is reliable; if the scores tend to fluctuate for no apparent reason, the test is unreliable.

2. Reliability and validity. Validity is not possible unless the scores we deal with are stable, that is, reliable. Reliability and validity, however, must not be confused. An intelligence test may be very reliable, i.e., it may yield stable scores, but it would be invalid as a French test. Validity refers to whether or not a test measures what it purports to measure. Reliability is a general quality of stability of scores regardless of what the test measures. Thus a test cannot be valid unless it is also reliable, for an unreliable test does not measure.

Interviews as tests of oral proficiency in a foreign language have obvious face validity, but they have low reliability. Written essays as tests of writing or of general proficiency have varying degrees of validity, but they are generally of low reliability. As a result their face validity is not supported empirically by validity coefficients with a valid criterion.

24.2   SOURCES OF UNRELIABILITY

The instability of test scores may be due to a great variety of possible factors and it is useful to separate at least three main sources for later estimation of reliability. First, there is instability or variability that results from time and circumstances. The skill we are testing may normally vary with time and with various circumstances that may be considered normal for the

330

performance of the skill. This might be called true variance of the skill. Also, the performance of the skill may vary as a result of irrelevant circumstances and time change.

Second, there is instability that results from limitations and imperfections of the test. No test or measure ever yields in practice absolutely identical results except in abstract mathematical operations. Some fluctuation in the scores obtained with a foreign language test may be due to inadequacy of sampling, lack of homogeneity in the items, etc.

And third, instability or unreliability of test scores may be caused by scorer fluctuation or even examiner fluctuation. In objective tests, scorer fluctuation is practically nil and need not be considered a factor. In various production tests and essay or long response tests, scorer fluctuation can be a major factor of the unreliability of a test.

It would be more meaningful to the test user to know not only the reliability of the test itself, but also the reliability of typical scorers and examiners as well. If time and conditions are potentially significant, it would be meaningful to the test user to have some index of the reliability of the test under the time and circumstances in which it must be expected to perform.

24.3 MEANINGS OF RELIABILITY COEFFICIENTS

The reliability of a test can be estimated by statistical means and is usually expressed in terms of the correlation of two sets of scores by the same students on the same test or equivalent forms of the same test. A perfect correlation would indicate perfect reliability and would be expressed as 1·00. Such a reliability would mean that each student made identical scores on both sets or that the differences if any were completely regular and exactly predictable. On the other hand, the absence of correlation would indicate complete unreliability of the test and would be expressed as ·00. These ratings or coefficients are not per cents and cannot be interpreted as such. They have meaning in relation to each other, that is, a higher coefficient indicates higher reliability, and for particular skills experience shows that particular correlation coefficients are good or poor depending on the skill and the use to be made of the test.

In practice, no language test shows a reliability of 1·00 or ·00. They range between these two extremes. The reliability coefficient of a given test is considered high or low not only according to how near it is to 1·00 but also according to how difficult to test that activity is and how stable the actual performance of the students in real life situations. A person does not always write even his native language with equal lucidity, and he does not always understand what is said to him with the same accuracy. Such differences, then, will be expected to appear in the scores and a reliability of less than 1·00 could theoretically be a perfect reliability as far as the test is concerned. In general, written tests may be expected to show a higher coefficient of reliability than oral and auditory tests. Good vocabulary, structure and reading tests are usually in the ·90 to ·99 range. Auditory comprehension tests are more often in the ·80 to ·89 range. And oral production tests may be in the ·70 to ·79 range. Thus, for example, a reliability of ·85 might be considered high for an oral production test but low for a reading test.

24.4 METHODS OF ESTIMATING THE RELIABILITY OF A POWER TEST

There are three widely used practices in estimating the reliability of a test. One consists in giving the test twice to the same students and computing the correlation between the two sets of scores. This is called the **retesting method**. Another method consists in giving two equivalent forms of the same test to the same group of students and correlating the scores. This is the **alternate-forms method**. And the third consists in giving the test only once, counting separate scores for each half of it, and computing the correlation coefficient between the two sets of scores thus obtained. Since this approach gives the reliability of half the test, an empirical formula known as the Spearman-Brown formula is then used to estimate the reliability of the whole test. This last approach is known as the *split-half* or **chance-half method**.

A fourth method of estimating reliability is based on the calculation of *inter-item consistency*. This method gives a measure of equivalence homogeneity. The inter-item reliability is estimated from a single administration of the test and the application of a formula that takes into account the proportion of students who passed and failed each item.[1]

These methods are applicable in estimating the reliability of power tests, that is, tests that measure the ability of students to pass every item. Speed tests measure the number of passable items that a student can manage in a given time. The estimation of the reliability of speed tests is discussed below.

With power tests each of the methods mentioned has its advantages and shortcomings. The retesting method seems more meaningful from a practical point of view but less valid from a theoretical one. From a practical point of view we want to know how variable our scores are both as a result of imperfections in the test and as a result of normal changes in conditions from day to day. The retesting coefficient of reliability being based on readministration of the test, includes the effect of changes in conditions. As a result, the retesting coefficient is usually a shade lower than the chance-half coefficient for the same test.

From a practical standpoint in the use of tests that have equivalent forms, the alternate-form method also has the advantage of including the fluctuation that may result from different samples of content and different context in the items. Though theoretically these variables are not part of the fluctuation of the skill we wish to measure, in practice the test user must reckon with scores that include this fluctuation along with the fluctuation of the skill.

From a theoretical point of view we are more interested in knowing the "real" reliability of the test. We may therefore find advantage in a method that eliminates such variables as the fact that some students may lose interest when asked to repeat a test while others may not, they may be occupying different seats on

---

[1] The most familiar formula is one developed by Kuder and Richardson,

$$r_{11} = \left(\frac{n}{n-1} \right) \frac{\sigma_t^2 - \Sigma pq}{\sigma_t^2}$$

where r_{11} is the estimate of the reliability of the whole test. n is the number of items in the test. Σ means 'the sum of.' p is the proportion of students passing an item. q is the proportion failing the same item. σ is the standard deviation of the test.

the retest and this may affect their performance, there may be a difference in noise and other disturbing elements at the time of the two administrations, etc. For this purpose, the chance-half method, which uses scores on halves of the test taken at the same sitting, yields a reliability coefficient more directly dependent on the test itself.

There is one practical advantage at least to both the chance-half method and the inter-item consistency method in the fact that a single administration of the test is sufficient. In the other methods a second administration is necessary, and it is not always a simple matter to have the same students take a test a second time without intervening instruction.

In view of the fact that the various methods of estimating the reliability of a test give us different kinds of information rather than being different ways of computing the same thing, it is probably wiser to estimate the reliability of a refined test by more than one method. It is meaningful to know the retesting reliability of a test that has only one form, and the alternate-form reliability between each pair of forms of a test that has more than one form. It is also meaningful to know in addition the split-half reliability of each form of a test. And if homogeneity is deemed desirable in a particular test, it is important to know the inter-item consistency reliability of the same.

Coefficient of scorer reliability. The problem of variations among different scorers in tests or production in language is a major one. In the various chapters on the preparation of tests we have discussed means of controlling the content and the scoring to minimize the effect of this variability among scorers. In addition to these steps, it would be meaningful to examiners and users of the tests to have some inkling of the coefficient of scorer reliability. Such a coefficient of reliability can be estimated for typical scorers who follow instructions by computing the correlation between the sets of scores given by two scorers to the same responses by the same students. With the development of recording equipment it is a simple matter to record the responses of the students and to have different scorers grade them independently. An estimate of how representative the particular coefficient obtained may be in relation to others that might be computed can be made by computing also the standard error of the obtained coefficient.

24.5 RELIABILITY OF SPEED TESTS

A speed test measures how fast a student can solve problems that are within his power. Typing tests are primarily speed tests. Reading tests are often speed tests or have a heavy speed factor. Auditory comprehension tests of a foreign language are not speed tests ordinarily, because every student is permitted to attempt every item. Most speed tests are characterized by having more items than can be finished by most students in the allotted time. Speed may be scored separately by the amount of material finished or it may become a factor in the total score of the test.

With tests in which speed is important enough to influence the scores, the chance-half reliability coefficient will be raised above its proper level by the fact that the unanswered items count the same on each half. This can be understood by observing that if, say, 90 items out of a 100-item test are not done by a student, 45 of these would fall on one half and 45 on the other. Any differences in the remaining 10 items would be outweighed by this perfect uniformity of the 90 items not tried.

Not all timed tests that are not finished by substantial numbers of students are speed tests. If the items of a test are scaled as to difficulty with the easy items first and items of increasing difficulty following, the point where the student stops working may indicate the top limit of his power to solve problems rather than an indication of his speed in solving problems, in which case the test would be a power test and not a speed test.

When there is evidence that speed is a significant factor in a test, the coefficient of reliability by the split-half method can still be applied, but in this case the two halves must be printed separately and timed. This method thus becomes the same as the alternate forms method.[1]

24.6 STEP-BY-STEP CALCULATION OF A CHANCE-HALF COEFFICIENT OF RELIABILITY

Step 1. Administer the test under normal conditions to about 100 students typical of those for whom the test is intended. If

[1] Other variations and methods are presented in the standard works on psychological and educational measurement and in the statistics manuals.

the test has already been given to a representative sample under normal conditions, use the papers available or select a random sample of about 100. One way to select a random sample consists of arranging all test papers alphabetically and then choosing systematically one every so many. If we have 1,000 papers for example, we would choose every tenth one to obtain a random sample of 100.

Step 2. Divide the test in halves and obtain the scores made by each student on each half. It is usually safe to take the odd items as one half of the test and the even items as the other half. This practice has the advantage of distributing evenly between the halves any factor such as fatigue at the end of the test. List the pairs of scores in two columns; label the column to the left, X, and the column to the right, Y. Each score under X has a corresponding score under Y for the same student.

Step 3. Calculate the following statistics:

   (*a*) the sum of the X scores,
   (*b*) the sum of the Y scores,
   (*c*) the sum of the squares of the X scores,
   (*d*) the sum of the squares of the Y scores,
   (*e*) the sum of the products of each X score with its corresponding Y score for the same student.

These data are needed in order to compute the correlation between the two sets of half scores by means of the formula presented in Step 4.

Step 4. Apply the following formula:[1]

$$r_{xy}{}^2 = \frac{[N \cdot \Sigma XY - (\Sigma X)(\Sigma Y)]^2}{[N \cdot \Sigma X^2 - (\Sigma X)^2]\ [N \cdot \Sigma Y^2 - (\Sigma Y)^2]}$$

where $r_{xy}{}^2$ = the square of the correlation of the scores on the two halves of the test.

   N = the number of students in the sample.

   ΣX = the sum of X scores.

---

[1] There are many ways to compute the Pearson Product-Moment coefficient of correlation. This formula is a convenient one especially when a machine calculator and a table of squares and square roots are available. The formula is from J. P. Guilford, *Fundamental Statistics in Psychology and Education.* Third edition. (New York: McGraw-Hill Company, 1956.) p. 141. See also his Chapter 13 for other correlation methods.

ΣY = the sum of Y scores.

ΣX^2 = the sum of the squares of X scores.

ΣY^2 = the sum of the squares of Y scores.

ΣXY = the sum of the products of X and Y scores for each student.

Step 5. Compute or find the square root of r_{xy}^2. The result is the obtained reliability of half the test.

Step 6. Use the Spearman-Brown formula to estimate the reliability of the entire test. The formula is

$$r_{11} = \frac{2r_{\frac{1}{2}\frac{1}{2}}}{(1 + r_{\frac{1}{2}\frac{1}{2}})}$$

where r_{11} = the obtained reliability coefficient of the entire test.

$r_{\frac{1}{2}\frac{1}{2}}$ = the obtained reliability of half the test.[1]

It is sometimes advisable to give estimates of the degree of confidence we can place in the coefficient thus obtained by computing the standard deviation of the correlation.[2] If this is not done we should report the number of cases and the method of selection of the sample used in estimating the reported reliability.

An oversimplified example will serve to illustrate the procedure. Let the number of students be ten. In Step 1 we would select ten papers randomly. In Step 2 we would score the odd items and the even items separately as if the two halves were two separate tests. We would also write the scores as follows:

Student (Names not necessary)	Odd Items Scores X	Even Items Scores Y
(1)	8	10
(2)	5	7
(3)	4	6
(4)	3	5
(5)	0	2
(6)	6	8
(7)	1	3
(8)	0	2
(9)	3	5
(10)	2	4

[1] For other methods see J. P. Guilford, *ibid.*, and Anastasi, *ibid.*

[2] For the calculation of the reliability of a coefficient of correlation see any standard textbook on statistics applied to psychology and education, e.g., J. P. Guilford, *ibid.*

In Step 3 we would compute the following statistics from our data:

$N = 10$

$\Sigma X = 32$ [the sum of column X: $8+5+4+3+ \ldots = 32$]

$\Sigma Y = 52$ [the sum of column Y: $10+7+6+5+ \ldots = 52$]

$\Sigma X^2 = 164$ [the sum of the squares of column X: $8^2 + 5^2 + 4^2 + \ldots = 164$]

$\Sigma Y^2 = 332$ [the sum of the squares of column Y: $10^2 + 7^2 + 6^2 + \ldots = 332$]

$\Sigma XY = 228$ [the sum of the products of X and Y scores for each student: $(8 \times 10) + (5 \times 7) + (4 \times 6) + \ldots = 228$]

In Step 4 we apply the formula:

$$r_{xy}^2 = \frac{[N.\Sigma XY - (\Sigma X)(\Sigma Y)]^2}{[N.\Sigma X^2 - (\Sigma X)^2] \quad [N.\Sigma Y^2 - (\Sigma Y)^2]}$$

$$= \frac{[10 \times 228 - 32 \times 52]^2}{[10 \times 164 - 32^2] \quad [10 \times 332 - 52^2]}$$

$$= \frac{[2280 - 1664]^2}{[1640 - 1024] \quad [3320 - 2704]}$$

$$= \frac{616^2}{616 \times 616}$$

$$= \frac{379456}{379456}$$

$$= 1 \cdot 00$$

In Step 5 we extract the square root of r_{xy}^2:

$$r_{xy} = \sqrt{1 \cdot 00} = 1 \cdot 00$$

The obtained coefficient of reliability based on these data is $1 \cdot 00$, a perfect reliability. This result could have been foreseen from the fact that every Y score was exactly two points higher than the corresponding X score.

Effect of range of scores on the coefficient of reliability. When the sample used in obtaining the reliability of a test is not typical of the levels of students who will be taking the test the obtained reliability may not be fully satisfactory. If the test is designed for a wide range of ability but the sample is of a narrow range, the obtained reliability will be lower than it actually should be. On the other hand, if the sample is arbitrarily selected to represent a wider range of abilities than that for which the test will be used, the obtained reliability may be higher than it should. A safe rule is to use a typical sample, or a random selection from a typical sample, and to report the range and other characteristics of the students tested.

24.7 HOW TO INCREASE THE RELIABILITY OF A TEST

If the reliability of a test is found to be too low for the use that will be made of the scores, we can increase the reliability in three ways: (1) by increasing the number of items; (2) by increasing the number of choices per item, and (3) by editing the items so as to make the choices more effective and thus reduce the factor of guessing.

1. Reliability and the length of a test. Lengthening a test with items that are homogeneous in interrelations and general level of difficulty with those of the shorter test results in increased reliability. By using a formula derived from the Spearman-Brown formula used to estimate the reliability of a test from that of its odd and even halves we can estimate how many additional items will be necessary to attain a given reliability. The formula is:

$$A = \frac{r_{AA}(1 - r_{11})}{r_{11}(1 - r_{AA})}$$

where A = the ratio of the new length to the old.

   r_{AA} = the reliability coefficient desired of the lengthened test.

   r_{11} = the reliability coefficient of the short test.

For example, if we have an experimental test of 50 items with a reliability of ·70, and we wish to raise its reliability to ·90, what will be the necessary length? Applying the formula we have $(r_{AA} = ·90.\ \ r_{11} = ·70)$

$$A = \frac{\cdot 90 \,(1 - \cdot 70)}{\cdot 70 \,(1 - \cdot 90)}$$

$$= \frac{\cdot 27}{\cdot 07}$$

$$= 3 \cdot 857$$

The 50 items of the short test would have to be increased $3 \cdot 857$ times to yield a reliability of $\cdot 90$. Multiplying the 50 items by $3 \cdot 857$ we find that the longer test would have to have 193 items.

A length of 193 items would take longer than the one hour allotted to the test and the fatigue on the part of the students resulting from such an increase in length would invalidate the results. We must therefore explore other means of increasing the reliability of the test.

2. Increasing the number of choices per item to increase reliability.

Rationale. An increase in the number of alternatives per item should increase the reliability of a test. To increase the number of choices per item is proportionately similar to increasing the number of items. A test of 50 items having two choices each represents 100 possible choices. Adding a third alternative to each item, the number of choices would be increased to 150 ($50 \times 3 = 150$). Adding a fourth alternative to each item would increase the total number of choices to 200 ($50 \times 4 = 200$). Therefore, a 50-item test of four alternatives per item is equivalent in number of choices to a 100-item test of two choices per item. Similarly a 97-item test of four choices per item is equivalent to a 194-item test of two choices per item.

Empirical evidence. The observation of the positive relation between number of alternatives and reliability of a test grew out of a study of a test of aural perception of the segmental phonemes of English for Spanish-speaking students.[1] This test had five parts, one with four alternatives per item, the other four with two alternatives per item. The part having four alternatives per item showed a reliability of $\cdot 70$. The parts having two alternatives per item

---

[1] R. Lado, *Measurement in English as a Foreign Language with Special Reference to Spanish-Speaking Adults.* (University of Michigan doctoral dissertation, 1950), pp. 60–1.

had reliabilities of ·42, ·40, ·39, and ·20. Since the problems tested were the same in all five parts, and since the type of item was also the same with only a slight difference in the part with a reliability of ·42, it was concluded that the difference in reliability between the part with ·70 and the others was related to the greater number of choices per item in this part. This conclusion was supported by a further check. An increase in the number of alternatives per item in the other parts from two to four resulted in an increase in the total reliability of the test from ·79 to ·90 even though the total number of items was reduced from 125 to 100 by eliminating one of the parts entirely.[1]

3. The effectiveness of the distractors increases reliability. If one alternative in a multiple-choice item of four alternatives is never chosen by the students who do not know the item, the item may be operating as if it did not have this alternative, or in effect, as if it had only three alternatives. If this is so, we can increase the reliability of the item by substituting an effective distractor as the fourth alternative, or by editing the alternative so that it becomes effective.

The distracting power of the alternatives is often attained in objective tests by unsystematically thinking up alternatives that seem plausible but are actually incorrect. A statistical check of the number of times each alternative is selected by students missing the item will show the effectiveness of each distractor. With this information and the selection of alternatives on the basis of the linguistic analysis of the problems being tested we can achieve maximum reliability from a foreign language test.

24.8   SELECTED REFERENCES

Anastasi, Anne. *Psychological Testing* (New York: The Macmillan Company, 1954). Chapter 5, Test Reliability.

Guilford, J. P. *Fundamental Statistics in Psychology and Education.* Third edition (New York: McGraw-Hill Company, 1956).

Thorndike, R. L. Reliability. In E. F. Lindquist, ed., *Educational Measurement* (Washington: American Council on Education, 1951). Chapter 15, pp. 560–620.

[1] *Ibid., loc. cit.*

Chapter 25

ITEM ANALYSIS, EQUIVALENT FORMS, SCORING

25.1   ITEM ANALYSIS

1. Introduction. At various points we have made reference to item counts of the performance of native speakers and of the performance of representative samples of students. Our attention on these occasions was on the total test as a measuring instrument. Since tests were made up of items, the effectiveness of a test is determined by its items and their arrangement. Sound test construction, therefore, requires that we study carefully each individual item. This is further required by the fact that testing time is precious time, and any item that is not contributing effectively to the purpose of the test contributes to its ineffectiveness.

2. What is an item? A helpful way to think of an item is to consider it a test in itself, a miniature test consisting usually of a single problem. A language item is a sample of the performance of students on a language problem. Another language item may be another sample of the performance of students on the same or on another problem. Recognition items provide a stimulus containing the problem and force the student to make a response that shows whether or not he has mastered the problem. A production item provides a stimulus that forces the student to express the problem utterance or parts of it. Items, like tests, can be of the objective or the essay types.

3. What is item analysis? Item analysis is the study of validity, reliability, and difficulty of test items taken individually as if they were separate tests.

4. Item validity. The validity of an item like the validity of a test is a complex quality. It is the degree to which it tests what it is said to test. This will depend on content and performance. We can thus study the validity of an item from the point of view of content and from the point of view of the performance of the item. The performance can be studied by comparison with the criterion which the item is said to measure or with performance on the test as a whole, which is assumed to be more valid than the individual item.

Content validity. Content analysis of a language item involves inspection of the item to determine if it contains a language problem that is valid and representative of the problems that students have in mastering the foreign language. This inspection includes the lead of the item and the alternatives, to see that the lead contains the problem and the alternatives force a decision based on the problem. It also involves the detection of any extraneous factors that may invalidate the item. The discussions in the various chapters dealing with testing the elements and skills of language deal with selection of the content of test items and are therefore relevant to the analysis of content of foreign language test items.

Other fields of testing such as human intelligence, personality traits, etc., do not have a body of content as neat and well analyzed as language today, and as a result such testing has had to rely heavily on statistically derived criteria for the determination and identification of factors. In foreign language testing, there is no substitute for content analysis. Statistical study of performance of items helps to refine and improve content and performance, but we should probably fall short of our capabilities today if we were to begin from statistical factor loadings rather than from specific linguistic content.

Native speaker performance as a means of detecting extraneous factors. Experience shows that extraneous factors easily creep into tests and test items. In language tests we can administer the experimental form of the test to native speakers of the goal language comparable in age and education to those students for whom the test is intended; if they stumble on an item, something extraneous to the language has probably crept into it.

Since the students for whom the item is intended will be those

343

who have studied a foreign language, it is desirable to choose native speakers of the goal language who themselves have studied or are studying a foreign language under comparable circumstances.

If the native speakers are given the experimental test as if it were intended for them, some may not take it seriously because it will be too simple for them. Reasonably good results are obtained by announcing the test as an experimental one and asking that they take the test as if they needed to make the highest possible score.

Occasionally, one of the test papers will show an unusually low score. An interview should be sought with the student to find out if there were any special circumstances connected with it. If the circumstances show that the score is not representative of the student's work, the test should be eliminated from the item count. Nothing is learned by including a test paper that we know is not what the student would normally do on the same test. If a second administration is feasible, it should be given to check the low score on the first administration. Should the score now go up to a reasonable level we may eliminate the first paper and the second with full confidence. The second paper is not valid either, because it includes some practice effect.

Item count of native speaker performance. The number of times that each item of the test was missed by the native speakers is computed. The number of times each item is missed can then be converted to the per cent of those missing it. Per cents are more easily compared and are more desirable for our purposes.

To make an item count, prepare a sheet of paper labeling five columns as follows: 1, No. of Item. 2, Tallies. 3, Number of Errors. 4, Number of Tries. 5, Per Cent of Errors. Next, write under column 1 the identifying numbers of all the items of the test: if the test has fifty items, write vertically numbers 1 to 50; if it has one hundred items, write from 1 to 100, etc. Then go through each test and write a tally in the tally column beside the number of the item every time an item is missed. This process seems more tedious than it actually is, since the items missed should be clearly marked in red and actually a rather small number of items are missed by the native speakers.

Add up the tallies for each item and write the numbers in column 3. Counting the tallies is speeded considerably if they are marked in groups of five as shown in Table 25.1, that is, with every fifth tally drawn diagonally across the other four.

The number of tries in a power test item count is usually the same as the number of tests, since every student is allowed to finish. The only reason the column is listed is that some experimental forms of a test may be so long that they require two sittings. In this case some students are often absent on the second sitting and the number of tries is not the same for all the items. Another case in which the number of tries will vary is one in which a student finds it necessary to abandon the test before he has finished.

When a student leaves an item blank in spite of instructions to answer every item, he poses a problem for the test maker. We assume that the student tried to answer the item as instructed but was not sure of the right response and left it blank. We still do not know if he would have marked the right response had he tried. If there is a high proportion of these unanswered items, our count will be off, because the blanks will be precisely among the items which would show a high number of misses. For this reason it is probably better to mark the item as if it had been answered wrong. When it is clear that a student stopped at a certain place and did not attempt any more items beyond this place, the remaining items have not been tried and should not be counted wrong or in column 4.

We are now ready to compute the per cent of errors under column 5. This is a simple division of the number of errors by the number of tries, converted to percentages. The conversion to percentages is accomplished by transposing the decimal point two digits to the right. For example, if an item was missed 3 times in 50 tries, we divide 3, the number of errors, by 50, the number of tries, and obtain a proportion of ·06. We then transpose the decimal point two places to the right and obtain a figure of 6, which is the per cent of misses.

Since we do not need any finer figure than whole per cents we can round off any decimals to the nearest full per cent. For example, if we have 3 errors in 49 tries, when dividing 3 by 49

345

we obtain a quotient of ·o61. Transposing the decimal point two places to the right to get the percentage we obtain 6·1. We round this off to the nearest percentage, which is 6. Any decimal fraction less than half a percentage point is simply cut off. Any decimal fraction which is half a point or more is rounded off by adding a percentage. Thus 6·49 per cent is rounded off to 6 per cent, and 6·5 is rounded off to 7 per cent. If one has to compute many percentages, it is more convenient and safer to prepare a double entry percentage table.

TABLE 25.1. Item count to obtain per cent of errors per item.

Item No.	Tallies	No. of Errors	No. of Tries	Per Cent of Errors
1	///	3	62	5
2	/	1	62	2
3	ЖЖ ///	8	62	13
4		0	62	0
5	//	2	62	3
6		0	62	0
7	///	3	62	5
8		0	62	0
9		0	62	0
10	/	1	54	2
11		0	54	0
12	//	2	54	4
13		0	54	0
14		0	54	0
15	/	1	54	2
16	/	1	50	2
17	//	2	50	4
18		0	50	0
19	ЖЖ ЖЖ /	11	50	22
20		0	50	0

Editing on the basis of performance by native speakers. At one end of the scale of errors in the example of Table 25.1 we have the items not missed by any of the native speakers. These are excellent from this test of validity. At the other end we have an item missed by 11 out of 50 native speakers, or 22 per cent of all those who tried it. This is not a satisfactory item. The best course of action is to eliminate this item altogether since we have prepared more items than we actually need and the same problem is tested by some other item.

We then have item 3 which was missed by 8 out of 62 native speakers. This is 13 per cent of the attempts. Again we should eliminate this item, without serious loss because the same problem is tested elsewhere in the test. If it should happen that the same problem is tested in both of these items in which native speakers have made so many errors, we should look very carefully at the matter. It may be that there has been an error in the analysis of the linguistic problem or it may be that the technique is not suited to test this particular problem. Some techniques that use ordinary spelling to test pronunciation do not perform well in testing the contrast between English /θ/ as in *think* and /ð/ as in *then*. Whatever the explanation, we are forced at this stage to eliminate an item if as many as 10 per cent of the native speakers miss it.

If we have no other items testing the same problem and if we cannot find another technique to test it, we use another avenue of validation that gets around this limitation of the performance of native speakers. Since our purpose is to discover if the student who is learning the foreign language hears the contrast, we can verify the technique directly with the students for whom the test is intended. We give the specific items to these students and then we interview them individually, checking to see if what they hear in the individual interview agrees with what they answered in the items under scrutiny. This "criterion validity" will be discussed below.

A foreign speaker has had to look at the goal language in a way that the native speaker usually has not, and therefore a technique that does not function well for a particular problem for native speakers could still be satisfactory for foreign speakers.

Between the two extremes, the items in which native speakers made no mistakes, and the items in which the native speakers made an unreasonable number of mistakes are the large number of items in which the native speakers made a moderate number of mistakes. If the number of errors by the native speakers is 1, 2, or 3 per cent, we can accept the items. A re-inspection of these items is necessary of course, but if we do not discover any reasonable cause for these few mistakes we can safely assume that the errors were due to clerical oversights. Even if the errors were due to some extraneous factor, the effect is so insignificant that we can disregard it with confidence that the item is still testing language primarily.

A good way to establish a judgment as to how high a percentage of errors by natives to permit without discarding the item is as follows: If 100 items were missed by 1 per cent of 100 native speakers, it would be equivalent to having each native speaker miss one item out of the 100 of the test. This would be a score of 99 per cent correct answers—a highly satisfactory score. Since in an actual test some of the items are missed by one native speaker and some are missed by none, the average score would be even higher than 99 per cent.

Similarly, if 100 items are missed by 5 per cent of 100 native speakers, it would be equivalent to having each native speaker miss five items out of the 100 of the test. This would be a score of 95 per cent correct answers—still a satisfactory score. This arithmetic equivalence can be verified by multiplying 5 errors per item times 100 items which gives us 500 errors. Similarly 100 native speakers times 5 errors each equals 500 errors. Actually we do not have to accept 5 per cent of errors by natives on every item but on a few items.

Criterion validity. In most of the items described, each item tested a specific language problem. With such items, the most precise type of criterion validation is possible: the proportion or per cent of cases in which the item correctly predicted the performance of the students on the same problem in the criterion.

The response to most items is counted either right or wrong in scoring. Therefore, from the point of view of item performance, the item has a 50–50 probability of predicting the performance of the students by chance alone. Items are valid as the per cent of correct predictions increases from 50 to 100. A margin of error is introduced in the calculation of this index of validity by the fact that chance variation will raise the per cent of correct predictions in some of the items and lower it in others. Thus an item that appears to have predicted 55 per cent of the cases may actually not have predicted any, while another item that appears to have predicted only 45 per cent of the cases may have some validity in fact but it may have been outweighed by the effect of chance. This error can be minimized by choosing the items that are closest to 100 per cent in the index and not using those that are close to the 50 per cent range, which is the zero range. We will thus eliminate the items that have no validity at the cost of items that have the lowest validity.

This kind of pin-point validation of test items permits the test maker to achieve maximum validity for the whole test, since even if an item does not correlate with the total test score of the students we are justified in keeping the item as part of the test provided the problem scored in both the item and the criterion is part of the skill we wish to test and is therefore valid.

In cases in which we do not have specific criterion performance on the very same problem tested by the item, we have to correlate performance on the item with general level of achievement as indicated by the total criterion scores. This is done on the assumption that students who are superior on the general criterion scores must also be superior on each individual item. Methods of estimating the correlation between items and total scores have been developed and are discussed elsewhere.[1]

Internal consistency. In practice most test makers are not able to collect criterion scores that are more valid or reliable than the total scores on the total test or on another test of the same skill. In foreign language testing, the recognition and perception techniques discussed in the various chapters above will usually yield more valid scores than any but the most elaborate schemes to obtain other criterion scores. In tests of auditory perception for example, the score obtained with the "same" versus "different" techniques are the most valid information we can gather. We will therefore discuss in more detail the estimation of item validity on the basis of the correspondence between item performance and total test scores.

The simplest case in the validation of the items of a test could be that of a teacher who prepares a test for his particular class, uses it once, and wishes to refine it for future use. In such a

[1] See any standard text on statistics applied to psychology, e.g., J. P. Guilford, (5) or specific treatments such as Flanagan (4), Davis (2) (3).

case the teacher might (1) score the papers, (2) arrange them from high to low according to their raw scores, (3) select the top 27 per cent of the papers and put them in a separate pile representing the superior group, (4) select the bottom 27 per cent of the papers and put them in a separate pile representing the low group. On a sheet of paper the teacher (5) lists the numbers of the items of the test and (6) marks a tally beside the number of the item every time the item is missed. The tallies for the superior papers go on one column, properly labeled, and the tallies for the low group go on another column. When the item count has been completed, a direct inspection of the number of times each item has been missed by the superior and the low groups will give a rough measure of the discriminating power, i.e., the validity, of each item. We say that this is a rough measure because chance variation and other factors will have distorted some of the figures considerably.

Those items that show a larger number of misses among the high group than among the low group are working at cross purposes with the rest of the test and are suspect of containing some extraneous factor that may render them invalid. The teacher should inspect each of these items carefully to discover the cause of its poor performance. In a surprising number of cases the defect can be found by such an inspection. Depending then on the importance of the imperfection and of the problem, the teacher might rewrite the item, leave it intact for another trial administration, or eliminate it altogether. An additional analysis of the performance of each alternative in multiple-choice items will be discussed below. Similar treatment is given those items that show the same number of misses by both groups and as a result are assumed not to be contributing to the power of the test.

A refinement of this method of estimating the discriminating power of an item is often used for tests intended for moderate circulation. The experimental test is administered to a representative sample of students. The papers are scored, arranged from high to low, and the top and bottom 27 per cents are separated.

The number of times the item is passed by the two 27 per cents is converted to percentages of those groups. The difference between these two per cents is taken as the discriminating power of the item. Obviously, when the per cent passing in the top group is less than that of the low group, the difference would be written with a minus sign, and the item would be unsatisfactory.

This method of estimating item validity has the advantage of ease of computation, and it is expressed neatly as a per cent itself. Essentially, however, it is the same as inspecting the number of times the item has been missed or passed by each group.

A more formal case in the refining of foreign language tests results when we prepare a test for medium-wide distribution and when large samples of students are not available or are economically inaccessible. In such a case, a group of 100 students of the general age range, educational level, and language background of the students for whom the test is designed is selected. The sample should be as representative as possible, including achievement level in the foreign language and any other variables that characterize the students.

The test is then given to this group of students with the same care and under the same conditions as if it were the final form.

The test is administered as a power test, that is, all the students are permitted to try every item. Exceptions are made when one or two students are confused or are so far out of the range of the population of students that they can be disregarded. Their papers can be eliminated without loss of validity. When the test is finished, all papers are collected and counted to make sure that none of the copies have disappeared.

Then proceed as follows:

(1) Score the test.

(2) Arrange the test papers from high to low on the basis of these scores. Divide the test papers into three equal groups.

(3) Prepare a sheet of paper for the item count with one column for the item numbers, another for the errors by the low group, a third for the errors of the middle group, and a fourth for the errors of the high group.

(4) Go through the papers of the high group and for each item missed write a tally in the high group column beside the number of the item missed. Do the same for the middle and low

groups, marking the tallies in the proper columns. A sample item count appears in Table 25.2.

TABLE 25.2. Item count to determine discriminating power of each item.

Item No.	Low Third N=20		Middle Third N=21		High Third N=20	
1	卌 卌 卌 卌	卌	////		卌	//
2	卌 //					
3	///					
4	卌 卌 卌 卌	卌 卌	卌 卌 卌 /		卌	卌
5	卌 //	////			卌	/
6	//					
7						
8	卌 /	卌	/			
9	卌	///			/	
10		卌	///		//	
11	卌 ///	卌			///	
12	卌 ///	卌	/		卌	/
13	卌 卌	卌	//		///	
14	卌	//				
15	卌 卌 卌 卌	卌 卌 卌 /			卌 卌	////

In interpreting the item count we assume that the performance of the entire test is more dependable, that is, more valid and reliable, than the performance of any individual item. This means that when the performance of the item is in contradiction with the performance of the whole test we accept the test and reject the item. This assumption implies a further assumption: when a group of students is better than other groups in hearing the problems of the entire test, it will also be better as a group in the recognition of any individual problem. As a result when an item shows that the high group made more errors than a lower group, we assume that the item is at fault.

Looking now at the item count of Table 25.2 we see that item 1 was missed by the entire low group, by nine of the middle group, and by seven of the high group. The item is a good one: it helps to separate all three groups.

Item 2 was missed by seven in the low group and by no one in the middle or high groups. This item does not help us distinguish between the middle and the high groups, but it does separate between the low group and the other two. This is a good easy item, and we keep it.

Item 3 is very similar, so we keep it also.

Item 4 was missed by everyone in the low and middle groups. It was missed by nine in the high group. It does not discriminate between middle and low but it does between high and the other two. We keep the item.

Item 5 was missed by six in the high group and by only five in the middle group; in other words, it goes against the classification based on the whole test. We eliminate the item even though it does discriminate between the low and the middle groups. We assume that some factor other than recognition of the sounds has crept in and confuses the high group. If we were very short of items or had no other item for this particular problem, we might re-inspect the item to see if there might be some correctable cause for this awkward performance. If there is, we might edit the item and try it again in a second experimental run.

By the same process we eliminate items 10 and 15 because some higher group made more errors in them than a lower one.

Although two levels score the same in items 6, 8, and 12, we keep them because they show a difference between the other two groups in each case.

We keep items 9, 11, and 13 because they test effectively at all three levels.

Item 7 does not test anything in this sample, but it does not go against the test as a whole, either. It is usually desirable to have the first item at a very easy level to give the students confidence in the mechanical operation of the test, and therefore the item might be kept. If there is any reason to believe that some of the students that will be tested in the future might be at a lower level of proficiency in sound recognition than the sample used for this experimental run, we would have an additional reason for keeping this and other easy items.

This item count contains the distortion caused by chance variation and other characteristics of this type of statistic. It has the advantage of simplicity of computation, and it is a fairly severe test of internal consistency validity. With this type of an item count based on a truly representative sample of students plus an analysis of the performance of the alternatives of each item, a test maker can refine a foreign language test with good content to a very satisfactory degree of sharpness.

For tests of very wide distribution and considerable permanence, especially if representative samples of 370 students are available, a more highly developed method of computing item validity is generally used. This method is based on the computation of coefficients of correlation between each item and the total score on the test, thus eliminating some of the errors inherent in the mathematically simpler methods.

Because the computation of correlation coefficients is laborious and time-consuming, excellent tables have been worked out by Flanagan (4) and others (2 and 3). The method is briefly as follows:

We score 370 test papers of a represenative sample. If there are more than 370 papers available, we eliminate the excess randomly so as to work with 370.

We arrange the papers from high to low on the basis of raw scores on the whole test and count the highest 100 papers. This constitutes 27 per cent of the 370 sample papers and represents the high group.

We count the 100 lowest papers beginning from the bottom to be the low 27 per cent of the papers.

We then count the number of cases in the high 100 papers that passed the item and the number of cases in the low group that also passed.

Using Flanagan's table[1] or Davis' chart[2] we enter the per cent of students passing in the highest 100 papers and in the lowest 100 papers and obtain an index of discriminating power for the item.

---

[1] J. C. Flanagan. "General Considerations in the Selection of Test Items and a Short Method of Estimating the Product-Moment Coefficient from the Data at the Tails of the Distribution," *Journal of Educational Psychology*, 30: 674–80, 1939.
[2] F. B. Davis. *Item-Analysis Data: Their Computation, Interpretation, and Use in Test Construction.* ("Harvard Education Papers," No. 2.) Cambridge: Graduate School of Education, Harvard University, 1946, p. 42.

Analysis of the performance of multiple-choice alternatives. Thus far we have analyzed the performance of items on the basis of the number of times that the right alternative was chosen by students who are known to be superior and by students who are known to be weak in the skill being tested. On the basis of the number of times the right alternative was chosen by these groups we have been able to identify items that are working at cross purposes with the rest of the test or which are not contributing to the purpose of the test.

In items that have more than one wrong alternative, a good deal can be learned by looking at the performance of the individual alternatives. Using the same assumptions as in analyzing the item, we tabulate the number of times that the highest 27 per cent of the students missed each alternative and the number of times that the lowest 27 per cent of the students missed each individual alternative. Comparing the two we can detect the alternatives that are working well and those that are not contributing to the effectiveness of the item.

If one of the wrong alternatives is chosen more frequently by the high group than the low group, the alternative is working at cross purposes with the item and should be edited or eliminated.

Alternative	No. of times chosen by High 27%	No. of times chosen by Low 27%
A (Distractor)	5	1
B (Right Alternative)	21	10
C (Distractor)	0	10
D (Distractor)	1	6

Distractor A in this item was missed five times by the high group and only once by the low group. If this alternative can be changed or edited so that it becomes more attractive to the low group who presumably do not know the item, the discriminating power of the total item will be improved.

If an alternative is not chosen by any students in either group, the alternative is not contributing to the purpose of the test.

Alternative	No. of times chosen by High 27%	No. of times chosen by Low 27%
A (Distractor)	5	10
B (Distractor)	0	0
C (Distractor)	1	6
D (Right Alternative)	21	11

Alternative B is not contributing to the effectiveness of the item. Revising it or changing it altogether might make the item more difficult and have greater discriminating power.

Items that are missed more often by the high group than by the low group and are therefore slated to be edited or eliminated may be improved on the basis of choice analysis. Analysis of an item missed more often by the high group:

Alternative	No. of times chosen by High 27%	No. of times chosen by Low 27%
A (Right Alternative)	10	11
B (Distractor)	10	7
C (Distractor)	3	4
D (Distractor)	4	5

The fact that distractor B was chosen ten times by the high group probably accounts for the lower number of correct answers by this group than by the low group. Editing or changing this distractor might increase the number of right choices by the high group and decrease them for the low group.

5. Arranging the items in order of difficulty. Modern tests usually have the items arranged in order of their difficulty from the easiest to the most difficult. This is good practice for several reasons; two will be mentioned. When the items are arranged according to difficulty the student can work rapidly through the simple ones until he finds them increasingly difficult and then devotes the proper time to solving them. When he finally is beyond his depth and begins to give up he will have ahead of him items which he would not answer correctly even if he did try them with full vigor. If a student does not finish in the allotted time he will leave untried that part which would be most difficult for him. Thus, the arrangement helps the student show his real level of achievement. Had there been easy items at the end of the test, the student who did not finish would not have a chance at them even though he would presumably pass them.

A second reason is one of mental set. Having passed an easy item, if there is a very difficult one immediately following, the student will tend to attack it with less than his full power. Similarly, having attempted a difficult item, if a very easy one follows immediately, the student will tend to attack it with more power than is necessary and will waste time and effort.

To arrange the items in order of difficulty we need to measure the difficulty of each item. The simplest way to determine the relative difficulty of the items in an experimental form of a test is to count the number of times each item has been missed by the students who take it. If all the students in the sample have tried every item, the raw number of errors on each item indicates its relative difficulty, provided also that the size of the sample is adequate and the selection of students is representative.

The use of the raw number of times an item is missed as an index of its difficulty is satisfactory for a test for medium-wide distribution. The necessary information is already available in the item count to test the discriminating power of the items. We simply add up all the tallies in all three columns for each item. In the example of Table 25.2 we simply add another column for the total frequency of the tallies, and from this information we find the new order of items according to relative difficulty.

The procedure is very simple:

(1) Cross out the items discarded because they did not discriminate effectively between levels or were defective in any other way.

(2) Find the item missed the least number of times and label it 1 in the New Item No. column. Write the old number and the number of times it was missed beside it to facilitate re-checking. List all remaining items similarly, i.e. according to difficulty.

From the new list we can cut up an unused copy of the test, or a used one, and staple or paste the items in their new order.

TABLE 25.3 Arranging items according to relative difficulty.

Item No.	Total Number of Errors	New Item No.	Old Item No.	No. of Errors
1	36	1	(7)	0
2	7	2	(6)	2
3	3	3	(3)	3
4	50	4	(2)	7
5	18 (discarded)	5	(14)	7
6	2	6	(9)	9
7	0	7	(8)	12
8	12	8	(11)	16
9	9	9	(12)	20
10	10 (discarded)	10	(13)	20
11	16	11	(1)	36
12	20	12	(4)	50
13	20			
14	7			
15	55 (discarded)			

Cutting and pasting or stapling are preferable to retyping because we thus avoid introducing new typing errors at this stage.

If the number of students that tried each item is not the same and if these differences do not introduce a heavy error in the estimation of the difficulty of the item, we can reduce to a per cent the number of times each item has been missed. Raw per cent of errors on an item can be used the same as raw difficulty numbers above.

With tests intended for very wide distribution and considerable permanence some further considerations need to be taken into account. The raw per cent of students passing an item includes an error caused by chance variation from guessing, and items not tried or not reached further distort the results. Increasing the size of the sample to 400 cases and applying a formula that allows for items not tried will tend to reduce the effect of these factors.[1]

6. Recording important item information in convenient form. Various card systems for recording the information gathered from item analysis have been suggested and used. Each individual worker may develop his own system on the

[1] See Davis (3) for a discussion of these problems.

basis of his own work habits. A card format for foreign language test items is suggested here that differs from other formats primarily because it includes the problem being tested in addition to the item itself. A place for recording the native language of the students is also provided.

Test: ACTIVE VOCABULARY

Language: ENGLISH

Native Lang. of Students: SPAN.

Part: I   Item No.: 16

Validation with TOTAL SCORES

Validation with *

	High Group (27%)	Low Group (27%)
No. in Group:	27———*	27———*
Choices:		
A:	5———*	10———*
B:	21———*	11———*
C:	0———*	3———*
D:	1———*	3———*
Omitted:	(0)———*	(0)———*
% Right:	78———*	41———*
Difficulty:		60%———*
Discrimin. Power:		r = ———*

*Use red ink for second validation if made.

Content Analysis:
Problem:
  VOCABULARY

Key word:
  BUTCHER

Difficulty: NORMAL
  SAME MEANING,
  DIFF. FORM.

Native language
form: CARNICERO
  'butcher'

Native language
meaning:
  CARNE 'meat'
  -ERO 'operator'

Form distractor:
  CARPENTER
  CARNIVAL

Meaning distractor:
  MEAT MAN

Item:

(Pasted or stapled)

A man who buys, cuts, and sells meat is a ———————.

(A) m - - t m - n
(B) b - - - - - r
(C) c - - - - - - - r
(D) c - - - - - - l

The card contains a great deal of information which can be grasped at a glance. The sample contained 100 cases since 27 per cent is 27 cases. The number of times each alternative was chosen by the high and the low groups is recorded. The per cent of right answers under the high group is obtained by dividing the 21 right answers by the 27 cases in the group. The result is 78 per cent of right responses by the high group. The 41 per cent of right answers of the low group was obtained by dividing the 11 right responses of this group by the 27 cases in it. The 60 per cent difficulty index was obtained by dividing the number of right responses by the entire 100 cases of the sample. In this particular sample the number of cases represented by 60 per cent is 60 because each case is 1 per cent of 100. The discriminating power is the estimated correlation using Flanagan's tables. The content analysis is given in sufficient detail to be self-explanatory.

| 25.2 | **EQUIVALENT FORMS** |

1. Need for equivalent forms of a test. When a test must be used more than once by the same students we should develop equivalent forms of it. Using the same form again tends to increase the amount of practice effect—the increase due to familiarity with the items particularly selected for this one test. Also, tests that are widely used year after year need to have more than one form to discourage attempts by students to collect the answers and thus invalidate the results. If the students do not know which form is going to be used, they will be less apt to have the answers ready-made, and if they do they are less apt to have the right ones.

2. Preparing equivalent forms of a test. The basic scheme in developing equivalent forms of a language test consists of (1) preparing duplicate sets of items for each language problem in the test list and (2) dividing the duplicate items according to performance by the students so that the difficulty of the two forms will also be equivalent. What we try to do then is to prepare two forms of the test, each form testing the same linguistic problems as determined by content planning and analysis and at the same level of difficulty as determined by student performance.

For the development of items that are equivalent in content the material of Parts II, III, and IV of this book is pertinent. For the equating of items that are equivalent in student performance, the section on item analysis in this chapter is pertinent. The simplest and in many ways the most satisfactory approach to the preparation of parallel and equivalent forms is to try duplicate sets of items in one combined test on exactly the same students the same day or on consecutive days.

If each form of the test is to have for example one item testing each problem we should prepare perhaps four items per problem to be sure that after eliminating those that are unsatisfactory we may still have two good ones that are nearly alike in difficulty. In preparing the experimental items we not only devise them to test a problem but we try to keep all other factors as nearly on the same level of difficulty as possible. If the items test the same pronunciation problem, for example, the vocabulary and structure must be kept as nearly on the same level as possible.

Let's say that we have prepared enough experimental items for two forms of a test. We then administer this double-sized experimental form to a representative sample of the type of students for whom the test is intended. We analyze the performance of the items and once the unsatisfactory ones have been eliminated the number of students failing each item as the measure of its difficulty can be tabulated. The two items which are the nearest in difficulty for each problem are used for the two forms of the test. As we progress from one problem to the next we alternate the order so that the easier item of each pair falls now on one form of the test and now on the other. Occasionally when a pair of items is somewhat unequal as to difficulty we put two easier items consecutively on the form that took the higher item of the unequal pair. If necessary to restore balance, we go back to preceding problems and reverse their placement in the two forms to compensate further for the unequal pair.

A cumulative sum of the number of errors on all the items of each form should be kept as new items are added. The cumulative sum of errors should be as nearly equal as possible through the length of both forms. Compensations by putting the easier item of a pair in the form that shows the higher cumulative sum of errors should be made as near the level where the imbalance occurs as possible. The reason for this is the fact that compensations at a high level will not operate for students who are at a low level.

The separation into two equivalent forms may not always be

possible on the basis of equivalent items for each problem tested. In tests of the integrated skills where only a few problems may be selected for each of the language elements, i.e., pronunciation, grammatical structure, vocabulary, etc., we equate pronunciation with pronunciation, grammatical structure with grammatical structure, etc., on the basis of student performance but not a specific pronunciation problem with the same problem in the other form of the test.

Once the two equivalent forms have been separated, the items are usually arranged from easy to difficult on the basis of the number of errors made by the students on each.

3. Cross-validation of equivalent forms. Because of various cross influences of items in a particular arrangement on the experimental test and because of differences introduced by judicious editing based on the analysis of the items and alternatives, it is good practice to give the separated and presumably equivalent forms a second experimental administration to a different group of representative students. An item analysis of the separated forms may confirm the equivalence of the forms, or it may more probably show minor changes in difficulty. Adjustments can be made by switching items between the two forms where imbalances appear until once more a balance of difficulty is achieved throughout the scale of both tests.

25.3　　　　SCORING TECHNIQUES

1. The use of objective tests in large numbers has brought with it the development of improved methods of scoring the test papers. The net result of these improvements has been a great saving in scoring time and the maintenance or improvement of accuracy in scoring. A considerable variety of scoring techniques are currently in use. We will describe those that seem either most useful to teachers or most generally accepted. For convenience the scoring techniques will be divided into two groups: those that have the responses marked on the test booklet and those that require a separate answer sheet.

2. Scoring test booklets. For a variety of reasons there are still many tests that permit the student to mark his responses in the test booklet itself. We need not go into the advantages and disadvantages of this practice here. The scoring of such tests can be done by means of a scoring key that merely records in paragraph form the right answers, or one that presents the answers in some form that facilitates scoring.

Answer keys in paragraph arrangement are the least helpful. It is laborious and inaccurate to go back and forth from the test booklet to the answer key finding the place each time. The scorer should attempt to memorize the sets of answers if any considerable speed is to be attained. When several scorers are working at the same time, it is sometimes advantageous to have one of them read out loud the answers while he and the others score several papers simultaneously.

To overcome the slowness and inaccuracies of these answer keys a number of devices have been developed that attempt to adapt the answer key to the format of the test booklets and the position of the answers. With this ordering of the format of the answer key goes an effort to arrange the test questions and responses so that they are conveniently accessible for the answer key.

Accordion key. This key gives the right answers in vertical columns, several columns to a page. The answers are placed to match the height of the responses on the test booklet. Each column matches a separate page. In using this type of scoring key the vertical column that corresponds to the page being scored is placed as close to the answers as possible. The right responses on the key will appear close to the corresponding student responses and these can be scored at a glance, often taking in both the student response and the correct answer in one eye fixation. As each page is scored, the scoring column is folded back to avoid interference and permit the next column to be placed equally close to the student answers on the following page.

Strip key. This key is the same as the accordion key except that each vertical column is cut out into a strip.

Cut-out key. For completion and short answer tests the cut-out key has the right responses placed directly contiguous to the position of the responses in the test booklet. For this purpose the answer sheet has a cut-out or window for each response that permits the scorer to see the student's response through it and compare it with the right response which appears contiguous to it.

Any one of these scoring keys that attempts to match the position of the answers on the test booklet will result in a considerable saving of time and improvement in accuracy. For tests prepared and scored by the same teacher in numbers up to the hundreds they are highly satisfactory.

3. Scoring separate answer sheets. The use of a separate answer sheet for the student's responses is a general practice in tests that are administered in large numbers. The advantages are the compactness of the position of the answers and consequent speed of scoring and the saving in materials resulting from the re-use of the test booklets. The students are instructed to record their responses on a separate answer sheet and not to mark their booklets. Disadvantages are the additional mechanical complication for the student in manipulating his test booklet and the separate answer sheet. With proper instructions and sufficient examples, students are able to use separate answer sheets on power tests without any noticeable decrease in efficiency.

The gain in speed is such that hundreds of tests can be scored in an hour by a single scorer. Busy teachers will be able to test their students more thoroughly and more often with the use of separate answer sheets without adding to the time they must devote to testing and often even reducing it. This advantage alone seems to be decisive in the wide preference for this type of scoring system.

Punched stencil. The punched stencil key matches the answer sheet and has punched holes at the places where the right answers must appear in the answer sheet. The student is instructed to make a heavy mark in a place identified by a number or letter with the alternative that he considers best. The answer sheet has separate spots for the separate alternatives.

In scoring the answer sheet the scorer superimposes the punched stencil on the answer sheet so that the marks in the right places show through the punched holes in the key. The scorer counts the number of holes which do not have a mark, indicating that the student did not mark the right answer. The scorer may also count the number of marks that do appear through the punched holes as a check on his scoring.

Various ingenious devices are in use to facilitate the super-imposing of the key on the answer sheets to speed the process of scoring, and to mark the right answers on the answer sheets for classroom discussion by teacher and students. They will be left to the ingenuity of the teacher here. For tests that must be scored in the tens of thousands the reader is referred to the excellent discussion by A. E. Traxler (6).

Machine scoring. IBM (International Business Machines) has produced a machine that scores answer sheets marked with special electrically conductive lead. Once the scoring electrical board has been set for a particular test, it takes only seconds to introduce the answer sheet in the proper slot of the machine and read the score on a dial. The machine also keeps an accurate item count and gives the score in terms of a conversion formula that may be set into the proper channels.

For very large testing programs operated by a small number of persons, this machine offers some interesting possibilities. It requires competent operation and is an expensive piece of equipment not always available unless fairly permanent rental is contemplated. For most testing purposes, hand scoring with punched stencils is fully satisfactory, and there are examples in which extremely large numbers of tests have been handled with punched stencils with superb efficiency and speed.[1]

Miscellaneous scoring devices. Various other scoring devices have been evolved that attempt to improve one or another aspect of scoring. Their advantages are usually accompanied by additional complications of production or use that restrict their general usefulness. Some of the better-known systems will be mentioned.

Carbon paper answer sheets. The Clapp-Young Self-Marking Tests introduced a patented scoring device that used a folded answer sheet with carbon paper inside.[2] The student marks his

---

[1] For example, the program developed by Lindquist for the Iowa Tests of Educational Development. See the discussion in Traxler (6).

[2] See for example *The Henmon Nelson Tests of Mental Ability: the Clapp-Young Self-Marking Tests*, by V. A. C. Henmon and M. J. Nelson. The Houghton Mifflin Co.

response on one of the small spaces numbered to coincide with the alternatives of the item. The marks are reproduced on the inner side of the answer sheet by means of the carbon paper. The student or teacher then opens the answer sheet and sees the right responses marked inside the squares printed for the purpose and wrong responses marked outside these spaces. This is an ingenious device, but it involves additional expense for the answer sheets, messy carbon paper, and it is doubtful that the process involved in opening the answer sheets and counting the right and wrong responses is much of a saving if any on superimposing a punched stencil on an answer sheet and counting the number of right and wrong responses. The Clapp-Young Self-Marking Tests are available with answer sheets for machine scoring as well as with the carbon paper answer sheets. Similar devices have been used by others.[1]

Punch pad self-scoring technique. Troyer and Angell[2] describe a self-scorer published by Science Research Associates by means of which the student perforates the cover sheet of the answer sheet and sees whether or not he has chosen the right answer. The under-sheet has a red dot which appears when the student cuts out the right hole on the cover sheet. If the student does not perforate the right hole on his first try, he perforates another hole, and so on, until he finds the red dot that indicates the right response. The student's score is given by the number of perforations he had to make to find all the right answers. Naturally, the lower the number of perforations the better the score. The advantage of this system is that the student learns as he takes the test. It also shows a distinction between the student who almost knows the item and makes only one error in it and the student who has no idea of the right answer and no general judgment as to approximate answers.

4. Correction for guessing. In true-false and multiple-choice tests a certain per cent of the items can be answered right by chance alone. As a result it is assumed that in the score of a

[1] Science Research Associates use carbon paper answer pads in their tests of "Primary Mental Abilities." A. L. Davis uses carbon answer sheets for self-scoring in his *Diagnostic Test for Students of English as a Second Language.* (Washington: Educational Services, Inc., 1953.)

[2] M. E. Troyer, and G. W. Angell. *Manual for the SRA Self-Scorer.* (Chicago: Science Research Associates, 1949.)

student there is an amount due to chance in addition to the score which the student actually earned. The standard formula to subtract this amount which is presumably due to guessing is

$$S = R - \frac{W}{n-1}$$

where S = the score
R = the number of right answers
W = the number of wrong answers
n = the number of alternatives per item.

Thus in a true-false test in which the number of alternatives is 2, we substitute 2 in place of n and have

$$S = R - \frac{W}{(2-1)} \text{ or } S = R - W$$

There are two main objections to this type of mechanical correction for guessing. First is the fact that good test items contain distractors that represent true interference for the students, so that they may be selected by students because they seem right to them rather than by sheer guessing. And second, even if the student guesses wildly at the items the number of times he will hit the right answer by chance will vary from case to case so that on one occasion he guesses more right answers than what the formula indicates and on another occasion he guesses less right answers than the formula indicates. As a result the correction for guessing has little validity for the individual student. For evaluation of group performance it probably tends to over-correct.

25.4   SELECTED REFERENCES

1. Anastasi, Anne. *Psychological Testing.* (New York: The Macmillan Co., 1954.) Chapter 7, Item Analysis.
2. Davis, F. B., Item-Analysis Data: *Their Computation, Interpretation, and Use in Test Construction.* (Harvard Education Papers, No. 2.) (Cambridge: Graduate School of Education, Harvard University, 1946), p. 42.
3. Davis, F. B. Item Selection Techniques. In Lindquist. (ed.). *Educational Measurement.* (Washington: American Council on Education, 1951.)

4. Flanagan, J. C. "General Consideration in the Selection of Test Items and a Short Method of Estimating the Product-Moment Coefficient from the Data at the Tails of the Distributions." *Journal of Educational Psychology*, 30: 674–680, 1939.
5. Guilford, J. P. *Fundamental Statistics in Psychology and Education*. (Third edition.) (New York: McGraw-Hill Book Company, 1956.)
6. Traxler, A. E. Administering and Scoring the Objective Test. In Lindquist, E. F. (ed.). *Educational Measurement*. (Washington: American Council on Education, 1951.)

Chapter 26

ACHIEVEMENT, DIAGNOSTIC, AND APTITUDE TESTING

26.1 WHAT ARE ACHIEVEMENT, DIAGNOSTIC, AND APTITUDE TESTS?

1. Achievement and diagnostic tests. The tests we have discussed in this volume attempt to measure how much of a foreign language a student knows. Such tests are usually called *achievement tests*, making reference to the fact that students have to struggle through a course or a learning experience of some sort to "achieve" a certain amount of control of the language. When the same tests are thought of independently of the learning experience, they may then be referred to as *proficiency tests*. Proficiency tests measure how much of a foreign language a person (not necessarily a student) knows.

Sometimes, achievement or proficiency tests are employed to "place" students in first, second, or third year courses in foreign language. The tests are then called *placement tests*, but they are still achievement or proficiency tests.

Diagnostic tests are also achievement tests, but they are characterized by one distinctive feature, namely that they are designed to show specific weaknesses and strengths within the skills or elements measured. These weaknesses and strengths may be as specific as the individual phonemes of the foreign language, e.g., when a test yields part scores on each consonant and vowel, or they may be as general as reading speed versus power reading, listening, and writing in a general foreign language test. When the partial scores become very broad in coverage it is probably not useful to speak of them as diagnostic scores.

2. Aptitude tests. Achievement and diagnostic tests differ fundamentally from *aptitude tests*, which are designed to predict the degree of success that individual students will have in studying a foreign language. Because of this predictive purpose of aptitude tests they have sometimes been called *prognostic tests*. The name "aptitude tests" emphasizes the fact that prediction is sought through measuring the ability (aptitude) that individuals have for learning a foreign language.

26.2   THE USE OF APTITUDE TESTS

Aptitude tests are useful for the selection of students for foreign language training when final mastery rather than educational growth of the students is a primary aim. The Armed Services of the United States used aptitude tests in selecting personnel for foreign language training. Professional schools for foreign language careers (teaching and translation) that have to limit the number of students they can accept might use aptitude tests as an additional criterion of selection, although achievement tests in the foreign language seem better indicated in such cases, and the use of language achievement tests in selection of students is common practice.

Aptitude tests can be used to decide how long it will take a student to achieve sufficient mastery of a foreign language to study in the country where the language is spoken. This information is crucial when we consider the fact that some students with apparently the same education and general ability as others learn three times as much as others in the same intensive language course of instruction over a short eight-week period. With a good language aptitude test we can tell a student that since his present achievement is X and his foreign language aptitude is Y, if he applies himself to the task of learning the language in a given course he can be ready for study abroad in so many weeks or months. Without a measure of his foreign language aptitude we have to depend on our progress norms alone and can only tell the student that if he is at least an average learner of a foreign language he will be ready in N weeks or months, thus leaving the decision up to what opinion the student has of himself as a language student, an opinion that will reflect personality attitudes more than language learning facts.

A questionable use of foreign language aptitude tests is made when students are not allowed to study a language because of lack of aptitude. If the foreign language is being taught primarily for its educational value, it may be an extremely valuable experience for a student with little aptitude to take a course in the language. Aptitude testing might be used, however, to group the students into fast and slow sections according to their proficiency and ability to learn.

26.3 PREPARATION AND VALIDATION OF APTITUDE TESTS

The preparation of aptitude tests consists of selecting types of items and problems that "might" indicate foreign language aptitude and correlating the scores made on these items with degree of success or failure in the study of a foreign language. We therefore have two chief variables: the items to be used in the test, which we will refer to as *the test*, and the degree of success or failure in studying a foreign language, known as *the criterion*. The correlation coefficient between the test and the criterion is *the validity* of the test.

1. The test. In planning the test, since relatively little is known about the specific aptitudes that contribute most to foreign language learning, we have to rely chiefly on insights and opinions of the test makers to think up problems and tasks that might prove valid predictors of success in the criterion. We can survey the chief learning activities involved in foreign language learning and/or try to abstract the psychological factors most heavily involved. For example, since learning to discriminate between strange sequences of sounds is usually involved in foreign language learning, the test should include a sample performance set of items testing the students on their ability to learn to hear samples of strange sequences of sounds.

Or we can abstract a factor of hearing accuity, or of flexibility of listening set and attempt to test this factor independently of any foreign language learning task. Factor analysis and the study of differential aptitudes in psychology are of considerable promise in the latter approach.

Once the learning tasks or the factors or both have been listed on the basis of the insights and opinions of the test makers, it is necessary to find tests that already measure these tasks and factors and proceed to construct items when promising tests are not available.

With an experimental battery of potential aptitude tests, we now seek to validate the tests, that is, to discover if the tests are actually valid in predicting criterion success and how valid each test or task is.

2. The criterion. The criterion has usually been the grades obtained by the students in a typical foreign language course, as for example in Henmon (2). More recently Carroll (1) added success in completing a highly controlled selection course of instruction in a foreign language including oral and auditory training. These criteria for the validation of foreign language aptitude tests are very practical and realistic. If the problem is to predict success in foreign language courses, let the criterion be success in foreign language courses.

Its practical and realistic basis, however, introduces the problem of variety in foreign language instruction and the complexities of the meaning of course grades. Course grades are more than indices of proficiency; course grades often represent a composite evaluation of proficiency, effort, cooperativeness, adaptability to the particular routine followed in the course, previous training in the subject, etc. The use of proficiency scores or achievement tests, however, is from a theoretical point of view at least, a more highly refined criterion. These achievement scores will have to be corrected for previous training in the language; and much better still, the criterion might be improvement scores adjusted for the factor of entrance level, e.g., expressed in *meanims*.

The use of achievement test scores instead of course grades would give us a purer criterion and a finer differentiation than the usual categories found in ordinary course grades. To be sure, the correlation of aptitude test scores with achievement test scores would not eliminate the fact that learning takes place in connection with courses of instruction which vary according to method and teacher, but the criterion is amount of learning according to a reliable testing instrument and not the composite grade given by the teacher for a variety of things.

3. **Validation.** The validity of an aptitude test is expressed by the correlation coefficient between test scores and criterion grades or success or both. The higher the correlation coefficient the more valid the test is taken to be. The higher the validity the more precise is the predictive power of the aptitude test. In a skill which is difficult to predict and to measure any positive correlation between the test scores and criterion scores would be considered good. In foreign language aptitude tests a high correlation has been achieved by Carroll (1).

There are two operational ways to validate an aptitude test. One is called the *predictive validity* method and consists of giving the experimental aptitude test to a representative sample of students before they study a foreign language. When these same students have completed a certain amount of work in the foreign language, criterion scores are obtained for correlation with the aptitude test scores obtained before study. This method of estimating the validity of an aptitude test parallels actual use of the test in predicting degree of success of students who plan to study a foreign language.

The other method also employed in estimating the validity of an aptitude test is called *concurrent validity* method because the test scores and criterion ratings are obtained simultaneously. This second method saves a good deal of time. In both approaches one must consider the fact that some students drop out or are eliminated from the course for various reasons which may or may not be linguistic in nature. In the concurrent method, it is difficult to find those who have dropped out and give them the aptitude test. The error which these circumstances introduce can be minimized by selecting samples that represent typical selection and typical competition.

Once the correlations between test scores and criterion ratings are obtained, we study them to discover the items and subtests which correlate most highly with the criterion ratings. These items and subtests are the most valid. We further compute the intercorrelations among the various subtests and select those that show the least correlation with the others since those that correlate highly with each other are probably testing the same factors and are therefore merely duplicating each other. By selecting those items that correlate most highly with the criterion and least highly with each other we include in a test of minimum length a maximum of measures of the various factors that seem to be responsible for criterion success.

4. Item validity. The validation of the aptitude test should be carried out with the whole test battery, the subtest scores, combinations of the subtest scores, and in addition, within those subtests that show high validity coefficients and are selected for the final test. An analysis of the validity of the individual items will permit the refinement of the successful subtests themselves with consequent improvement of the validity and compactness of the test.

5. Cross-validation. When the samples used to validate an aptitude test, or any test, are not very large, it is possible that factors irrelevant to language learning may be unusually heavy in the groups of successful students. Since the tests are selected on the basis of correlation with the performance of the sample, the highest coefficients may reflect this extraneous factor and obscure the language learning factors. To counter this possibility of error the usual procedure is to validate the revised test with a new sample. If the correlations are similar, it is concluded that no major extraneous factor has influenced the validity coefficients obtained.

26.4 THE HARVARD LANGUAGE APTITUDE PROJECT

The most recent and most productive study of foreign language aptitude is that of the Harvard Language Aptitude Project under the direction of J. B. Carroll (1) (2) (3) (4). This investigation had as its main objective the development of aptitude tests that would predict the probability of success in learning a spoken foreign language on the part of English-speaking students.

An extensive battery of tests were collected or developed on the basis of their power to test factors in the verbal domain and traits deemed requisite to learning a foreign language. The experimental forms of the test were administered to about five thousand persons including high school and college students and persons in foreign language courses under the U.S. military forces and Government.

Carroll and Sapon (3) report very high predictive correlations between test scores and, in one case, a five-day "trial course" in Mandarin Chinese for Air Force personnel. Four tests of the experimental battery yielded a multiple correlation of ·75. Another sample yielded a multiple correlation r = ·77. The highest predictive validity, ·84, was obtained with an improved group of four tests.

There was 82·5 per cent agreement between the aptitude test battery scores and the five-day "trial course." And there was a correlation of ·51 with grades for these students at the end of five weeks of study (2). Good results, though not as high as these, were obtained with other groups.

Equally interesting was the identification of six factors interpretable as components of foreign language aptitude. The interpretations made of the factors by Carroll (4) are as follows:

"*Factor A:* Verbal Knowledge. Knowledge of the vocabulary and structure of one's native language.

Factor B: Linguistic Interest (?). This is tentatively identified as an increment of test performance ascribable to a specific motivation, interest, or facility, with respect to linguistic materials.

Factor C: Associative Memory.

Factor D: Sound-Symbol Association. This factor is conceived as representing the extent to which the individual possesses a knowledge of sound-symbol correspondences in language, or can learn a novel set of such correspondences. It is proposed that this is the same as what has previously been identified as Factor *W* ("Word Fluency") and that the description of the factor as sound-symbol association ability is more accurate and descriptive than "word fluency."

Factor E: Inductive Language Ability: This is the ability to induce the grammatical rules and properties of a language when suitable learning materials are presented. It is uncertain whether this factor can be cross-identified with the inductive reasoning factors found by other investigators.

Factor F: Grammatical Sensitivity or Syntactical Fluency. Sensitivity to the functions of words in sentences and facility in producing syntactically coherent verbal materials.

"Consideration of the factor loadings of the criterion variable and of the tests predictive of the criterion leads to the conclusion that all of the above factors ... play a significant role in foreign language learning. Factors B, C, and E are probably more important than Factors A, D, and F, however.

Some of the results reported here may be of limited generality, owing to the relatively small samples on which they are based and the somewhat special circumstances in which the data were obtained." (4).

26.5   SELECTED REFERENCES

1. Carroll, John B., and Sapon, Stanley M. *Modern Language Aptitude Test, MLAT Manual,* 1959 edition. (New York: The Psychological Corporation.)
2. Carroll, J. B., Sapon, S. M., and Richards, S. E. *Construction and Validation of a Test Battery for Predicting Success in Spoken Language Courses.* The Harvard Language Aptitude Project. Report No. 1, June 1954. (Hectographed for private circulation.)
3. Carroll, J. B., and Sapon, S. M. "Prediction of Success in a Work-Sample Course in Mandarin Chinese." *American Psychol.,* 1955, 10, 492–493. (Summary of a paper.)
4. Carroll, J. B. "A Factor Analysis of Two Foreign Language Aptitude Batteries." *Journal of General Psychology,* 59: 3–19, 1958.
5. Frith, J. R. "Selection for Language Training by a Trial Course." *Monograph Series on Languages and Linguistics.* (Washington: Institute of Languages and Linguistics, Georgetown University, 1953.)
6. Henmon, V. A. C., *et al. Prognosis Tests in the Modern Foreign Languages.* (New York: Macmillan, 1929.) (Publications of the American and Canadian Committee on Modern Languages, Vol. 14.)

Chapter 27

DESIGNING EXPERIMENTS IN
FOREIGN LANGUAGE LEARNING

27.1 THE PROBLEM OF COMPARING RESULTS
IN A COMPLEX FIELD

1. Need for dependable evidence of effectiveness. When one looks at the hundreds of foreign language textbooks available he is struck by the claims that most of them make to representing some new method and producing wonderful results. The "method" usually receives a descriptive name or the author's name, and so we are faced with a parade of methods labeled "natural," "psychological," "direct," "universal," "functional," "extensive reading," "intensive reading," "conversational," "essential," "basic," "phonetic," "Hamilton," "Berlitz," "Cortina," "Mase-Dixon," "Army," "clinical," "audio-visual," "oral," "oral-aural," "new," "translation," "grammar-translation," etc. To be sure, the label often bears little relation to the content of the book itself or to the procedures used in teaching it in the classroom. Yet whatever the label and whatever the content, the student is usually assured of quick results. The observer has no way of knowing which of the claims are founded on solid evidence, which are well meaning but without foundation and which are mere advertising slogans. In fact, the writers and developers of the methods and textbooks have not had at their command the means for verifying their own impressions as to the success of their materials.

The parade of methods and textbooks and the confusion of their conflicting claims emphasize the magnitude of the task of learning a foreign language and the difficulty of verifying or exploding such claims. There is indeed need to evaluate the effectiveness of learning materials, techniques and methods by

377

the finest objective means at our command. Unless we can show by objective, scientific means which techniques and materials are the more effective for particular students we run the risk of rejecting the good and helping the bad with consequent loss to our students and ourselves.

2. Mass experiments of whole methods versus small experiments of single elements. The widely felt need for dependable evaluation of foreign language teaching and learning culminated in two nation-wide objective studies in the United States since the 1920's. The first was the Modern Foreign Language Study of the 1920's which began with the production of *New York Experiments with New-Type Modern Language Tests* by Ben D. Wood and ended with *Studies in Modern Language Teaching* by A. Coleman with fifteen intervening volumes. The second was the Chicago Investigation of the Teaching of a Second Language which produced *An Investigation of Second-Language Teaching* by F. B. Agard and H. B. Dunkel and the companion volume, *Second-Language Learning* by H. B. Dunkel in 1948.

Although the Modern Foreign Language Study and the Investigation of Second Language Teaching are of unquestionable significance in themselves and although the Modern Foreign Language Study produced nearly a score of outstanding volumes, the results of the final evaluations themselves were less meaningful and helpful than their magnitude might lead us to expect. These weaknesses are probably inherent in the mass approach to evaluation and research and should be considered critically for future evaluation and research.

Whatever value a large-scale study involving the entire profession may have for stirring up activity and presumably achieving progress is minimized or checked by the following disadvantages:

(1) Mass experiments are extremely difficult to control, and as a result the mass of data obtained embody unknown amounts of extraneous factors. The reports of both investigations emphasize the problems of controlling such experiments.[1]

[1] "Where so much uncertainty prevails and so many variables are involved it is the part of wisdom merely to offer these pages as a report of an undertaking and as a warning to those who believe that it is relatively easy to establish by experimental means the pros and cons with respect to teaching procedure.

(2) The differences between the methods that are defended and attacked are not always made clear by the labels given to the methods and the descriptions of the actual activities and procedures. In mass experiments these differences or the lack of them are even more difficult to ascertain. There is actually much duplication in what are purported to be very different methods, and there are many fundamental differences within what is labeled the same method but is practiced according to the individual tastes and experience of teachers who are not interested or trained in scientific investigation.

(3) Even if significant results are obtained by a mass experiment showing that one method is more effective than another for a particular purpose, the vested interests of those who derive their income from the less effective methods as teachers, writers, or publishers will not adopt the presumably better method, especially since the evidence is not specific as to which practices are most effective within the better method. Why should they abandon practices and materials that may actually be superior

And, finally, it is not out of place to draw the conclusion that, until modern language teachers are ready to take part wholeheartedly in experimental enterprises, we may expect only inconclusive and bewildering outcomes to such as are launched." (A. Coleman. *Experiments and Studies in Modern Language Teaching.* University of Chicago Press, 1934, p. 188.) (As quoted in *Second Language Learning* by H. B. Dunkel, Boston: Ginn and Company, 1948, pp. 4–5.)

"*Control of Non-Linguistic Factors.*"

"Data on many of these points is admittedly difficult to obtain under any circumstance: e.g., the effectiveness of the teacher (especially the reaction between his personality and the type of student found in that particular class). But even for relatively objective materials, precise data were often hard to obtain. Many teachers and students failed to give the information requested. Sometimes when the information was given, further checking showed that it was inaccurate. Even with the greatest possible care and trouble, the data available ran out before the theoretically desirable limit was reached. For example, some idea of the students' general intelligence was highly desirable. Yet the variety of tests used by different institutions for this purpose, the number of transfer students, and the many individuals who somehow failed to take the tests presumably required of all students, produced many cases for which satisfactory data were not available. The size of this group will be astonishing to anyone who has never sought to track down this kind of information. In any case, perfect control of these factors would be possible only for an organization which could dictate (to fifty or sixty institutions) the full detail of their entrance applications, placement tests, and registrar's records. Similarly, it was impossible to control adequately the student's previous experience with the language. Often registrar's records did not cover incomplete courses or courses which had been failed. Likewise foreign residence or the opportunity to speak the language with family or friends could not be ascertained with the precision which was theoretically desirable." (F. B. Agard and H. B. Dunkel. *An Investigation of Second-Language Teaching.* Boston: Ginn and Company, 1948, pp. 11–12.)

in many respects because they are inferior for the mass and as a whole?

(4) The security of teachers who have learned to teach by one method and who may be quite ineffective in learning to teach by a new method will also militate against adoption of the over-all better method. This security in sticking to old practices that they know well will be supported by the natural inertia of many human beings, who feel more comfortable doing their work the same way. And a further reason against accepting any total new method is the problem of face saving by a teacher who has for years used one approach and must admit he has been wrong all along and must now change over completely.

For these and other reasons, the smaller, highly controlled experiment, dealing with the effect of one variable at a time, disassociated from any particular method, but framed in a total rationale of the dimensions of foreign language learning and teaching seems to offer greater promise of effectiveness in (1) the discovery of the most effective elements and techniques, (2) the incorporation of such discoveries in the practices of teachers who would not then be changing from one method to another but merely keeping informed on progress and incorporating into their own practices such changes as seem appropriate and convincing to them. And (3) the incorporation of discoveries into the publication of new textbooks which might continue to bear the same labels but keep up-to-date on language learning knowledge.

Progress is more likely to come not through wholesale change from an oral to a translation or to a reading "method," since such a label change refers only to one oversimplified aspect of the problem, but through articles and reports and demonstrations showing how many attempts under what conditions produce optimum results in learning such and such a problem for given ages and educational and cultural groups. Such experiments can more easily and less expensively be planned, executed and repeated by the teaching profession than the mass experiments which cannot be repeated because of expense and the complexity of the factors involved.

3. Dimensions of foreign language learning of particular interest in experimental investigations. Some of the crucial things we do not know, which foreign language teachers would appreciate knowing might be the following:

(1) If grammar is to be learned, is it more effective to teach it incidentally, or formally before the student learns the language, or formally after the student learns the language, or concurrently and systematically as the student learns the language? Is it more effective to teach the grammatical patterns systematically but inductively, or systematically but deductively? Is it more effective to teach a set terminology with the teaching of grammar or to avoid any technical terminology?

(2) How effective for particular learning problems for particular groups of students are such drill devices as memorization of sentences, translation from native to foreign language or vice versa, fill-in exercises, oral substitution of various types, picture exercises, etc. etc.?

(3) How effective are different techniques at different age levels, for immediate recall, for long-term recall, for habit formation, etc.?

(4) What is more effective in learning to read: to master the basic sentences orally first and then go on with reading after a certain level of oral mastery is attained? to begin reading from the beginning without attaining speaking proficiency of the material? to attain speaking and reading proficiency simultaneously? to have the reading precede the speaking? to have the speaking precede the reading?

(5) Is it more effective to master the sound patterns and grammatical patterns of the foreign language first within a very limited vocabulary than exposing the students to large amounts of vocabulary from the beginning?

(6) Is it more effective to have the students merely listen for a given length of time to avoid mistakes, or is it more effective to have the students attempt to recite from the beginning?

These are questions concerning method more than content. Questions of effectiveness of content and order of presentation of content can be explored with small-size, well-controlled experiments.

(7) Is it more effective to devote considerable time to the

present tense alone or to introduce several contrasting tenses early?

The questions asked in an experiment need not and probably should not be limited to problems directly concerned with language mastery. The chapters dealing with problems of testing matters beyond language, Part IV, are within the scope of the small experimental design.

An experiment cannot prove anything beyond the validity and reliability of the tests used to measure the amount of learning. As a result, highly controlled experiments will usually require the preparation of special tests for concentrated measurement of the particular variable being investigated and for the control of extraneous factors.

27.2 CONTROL-TYPE EXPERIMENTAL DESIGN

The control type of experiment has produced extremely valuable results in medicine, psychology, education, and other fields of scientific research. The effectiveness of the Salk vaccine for polio was demonstrated by a large but simple control-type experiment. In this type of experiment we control every possible factor except the one we want to test. By this device we are able to measure the effect of this experimental factor on learning.

Within this single method there are many variations of design possible. Some of the simpler ones will be discussed and illustrated.

Design 1. C X. " C " represents the control group, a group of students taught by a non-experimental method. " X " is the experimental group, a group taught by the experimental method being tested. This is one of the simplest types of control experiment.

In this type of experiment we take two groups of students as nearly equal in learning factors as possible, that is, in age, intelligence, previous knowledge, and even personality type, if possible. A refinement in equating two groups is to pair the students so that each student in one group is paralleled by a student in the other group who matches him as nearly as possible in the various learning factors.

Both groups are taught the same material, the C group by a

non-experimental method, the X group by the experimental method. The experimental method should preferably differ only as to one feature or technique from the control method.

Test both groups before and after teaching with the same testing instruments and ascertain the amount of learning of each group by the difference between the entrance and final scores. Testing before teaching should be used to equate the two groups, since amount of previous knowledge is an important learning factor.

Compare the increases, i.e., the amount of learning, of the two groups. Amount of learning may be determined in various ways other than by a difference in test scores. Some of these other ways to measure learning will be mentioned below under " 1, Dimensions of goodness."

Find out if the difference between the two groups is statistically significant, i.e., if it is probably a real difference or if it might reasonably be the result of chance variation.[1]

If the difference between the two groups is significant, it is tentatively ascribed to the feature or technique of the experimental group that differs from the control group.

Design 2. X Y. This design is the same as the C X design except that both groups are experimental. This design is applicable when we have two experimental factors to test for comparative effectiveness. Two equal groups are chosen, each is taught by one of the experimental techniques, the learning of each group is computed by testing before and after teaching, and any differences are checked for statistical significance. We then tentatively conclude that X or Y is superior, or that there is no evidence of superiority for either.

Design 3. C X/X C. Since it is not always feasible to set up two equal groups in language experiments because so many possible factors are involved, and since even if we succeed in equating two groups on the basis of the known factors we cannot be entirely certain that other factors not yet identified may have rendered

---

[1] Methods of determining whether or not a difference in arithmetic means is significant (chance factors of 5 per cent or less) or very significant (significant at the 1 per cent level) are presented in the standard textbooks on statistics applied to psychology and education. Cf. J. P., Guilford, *Fundamental Statistics in Psychology and Education.* (Third edition) (New York: McGraw-Hill Book Company, 1956.)

the groups unequal, we may use this design which introduces rotation in order to equalize the student and teacher factors.

With this design (1) we test and equalize the C group and the X group. (2) We teach both groups, using the control factor with the C group and the experimental factor with the X group. (3) Both groups are tested and the learning of each is computed. Then (4), both groups are tested on another problem of the same type. (5) The factors are reversed so that the C group now becomes the X group and is taught with the experimental factor and vice versa. (6) The materials of the experiment are taught. (7) We test both groups again to measure learning in this second round. (8) We add up the amount of learning of both groups with the experimental factor, and we compare it with the amount of learning of both groups with the control factor. (9) We check the difference, if any, for statistical significance; and (10) tentatively ascribe any significant superiority or inferiority to the factor being tested.

The experimental factor might be the method, in which case the content would be the same for X and C; it may be the content, in which case the method would be the same for X and C; or it might be the teacher, in which case the method and content would be the same. The specific problem taught must be different for the second round or the results would be invalidated.

Design 4. X Y/ Y X. This design is the same as the previous one except for the fact that two experimental factors are tested and compared instead of one experimental factor and a control.

Design 5. CX. When the experimental factor is some difference among the students themselves, this very simple design is possible. In it both types of students, those with the experimental characteristics and those without, are taught together. Their learning is computed and averaged separately, however, and it is compared and tested for statistical significance.

Design 6. C/X. When only one group of students is available this less satisfactory design might be used. In it the same students are taught one problem with the non-experimental factor and a comparable problem with the experimental factor. The students are tested before and after the teaching of each problem, and the amount of learning is compared.

This is a weaker design because any difference that may appear could easily be attributed to the problem itself as well as to the experimental factor. This shortcoming is resolved when we know the difficulty rating of each problem with precision.

A refinement of this design consists in repeating the experiment with another pair of comparable problems, reversing the order of teaching on this second round so that if the control lesson was taught first on the first round it is taught last on the second round.

Design 7. X Y Z/Y Z X/Z X Y. This design provides for the comparison of three experimental factors. It involves three rounds equal to each other except for the rotation of the experimental factors so that each group tries all three factors.

In this design we form three groups as equivalent as possible as to learning factors. Then for each round we test, teach, and test the groups and compute the amount of learning for each. Then the learning of all three groups is averaged on each of the factors so that there are three final averages of learning, one with the X factor, another with the Y factor, and the third with the Z factor. The differences are checked for statistical significance and it is tentatively concluded that there is or is not a factor that is superior to the others.

More factors can be tested by extending this design to four, five, or N rounds, but there is a point of diminishing returns as the design becomes more and more complicated. If enough students are available it may be more economical to extend the number of factors in design 2, X Y, with designs that might involve W X Y Z or more groups. If not enough students are available for experimental comparison of all the factors simultaneously, we can work with whatever number of groups are available. For example, if there are three groups but nine factors, the factors can be divided in three clusters of three factors each. Each three factors are compared leaving the most effective factor from each cluster for a second round. The second round compares the three best from the three first-round groups.

1. Dimensions of goodness in designing and interpreting experiments. Valid and reliable testing is essential in any experiment. Obviously no matter how carefully planned an experiment or how refined its design, if the tests used are not valid and reliable, the entire experiment collapses. We have devoted this book to the production of better language tests. Although the kind of tests discussed were rather general ones to be used as separate measuring instruments independent of any particular experiment, the linguistic criteria and statistical techniques apply to tests prepared for a specific experiment as well.

Evidence of learning need not be the number of correct responses on a test, however. Greater learning may be evidenced by (1) less time needed to learn something to a certain degree of mastery, (2) fewer repetitions or exposures required to achieve criterion level of mastery, (3) increase of number of students desiring to continue studying the language or a language, (4) more permanent learning, i.e., better retention, (5) less review time needed to regain mastery to a given criterion, (6) greater understanding of the other culture, (7) fuller understanding of language, (8) richer individual meaning of native language, and (9) learning more of the foreign language in the same amount of time.

2. Some problems that lend themselves to investigation by the control type of experiment. The following are some language learning problems that seem accessible to experimental investigation by the control type of experiment.

(1) Presenting the language systematically versus presenting it as it occurs.

(2) Practice on the elements that are different in the native and the foreign language versus practice on all the elements of the foreign language with equal emphasis.

(3) The use of a live voice versus a transcribed voice.

(4) The relative effectiveness of language learning through the ear, the eye, the hand, the mouth, and combinations thereof.

(5) The use of a phonemic transcription versus ordinary spelling in learning the pronunciation of a foreign language.

(6) Explanation as a medium of instruction versus imitation and analogy.

(7) Relative effectiveness of various ways to learn meanings in a foreign language.

(8) Relative effectiveness of various ways of practicing the retention of meanings.

(9) Relative effectiveness of various techniques of establishing instantaneous meaningful recall of forms and patterns.

27.3 CORRELATION TYPE OF EXPERIMENTAL INVESTIGATION

1. **Correlation as a means of discovering significant factors.** Another general method of investigation is that of statistical correlation. This method consists of finding the coefficient of correlation between amount of learning and various potential factors. To use this method we simply teach an adequate number of students under equal conditions. We test them before and after the teaching to find the amount learned by each student. We convert these raw improvements to mean improvements to minimize the effect of entrance level differences. We then compute the correlation between the learning scores and various factors such as age, hearing accuity, general ability, etc.

For any factor, if the correlation obtained is positive and not explainable as a chance happening, we conclude tentatively that the factor is positively related to amount of learning so that the greater the amount of the factor present for a student the greater the learning expected on the average.

If as in the case of age the correlation is negative and cannot be explained as a chance occurrence, we say that the factor is negatively related to amount of learning so that the greater the amount of the factor present the less learning can be expected.

2. **Some variables that seem accessible to correlation-type investigation.** Student factors are accessible to correlation study. Some of these are will, interest, previous grades in language or in other subjects, memory, hearing acuity, general intelligence, age, energy, health, education, knowledge of other languages, etc.

27.4 OTHER DIMENSIONS OPEN TO STUDY

Not necessarily requiring separate experiments but rather to be observed in almost any of the experiments indicated above are the attitudes that particular approaches encourage in the students. In addition to comparing various techniques as to amount of learning, we can check for differences in these attitudes.

Do the students want to learn more? Do they want to continue the study of the language? Do they think studying the language is worthwhile? Do they think others should be taught the same way? Do they attend class more regularly? Are they more punctual? Is the class interesting to them? Can they guess how many minutes the class lasted? Any significant differences in these and other attitudinal matters would be helpful although not decisive in choosing a teaching approach.

27.5   IN CONCLUSION

1. Progressive improvement of foreign language teaching. As the results of experiments such as those suggested and others become known, teachers and textbook writers who wish to use the best materials and the best techniques would want to incorporate them into their teaching and their textbooks. The artistic performance of the actual teaching would be supported with scientific tools and knowledge for the highest professional standards.

The experiments listed are directed to the comparison of various possible ways to proceed in teaching a foreign language. When the results of such experiments become known, it will be important to explore then the maximum limit of effectiveness of those techniques that are found to be superior. In other words, in the experiments suggested we would inquire only which technique among several is most effective: we should then experiment with various amounts and conditions in using the best technique so that the profession may know not only that such and such a technique is effective, but that it is most effective under such and such conditions.

As language yields its secrets to linguistic analysis, lexicographical study, and quantitative research it is more and more feasible to define specifically the task of learning a foreign language. As we identify more precisely the elements and patterns to be acquired by the speakers of a language in learning another we will be able to test more precisely the progress made by the student under given conditions. We will thus be able to establish the maximum amount learned by a given means under given conditions. With this information, single individuals may attempt to better the record of other individuals, and groups may compete with groups. Precise knowledge of the task and precise testing of the amount learned under clearly defined conditions can bring language teaching out of the confusion of thoughtless or interested opinionism into the more productive realm of scientific investigation.

This may be an overly idealistic view of the future, yet any progress in this direction that the book may help to encourage would be well worth the effort spent by the writer in preparing it and by the reader in struggling through it to the end.